UNIONS
AND
WORKPLACE
REORGANIZATION

UNIONS
AND
WORKPLACE
REORGANIZATION

EDITED BY
BRUCE NISSEN

 WAYNE STATE UNIVERSITY PRESS   DETROIT

Library of Congress Cataloging-in-Publication Data

Unions and workplace reorganization / edited by Bruce Nissen.
        p.   cm.
    Includes bibliographical references and index.
    ISBN 0-8143-2703-6 (pbk. : alk. paper)
    1. Industrial relations—United States.   2. Organizational
change—United States.   3. Trade-unions—United States.
4. Industrial management—Employee participation—
United States.   5. Quality of work life—United States.
I. Nissen, Bruce, 1948–   .
HD8072.5.U5   1997
331.88′0973—dc21   97-15001
                                                                    CIP

The New American Workplace: A Labor Perspective was originally
published in 1994 by the AFL-CIO Committee on the Evolution
of Work (Washington, D.C.: American Federation of Labor-
Congress of Industrial Organizations).

Portions of "New Unionism and the Workplace of the Future"
were previously published in "A Workplace Strategy for Saving
Jobs and Enhancing Workplace Democracy," *Labor Studies Journal*
21, no. 2 (summer 1996).

CONTENTS

I

INTRODUCTION

1

UNIONS
AND WORKPLACE
REORGANIZATION

BRUCE NISSEN

THE ORGANIZATION OF THE WORK SITE

Ever since Henry Ford introduced the assembly line at the workplace and the "$5 a day" compensation system, U.S. employers have paid close attention to how the organization of the workplace and the relationships between managers and workers affect economic performance. Employers search for the most effective ways to harness employees' efforts to achieve the efficiency and profitability goals of their firms. (In the public sector, of course, the profit motive is absent, but budgetary constraints and public demands create roughly similar pressures to produce the best, the most, and at the least cost.)

Frederick Taylor's development of "scientific management" is well known as the most influential early attempt to systematize methods for managerial control to achieve maximum productivity (Taylor 1947; Nadworny 1955; Braverman 1974; Nelson 1975; Clawson 1980). By separating planning and execution, and by centralizing all knowledge in management, who then gave instructions to workers on the "one best way" to accomplish a task, scientific management attempted to obtain the maximum production of uniform quality products from the workforce. While scientific management in its most extreme form was seldom fully implemented, there is no doubt that American management widely utilized

9

time-and-motion studies and other Taylorist techniques throughout much of the twentieth century.

The discipline inherent in the assembly line, which Richard Edwards labels "technical control," also aided management efforts (Edwards 1979, ch. 7). In addition, sophisticated personnel departments with rationalized sets of "company policies," individuated job ladders, and hierarchical job structures all combined to institutionalize production into what Edwards calls "bureaucratic control" (Edwards 1979, ch. 8).

Throughout the century, some companies and schools of management thought have attempted to humanize labor-management relations as a way to improve productivity, profitability, workplace morale, product quality, and the like. Ever since Elton Mayo's famous Hawthorne experiments in the 1920s, there have been waves of enthusiasm and disillusion about the possible benefits to be had from new forms of employee relations. The "human relations" school of management in the 1930s and the "social relations" movement of the 1950s are two well-known examples (Appelbaum and Batt 1994, 5).

However, beginning in the 1970s, a new-wave of workplace reorganization began that continues to the present day. While some thought it merely a "fad" that would disappear in short order, the current wave has continued and has gone through several phases. It is clear that this is not a fad but is rather a long-term and permanent search for a new type of industrial relations system. One pertinent question is why U.S. management sought change at this time.

Why Management Sought Reorganization

Beginning slowly in the 1970s and steadily accelerating in the 1980s and 1990s, U.S. managers sought to reorganize their work sites and to rearrange their employee relations systems. It was becoming increasingly apparent to them that the old way wasn't working, or at least was not working well enough to keep their firms dominant in world markets. The breakdown was apparent on many fronts.

First, public opinion polls and widely reported stories about discontented workers at the GM plant in Lordstown, Ohio, and elsewhere showed that blue-collar workers were increasingly alienated from their jobs, their workplaces, and their employers. Absenteeism was high, drug usage was invading the work site, and rebellious acts of sabotage and wildcat strikes were on the increase. The "blue-collar blues" became a common phrase in the mainstream media. A special task force produced a widely discussed report to the U.S. Secretary of Health, Education, and Welfare on work in America and how to humanize it (Special Task Force 1973).

Second, the economic performance of U.S. facilities relative to those elsewhere in the world began to deteriorate. Imports from other countries, especially Japan and certain European countries, began to capture larger shares of important U.S. markets. U.S. exports as a share of all world exports began to fall. Various reasons were given for this shift, but many observers began to look at the labor relations systems in Japan and elsewhere for clues as to why their firms seemed to be doing better than their U.S. counterparts.

Ignoring all other factors, such as government macroeconomic policies and cultural differences, and concentrating solely on labor relations practices, at least three alternatives to the U.S. post–World War II model are apparent: the Japanese, the Scandinavian, and the German. Although this is an intentional simplification of complex differences among countries, these three models serve roughly to sketch out major differences in industrial relations practices. U.S. managers found a selective importation of features of the Japanese system to be most attractive: enterprise unionism or no unions as opposed to industry-wide unionism based on centralized or pattern bargaining; worker involvement in programs and processes carefully controlled by management; and employee involvement in improving efficiency, which might best be called "participative Taylorism." Other features, such as guaranteed lifetime employment to at least a portion of the workforce and limited compensation gaps between top management and the workforce, were largely ignored in the U.S. management enthusiasm for the Japanese model.

U.S. unions were more likely to find the Scandinavian model attractive. High levels of unionization, nationwide centralized bargaining, legislatively required institutions of codetermination at all levels of the firm, major union influence in national political affairs, and extensive job training and retraining made the Scandinavian model attractive to unionists and their sympathetic academic counterparts.

As a third alternative, many industrial relations experts and a small number of unionists favored the West German model: works councils as well as unions to provide worker representation, extensive tripartite bargaining at the national level among unions, employers and the government over defining features of economic policy, and high skill levels and extensive national training policies.

Whichever model one favored, or whichever mix of features from models one liked, these were alternatives that could plausibly be made to look as attractive as, or more attractive than, the previous practices prevalent in the United States. Pressures to experiment and change began in the 1970s and intensified throughout the 1980s and into the 1990s, as neoliberal, free-market policies swept the country and the world, making the U.S. economy ever more vulnerable to products produced abroad under different production systems.

The most widely accepted explanation as to why the American workplace underwent such rapid changes is that the mass-production system that made the U.S. economy the most productive in the world for two to three decades after World War II is no longer a viable option. Faced with intensified worldwide competition brought on by advances in production technology and telecommunications, U.S.-based production facilities are unable to compete on the basis of lowest cost for mass produced, standardized products produced under Taylorist or scientific management methods. Similarly, domestic Keynesian policies to stimulate demand fail to work well in a wide-open worldwide market (Piore and Sabel 1984; Marshall 1992).

Instead, it is argued, U.S. operations have two choices. They can attempt the "low road" of massive cuts in labor costs, "sweating" of labor, and the like, or they can move in the direction of utilizing a highly skilled, motivated workforce deployed in a flexible manner to produce for high-value-added specialized niche markets that change rapidly. Only by following this "high road" will high living standards be sustainable, according to the argument. Standardized mass production is either moving offshore to low-wage areas of the world or drastically cutting wages and costs domestically; only by moving higher on the learning curve through a high performance organization will U.S. producers be able to compete in a manner that sustains historical living standards. Although the specifics of the argument differ, similar arguments are made for the service sector and the public sector (for details, see Appelbaum and Batt 1994, ch. 7).

WHAT HAD HAPPENED TO THE OLD INDUSTRIAL RELATIONS SYSTEM?

The U.S. post–World War II industrial relations system, whereby large corporations in major industries bargained industry pattern contracts with their largely unionized workforces, had been deteriorating for some time. Even in the "Golden Age" of the 1950s and 1960s, when U.S. unions had a major foothold in most major U.S. production industries, employers were positioning themselves to lessen their dependence on union labor (Glyn et al. 1990; Klein and Wanger 1985). Through union avoidance investment patterns and the development of sophisticated non-union "human resource management" techniques intended to stabilize employee relations without unions, companies steadily shed unions on an accelerating basis from the 1970s on (Kochan, Katz, and McKersie 1994; Harrison and Bluestone 1988, ch. 2). The process of "deindustrialization" from unionized workforces and communities grew rapidly (Bluestone and Harrison 1982; Craypo and Nissen 1993).

Unions declined drastically in size and numbers (Goldfield 1987; Moody 1988; Craypo 1990; Freeman 1992). Industry-wide pattern bargaining broke down in major industries, leaving decentralized union locals bargaining against centralized firms. The ability of unions to "take wages and working conditions out of competition" deteriorated badly. Political power, economic bargaining power, and stature in the public's estimation all plummeted. At the same time, nonunion operations continued to take a larger share of many markets. Unions thus faced employer demands to transform industrial relations practices in the remaining unionized operations in a much weakened position.

Writing in 1986, Thomas Kochan, Harry Katz, and Robert McKersie were convinced that nonunion human resource management systems had successfully implemented the policies needed for success in the new environment (Kochan, Katz, and McKersie 1986). Flexible work design, worker and work group involvement, and high employee commitment to the firm had made nonunion companies the vanguard of progressive, successful adaptation. In contrast, unionized workplaces were seen as dysfunctional sites trapped in rigid work rules, destructive adversarial attitudes, and uninvolved workforces.

Subsequent scholarship has cast considerable doubt on this claim. Eaton and Voos present both empirical evidence and theoretical arguments that unionized workplaces have the more meaningful types of worker-participation programs. They conclude that the union sector actually leads the nonunion sector in workplace innovations that improve economic performance (Eaton and Voos 1992). Similarly, Kelley and Harrison (1992) find that in the machining industry, for example, nonunion worker participation programs failed to work, compared to their unionized counterparts. In a new preface to a 1994 paperback edition of their book, Kochan, Katz, and McKersie concede that nonunion employers have been less successful than they had previously believed (xvi).

WHAT PHASES HAVE WORKPLACE CHANGES GONE THROUGH?

Under the pressure of an increasingly competitive and frequently worldwide economic environment, managers of U.S. firms attempted to improve their organizational performance through what at first appears to be a bewildering array of innovations and programs with numerous titles. Without attempting to be comprehensive, one can list a representative number of these work site changes (Wells 1991; Eaton 1995). Examples include better communications systems between managers and workers, new styles of management involving more collaboration, expansion of job duties (job enlargement or enrichment, job rotation, and so forth), added skill acquisition (multiskilling), group problem solving, "self-managed" work teams, careful screening of new hires for compatible personality types, contingent forms of pay such as gainsharing and profit-sharing, "cell manufacturing" arrangements, just-in-time production, new quality control systems, and a wide array of formal and informal consultative arrangements on work site management issues.

Generally, changes of this nature have been partial in several respects. Companies may adopt only some of these arrangements, and they usually do so only in selected parts of their organization. Similar companies in the same industry may radically diverge in their adoption of any of these changes. And many innovations have been dropped as disappointing results occurred, often to be followed by renewed attempts with a different mix of features and a new name. Nevertheless, twenty-plus years of continuous innovation shows that the current wave is more than a fad; something more permanent is being established.

The first phase was largely experimental and was initially only undertaken by isolated companies. The most frequent label put on such programs was quality of working life (QWL). The explicit attempt was to make working conditions more humane so that workers would improve product quality, reduce absenteeism, and in similar ways improve their attitude toward the company, thus helping to make it more profitable. The focus, probably influenced by the "blue-collar blues" issue mentioned previously, was on worker satisfaction with the work environment.

QWL programs grew rapidly in the early 1980s, but the focus shifted as the decade wore on, and as many programs died after initial enthusiasm. Instead of "creature comfort" issues such as improved cleanliness, lunchroom facilities, and water fountains, the emphasis shifted to improvements in product quality or productivity. At this point, many programs were set up as quality circles (QCs) concerned solely or mainly with product quality improvements. Many QWL programs combined with QC programs, and a new terminology was introduced (using "involvement" and "participation," as in employee involvement [EI], employee participation [EP], labor-management participation teams [LMPT], and so forth).

Growing competition and economic stress led managements to emphasize productivity and product quality; worker satisfaction with the work environment became a secondary issue. Unions involved in these programs shifted emphasis from job satisfaction to job security. The accelerating pace of plant closures punctuated the dangers of inferior economic performance, and both sides shifted emphasis accordingly.

In the decade of the 1980s, emphasis shifted from strictly "off-line" programs such as earlier QWL or EI efforts to "on-line" attempts to reorganize the work process itself. In some cases, reorganization of production had no element of direct employee involvement, but some of the new programs extended participation to these reorganization efforts.

One such innovation that gained much prominence by the mid-1980s was team production. Teams take many forms, but they usually involve a major reduction in the number of job classifications, team members being at least potentially interchangeable because of cross-training, and work group responsibility for labor tasks not directly involved in production. In

14

some cases, teams are given much more responsibility over such matters as scheduling, admission to the team, and pay.

Particularly in the U.S. automobile industry, teams could be combined with "lean production" features of just-in-time delivery, constant improvement ("kaizen"), and elimination of job classifications (Babson 1995; CAW-Canada Research Group on CAMI 1993; Graham 1995). The team concept moved considerably beyond earlier quality circle and quality of working life programs. No longer were workers simply involved in meetings; the very organization of the work process was being altered, with varying rates of success.

In the late 1980s and early 1990s, the concept of total quality management (TQM) became prominent. TQM involves a reconceptualization of the organization to achieve high-quality goods or services. "Building quality in" to the product or service, viewing most relationships as "customer" ones (even relationships internal to the firm), and getting close and constant feedback from customers are among its chief features. In 1988, the U.S. government created the Malcolm Baldridge Award to reward companies fitting into a particular vision of TQM. The vision emphasizes management and customer service policies; human resource or employee-oriented criteria play a rather small role. TQM is mainly concerned with management vision and consequent marketing and operational activities. Worker involvement or "empowerment" are not essential to its conception or practice (Appelbaum and Batt 1994, 129–31).

The very latest stage of workplace reorganization involves the concept of "reengineering," or "reinventing." Going well beyond TQM, advocates of reengineering the firm call for basic restructuring of the very organization. Core activities are to be built around generalists, with special work contracted out (Hammer and Champy 1993). Downsizing, contingent employment relationships, and similar features supplying the headlines for the business press in the mid-1990s are the consequences.

Most management versions of TQM and reengineering provide no special role for unions and no empowerment of workers. However, an alternative conception of workplace reorganization involving more commitment to the workforce has recently been developed by researchers and practitioners who are friendlier to union goals. One version of a "high-performance workplace" involves the combination of continuous skills upgrading and training, worker participation and worker-management partnerships, employment security, compensation linked to performance and skills, and a supportive work environment, according to those supportive of the concept (Marshall 1992; U.S. Department of Labor 1994; AFL-CIO Human Resources Development Institute 1994).

As this summary of TQM, reengineering, and high performance workplaces indicates, a major debate in management and academic circles is whether independent worker representation is necessary for new forms of

15

production to be successful. The majority view is that it is not and that unions are therefore to be avoided, or at least weakened where they cannot be avoided. A minority view argues that successful new forms of flexible production built on a basis of employee trust are not sustainable without such representation (Adams 1995). Even some normally prounion intellectuals have carefully straddled the fence; former U.S. secretary of labor Robert Reich recently stated, "The jury is still out on whether the traditional union is necessary for the new workplace" (Uchitelle 1993, 32).

The many different programs and trends enumerated above often coexist; all of them can be found today, although the later ones tend to be most prominent in public attention and management theory. This wide array of programs can be confusing to the onlooker; it can also make it hard for unions to develop unified and coherent strategies, given the many variations in management programs. But the less effective programs continue to be dropped over time as managements and their academic counterparts learn more about what is working and what is not.

The level of sophistication in businesses and business schools about workplace reorganization has gone up dramatically in the last decade and a half. A quick comparison of the scholarly and business literature on the topic in 1995 with that of 1980 reveals stark differences. Both theoretical clarity and empirical knowledge of outcomes of various sorts have risen impressively. There is every likelihood that the future will bring a continued refinement in their strategies and knowledge base.

UNION REACTION TO THE NEW PROGRAMS

Unions initially reacted to the growth of worker participation programs in a wide variety of ways. A U.S. Department of Labor publication in the mid-1980s reprinted a number of statements from national unions and union leaders on the topic (U.S. Department of Labor 1984). Official union statements ranged from enthusiastic embrace to cautious ambivalence to outright rejection. The middle position was almost certainly the majority stance in the early 1980s, although prominent advocates of the pro and con positions were also clearly apparent.

Individual union leaders at the national level, such as Irving Bluestone of the United Autoworkers (UAW), Sam Camens of the United Steelworkers (USWA), and Glenn Watts of the Communications Workers (CWA), proselytized heavily within and outside the labor movement in favor of employee involvement programs. Early statements from these leaders often described such programs in glowing terms of human dignity, self-worth, self-fulfillment, and control over one's work process.

At the other end of the spectrum, then-president of the International Association of Machinists (IAM) William Winpisinger characterized worker participation programs as management maneuvers to divide workers, gain workers' knowledge without compensation, circumvent the union contract, and eliminate jobs in a context of antiunion offensives. The American Postal Workers Union (APWU) in 1984 passed a resolution at its national convention condemning QWL-EI programs in the postal service as attempts to create a union-free environment; it was "unalterably opposed" to union participation in such programs. Other unions, such as the Oil, Chemical, and Atomic Workers (OCAW), the independent United Electrical Workers (UE), and the Teamsters (IBT), following a changeover to reform leadership, have also been quite critical.

Initially the majority of unions either took no clear stance or adopted a cautious attitude that circumstances would dictate a proper union posture. Most developed no national union policy, leaving it up to union locals to deal with management programs on their own. While this may have had a few beneficial consequences, such as unfettered experimentation to see what works best, the main result was probably harmful to workers and unions. Union locals usually were not prepared on their own to deal with the program, national unions were often not even aware of what was going on in the locals, and many union locals drifted into disasters because of a lack of preparation or guidance.

Generalizations about the evolution of union attitudes over the decade of the 1980s and into the 1990s are difficult to make. Uniform patterns do not clearly appear. However, to this observer the following seemed to occur: initial confusion for the majority of unions gave way to clearer perspectives as experiences at the work site gave unions a more grounded perspective. Extreme optimists were forced to moderate their enthusiasm as programs failed at a high rate and as companies often continued making investment and production decisions undermining the union even as they engaged in "cooperative" programs. Total rejectionists likewise were forced to retreat; even hostile unions like the Machinists found the combination of employer pressure and interest from a portion of the membership impossible to resist.

Most of the experimentation happened at the local level. Battles raged inside unions as critics documented antiunion motivation and action in a number of the companies undertaking participation programs (Wells 1987; Grenier 1988; Parker 1985; Parker and Slaughter 1988, 1994; Rinehart 1984; Alexander 1987; Lever-Tracy 1990; Knauss and Matuszak 1994). Proponents pointed to successful examples and argued that unions were gaining influence and power (Cohen-Rosenthal and Burton 1993; Bluestone and Bluestone 1992; Klingel and Martin 1988; Whyte et al. 1983; Verma and McKersie 1987; Rosow 1986).

As the 1980s progressed into the 1990s, the level of union expertise rose. National unions such as the Communications Workers, the United Steelworkers, the Amalgamated Clothing and Textile Workers Union (ACTWU, now merged with the Ladies Garment Workers in UNITE), and

17

the Grainmillers developed specialized departments, internal education programs, and/or "strategic partnership" models with major employers. Unions moving both in more positive and more critical directions developed more complex understandings and strategies; the Machinists and the Teamsters unions are respective examples. Both unions developed programs and positions with more depth than they had previously; the main difference is that the Machinists became more positive about possibilities while the Teamsters became more critical. Union strategy guides with both a critical and a positive stance were developed (Parker and Slaughter 1992; AFL-CIO Human Resources Development Institute 1994). Perhaps surprisingly, both the ideologically critical and ideologically positive guides arrive at somewhat similar lists of "what to do" in relation to such programs.

Theoretical and practical discussion within the labor movement began to shift focus. A widely read article by Andy Banks and Jack Metzgar conceptualized participation programs as a terrain for union organizing. This article clearly separated the notions of "participation" and "cooperation" and argued for unions to maintain maximum control over shop-floor knowledge in such programs (Banks and Metzgar 1989). Others focused on union attempts to gain influence at higher strategic levels of business decision making, using highly publicized cases like the Saturn Corporation as examples (Heckscher 1988; Bluestone and Bluestone 1992).

Among proponents, a "trust management" perspective receded somewhat, as events repeatedly showed that simple trust frequently leads to betrayal and harmful consequences. Among critics, a "just say no" perspective likewise receded somewhat as it became clear that this trend toward employee involvement was not a short-term fad that would blow over in a short while. An evolution of emphasis from *job satisfaction* to *job security* in union goals for such programs is equally evident, as the shrinkage of well-paying union jobs and the wave of plant closings continued apace. And finally, unions have been focusing more on access to, or influence over, management decisions at levels higher than the shop floor, at least in theory. This is what underlies the "strategic partnership" model being pursued by some unions.

AFL-CIO PERSPECTIVES

The American Federation of Labor-Congress of Industrial Organization (AFL-CIO) was originally silent on the subject. A 1982 talk by AFL-CIO secretary-treasurer Thomas Donahue and a 1984 article in *AFL-CIO News* expressed considerable skepticism about management's intentions (Donahue 1982; *AFL-CIO News* 1984). In 1982, the federation set up the Committee on the Evolution of Work to examine the changing world of work and the labor movement's role within this changing context. In

18

1983, the committee issued an initial report, *The Future of Work,* which briefly surveyed technological and other changes. The 1985 document *The Changing Situation of Workers and Their Unions* followed; it critically evaluated changes in organized labor's environment and suggested a number of changes in federation and union practice. The suggestions concerned mostly issues of union organizing, new membership categories, membership involvement, union mergers, and the like.

It was not until February 1994, however, that the committee issued a report on U.S. workplace reorganization and organized labor's proper stance toward it, *The New American Workplace: A Labor Perspective.* The nine-year gap between the publication of *The Changing Situation of Workers and Their Unions* and *The New American Workplace* testifies to the difficulty the AFL-CIO had in arriving at a uniform statement on work reorganization. According to knowledgeable sources, a common strategy was almost achieved in the late 1980s, but AFL-CIO leaders were unable to reach agreement (Kochan, Katz, and McKersie 1994, xv).

The New American Workplace is reprinted in the second chapter of this book. As a consensus document on a very controversial subject, it is carefully crafted to avoid some of the most contentious issues within the labor movement regarding labor-management participation programs and new work systems. Both critics and supporters are likely to find phrases and arguments with which they thoroughly agree, as well as some that give pause.

The New American Workplace critiques the traditional Taylorist method of production and the authoritarian management that has accompanied it. It then outlines five principles that jointly define a model of work reorganization, together with four general guidelines to be used in the construction of labor-management partnerships to achieve such new workplaces. The five principles are: 1) rejection of the dichotomy between thinking and doing; 2) greater worker skills and responsibility; 3) flatter management structures; 4) decision-making roles for workers through unions at all levels of the employer; and 5) negotiated equitable distribution of rewards.

Based upon these five principles, *The New American Workplace* calls for a new labor-management partnership whereby independent unions would join with management in managing the new systems of work organization. Accordingly, the partnerships must be based on four principles: 1) mutual recognition and respect; 2) a collective bargaining foundation for the relationship; 3) equality of roles; and 4) focus on mutually agreed-upon common goals. If these four principles are satisfied, *The New American Workplace* sees the partnership as productive. The document closes by surveying obstacles to change, the role of organized labor and of the AFL-CIO, and two divergent paths ("low wage" vs. "high skill, high wage") that could be pursued.

Following a 1995 change in leadership, the AFL-CIO chose to restructure itself by breaking its former research department into four separate entities. One of these is the Center for Workplace Democracy, which will pursue initiatives in the area of workplace reorganization and democratization. At the time the writings in this book were completed, its exact role and staffing had not been finalized.

ASSESSMENTS OF THE AFL-CIO PERSPECTIVE

The authors of the remaining chapters in this book address themselves to *The New American Workplace*, assessing its adequacy or inadequacy as a guide for the U.S. labor movement in relation to new work systems. Each author brings to bear his or her understanding and experiences on the formulations of the AFL-CIO document, so there is a wide variety of perspectives. However, the unified focus on one document ensures that the same core issues are examined, and the chapters provide excellent complements to each other. They could be considered an ongoing critical conversation on organized labor's relationship with new work systems.

In chapter 3, Adrienne E. Eaton places *The New American Workplace* in a comparative international context. After noting its importance as a measure of some degree of consensus and as a stimulus to action, she compares it to similar documents in five other countries: Britain, Australia, Germany, Sweden, and Denmark. The comparisons, too detailed to summarize here, illustrate the importance of the national system of industrial relations in each country, with consequent differences in vulnerabilities and strengths in each country's labor movement.

In comparison to documents from other countries, Eaton finds *The New American Workplace* to have a stronger critique of Taylorism and more emphasis on the need for labor-management partnerships. It is comparatively weak, however, on issues of training and skills formation, safety and health and environmental protection, and the position of underrepresented groups (women and contingent or casual workers).

Beyond these direct comparisons, substantive issues are raised by this review of different systems. One is the relationship of workplace reorganization with collective bargaining. Workplace experimentation tends to decentralize collective bargaining, challenging centralized traditional union methods of protecting standards. This is particularly acute in the already relatively decentralized U.S. system. To avoid a drift toward enterprise unionism, Eaton states, the U.S. labor movement needs to confront this reality.

Even more fundamental, Eaton believes that workplace reorganization may require a complete reconsideration of traditional representation strategies and structures. American industrial unionism has been intimately tied to Taylorized production in the workplace (a fact not completely understood by the U.S. labor movement), and new models may be imperative in the changing workplace of the future. Perhaps a more political form or model of unionism is required of the U.S. labor movement, she writes, in light of the importance of strong legal rights and partnerships with Labor or Social Democratic political parties to labor movements abroad.

Finally, Eaton finds *The New American Workplace* a bit thin on context compared to comparable documents from other countries. However, a federation document in the U.S. may mean less than it does in other countries where central federations bargain nationally with the government and employer federations. Nevertheless, *The New American Workplace* has provided a beginning for organized labor's self-definition in relation to workplace reorganization.

In chapter 4, Jim Grattan places workplace change within the context of a democratic society professing to extend democratic processes to every aspect of its life. Traditionally the workplace has denied employees democratic rights granted in the public sphere, but economic changes are now forcing management to rethink traditional methods of work site organization.

However, Grattan finds the AFL-CIO document inadequate or incomplete in that it fails realistically to address major obstacles to attaining its goals of worker empowerment and union influence. According to Grattan several problems exist: 1) worker-empowering rights lack a legal (or quasi-legal) basis; 2) employer property rights and employer hostility are preeminent; 3) worker empowerment is highly constrained under the traditional National Labor Relations Act (NLRA) framework; 4) workers are manipulated under EI plans by employers using democratic terminology; and 5) workers are not appreciative of the need for a legal (or quasi-legal) basis for real empowerment. To counter these problems Grattan concludes that an amended NLRA framework represents the only practical path toward substantive worker empowerment. Employer goodwill alone will not do it, he argues, and the massive challenge facing the AFL-CIO is to build sufficient political power to enact necessary legal changes.

The broad overviews of Eaton and Grattan are followed by three chapters written by practitioners in the field. Peter Downs in chapter 5 evaluates the AFL-CIO document from the perspective of his experiences as a worker for General Motors. He argues that the realities of worker participation programs and team production bear little resemblance to the bright picture portrayed in *The New American Workplace*. Downs analyzes the "psychology of consent" fostered by such programs and concludes that they undermine worker solidarity and promote destructive competition between workers and between union locals.

The root of the problem, Downs asserts, is that labor-management

21

partnerships make "competitiveness" the central goal. Distinguishing "competitiveness" from high quality and productivity, he asserts that the former cannot be a legitimate union goal: it only leads down a slippery slope of speed-up, worsened working conditions, outsourcing, and loss of a strong grievance procedure. Downs concludes his piece by calling for a labor movement with broader goals, with an agenda independent of management's, and with a firm commitment to internal accountability and democracy.

In the next two chapters, Maureen Sheahan and Mae Ngai review *The New American Workplace* in light of their experiences implementing participative projects for unions. In chapter 6, Maureen Sheahan argues that critics like Downs are too simplistic. She agrees that "taking wages and working conditions out of competition" is a laudable goal, but she asserts that it is often unattainable and that it should not be seen as the *only* way to achieve workers' goals. Although agreeing that worker participation programs *can* be used to turn workers into "policemen" spying on each other or to increase the work pace and stress, she argues that these are not *necessary* consequences if unions structure the program properly. Independent union participation is the only workable approach, she asserts; noninvolvement is very harmful, and critics have no realistic alternative.

Sheahan lists ten strategic union goals in such programs and utilizes her experiences with UAW Region 1A's project as a case study. She illustrates a "distinct agendas" approach (as opposed to the "common agenda" rhetoric of many consultants and program advocates) and charts out the separate and common interests of managements and unions. By maintaining an independent yet constructive stance, Sheahan claims that UAW Region 1A has been able to make positive achievements through its employee involvement project, even if it has not scored any "glowing" successes.

Mae Ngai in chapter 7 depicts the "high performance workplace" as a contested terrain where negotiations will determine the actual contours of work organization, compensation, use of technology, and the like. Placing changes in a worldwide economic context, she argues that the AFL-CIO is correct to see a flexible, post-Taylorist workplace as potentially more humane and democratic. High skills, control over management rights, and employment security are additional potential benefits. However, citing the federation's opposition to the Dunlop Commission's call for altering the National Labor Relations Act section 8(a)(2) as an example, she feels the AFL-CIO is still wedded to conventional industrial relations practice without a proactive strategy of its own.

Ngai details the education and training programs for small and medium firms by the New York City-based Consortium for Worker's Education as an example of how education can aid unions in their struggle for power and influence on the new terrain. She outlines a model of education that is based on workers' knowledge while it strives to be both participative and integrated into life tasks. Education is seen as more than simply training, and the consortium strives to build three-way partnerships among labor, management, and educators.

Ngai argues that such education programs have helped union workers to define and clarify their goals and positions. Even when unions are willing to commit to quality, productivity, and cooperation, she asserts, companies often resist making a countercommitment to job security and just compensation. Unions then have to struggle for *real* cooperation, and education plays a positive supportive role in this struggle.

Chapters 8 and 9 examine workplace change in the public sector. In chapter 8, Edward L. Suntrup and Darold T. Barnum consider the federal government. They note a sharp change in the policy of the U.S. government since the advent of the Clinton administration. Both the Dunlop Commission report on changing federal labor law and federal encouragement of labor-management partnerships indicate that the present administration believes in mutual labor-management trust as a basis for industrial relations.

Noting that labor law in the private sector is premised on the assumption of adversarial or conflictual relations, Suntrup and Barnum read President Clinton's Executive Order 12871 in 1993 and its preceding commission on reinvention of the government, led by Vice President Albert Gore, as based on a model of labor-management cooperation and consensus. The executive order provides great gains for federal sector unions by making collective bargaining mandatory for many topics previously left to management discretion. However, collective bargaining is seen not as adversarial but as consensual ("interest-based" bargaining, rather than adversarial bargaining).

Suntrup and Barnum compare the Clinton administration view of labor-management partnerships with that of *The New American Workplace*. They are similar, they assert, in that they are firmly based on collective bargaining and on the full equality of the two partners. But, they differ markedly in a basic assumption: the AFL-CIO document is based on conflict theory and power politics, while the government position is based on a theory of cooperation the authors label "quasi-utopian."

They also assert that in the private sector, lack of legal protections and frequent management hostility make unions understandably reluctant to give up job protections and control. Hence, *The New American Workplace* is grounded in power politics assumptions. But the federal sector may provide more hospitable grounds for deeply and genuinely cooperative relations, the authors claim, although considerable skepticism about how far this can go or how long it could survive changes in administration is warranted. At minimum, federal workers and unions are likely to make permanent gains owing to the widened scope of bargainable issues, they state.

In chapter 9, Lee Balliet also argues that chances for union-management partnerships are better in the public sector than they are in the private sector. He points out that many private sector employers are offering a "kinder and gentler" workplace while at the same time engaging in downsizing, outsourcing, and plant closures. He finds the likelihood of less adversarial labor-management relations in most private sector companies to be severely circumscribed by such an environment.

However, Balliet finds that rising union density in the public sector (compared to severe declines in the private sector), greater employer acceptance, softer management attitudes, and the absence of the private profit motive make the dynamics of public sector labor relations somewhat different. The risks are lower for unions, and the potential gains often higher, because traditional public sector collective bargaining is already greatly constrained in terms of areas and influence.

Balliet reviews experiences around the United States and gives a more detailed account of a labor-management partnership program he has been administering in the state of Indiana. His account demonstrates both problems and advances, but he finds that gains in power are possible for workers and unions involved. He concludes that labor-management partnerships are one strategic tool that can be useful to state and local public sector unions under the right conditions. And those conditions are more likely to be present in the public sector than they are in private sector settings.

Chapters 10 and 11 present strongly opposing views on the "big picture." Peter Lazes and Jane Savage in chapter 10 state that unions are now struggling for their very existence as a meaningful force in the United States. In this context, *The New American Workplace* is a landmark document making a strong case for union involvement in workplace restructuring, they assert. But, the authors write, it does not go far enough or deep enough in showing the way to implement partnerships and workplace reorganization as a union *strategy*. Thoroughgoing transformations are necessary.

In Lazes and Savage's view, a new environment means unions need entirely new strategies. A globalized economy and free trade, combined with technological changes making mass production feasible in less developed countries, make for greatly increased competition. Institutions within the United States have been slow to change in meeting the new challenges, and domestic inequality is growing.

Unions have also been slow to change, they assert. Relying on traditional mechanisms of collective bargaining and contract administration, unions have counted on job classifications, seniority rights, and the grievance procedure to protect their members' interests. These have failed badly; they don't protect against plant closings or job loss.

Lazes and Savage argue that unions now need a new strategy to affect critical business decisions. They recommend that unions form "strategic alliances" with managements to protect their members and to build the union. Unions now need to help run the business if they wish to ensure their own survival.

They propose a five-point strategy for unions: 1) create an independent union agenda; 2) bargain to become management partners (the strategic alliance); 3) bargain for compensation increases tied to union and worker contributions; 4) change workplace structures, decision making, and technology; and 5) restructure internally.

Much of Lazes and Savage's chapter is devoted to explaining each of these five points, utilizing examples and suggesting action steps for both union locals and international unions. They also address a changed role for the AFL-CIO in relationship to workplace change.

Lazes and Savage admit that there are limitations to, and difficulties for, their suggested strategy. But they are convinced that unions have little choice. In their view, "only through participating in the management of the enterprises of which they are a part will unions be able to assure that their interests and those of their members are met." Otherwise unions remain mere bystanders witnessing further deterioration of living standards and job conditions/security.

In the final chapter, Mike Parker and Jane Slaughter present an opposing view that is highly critical of certain aspects of *The New American Workplace*. They endorse its five basic principles but believe it deepens certain illusions, or confusions, within the labor movement. The report calls for unions to develop strategic partnerships with employers on terms reasonably favorable to unions and workers, but employers overwhelmingly reject any such reciprocity, they assert. Guidelines such as mutual recognition and respect are routinely violated by employers engaged in cooperative programs at unionized sites while avoiding or breaking unions elsewhere.

The problem with *The New American Workplace*, Parker and Slaughter feel, is that it relies upon enlightened employer self-interest instead of pursuing union power as a way to build organized labor as a force in society as a whole. It thus relies on wishful thinking and misidentifies the main problems facing the labor movement. Parker and Slaughter do not believe that the programs currently being implemented develop organized labor's ability to build a powerful social movement. They analyze well-known examples in the U.S. automobile industry such as the New United Motor Manufacturing, Inc. (NUMMI) site in California and Saturn in Tennessee. They argue that NUMMI merely extends Taylorism to a continuous and self-imposed process while Saturn, even with its admittedly

25

positive features, fails to build either independent union power or union solidarity. It is trapped in an "enterprise union" mold tying the union local more firmly to its employer than to its own members or to other unionized workers.

Parker and Slaughter also examine other features of the AFL-CIO report, such as flatter management structures, skills issues, and equitable distribution of rewards, critiquing actual practice and suggesting alternatives that would be more beneficial. They conclude with a series of suggestions on how to function within participation programs, basing their suggestions on collectively bargained rights and procedures that protect union independence. They also suggest a number of issues for collective mobilization building solidarity within such a program.

The premise of Parker and Slaughter's chapter is that the labor movement can only move forward if it becomes a powerful social movement in battle against established centers of power currently controlled by capital. And that, they believe, is only possible when the membership is union-conscious and mobilized for struggle, not for cooperation.

CONCLUDING REFLECTIONS

From this brief summary of the chapters, it should be apparent that many of the most critical, defining questions involving unions and workplace reorganization are addressed by the authors. It is well beyond my intent to address all of them here or to resolve any. These concluding reflections will merely highlight a few of the questions raised by the analyses in this book.

One set of questions concerns the U.S. context into which workplace reorganization is being placed. All analysts believe context is extremely important, but the features chosen as critical and the conclusions drawn vary widely. All chapters relate current efforts at employee involvement or union-management partnerships to globalization of the economy, union decline, and new competitive pressures, but the similarity often ends there. What follows from these changes? A need for the labor movement to become more militant, more based on worker solidarity, more internationalist, as Downs and as Parker and Slaughter suggest? Or a need for unions to reorient the very meaning of what it means to be a union by taking on coresponsibility for running the company and reconceptualizing the adversary as primarily competitors and market forces, as Lazes and Savage advocate?

Beyond the big context, more specific contextual questions arise. Three particularly interesting ones are embedded in the readings: 1) differences between public and private sector settings; 2) the relationship of workplace reorganization to labor law and political representation; and 3) the relationship of workplace reorganization to the attitudes of U.S. workers. The public/private distinction is raised explicitly by Suntrup and Barnum and by Balliet. If public sector workers have more to gain, that is, more severe restrictions to overcome on bargainable topics, and if public sector management hostility to unions is less intense, as Suntrup and Barnum as well as Balliet suggest, it could be that labor-management partnerships will be easier to achieve here than in the private sector. At least, that is the intriguing possibility raised by the public sector chapters.

The relationship of workplace reorganization with labor law and political representation for labor is raised by Eaton, Grattan, Ngai, and Suntrup and Barnum. One question is how serious a blow to genuine independent unionism would the effective repeal of National Labor Relations Act Section 8(a)(2) (the ban on company dominated labor organizations) be. Both the "Team Act" introduced into the Republican-dominated Congress in 1995 and a recommendation of the Dunlop Commission would have strongly modified or destroyed 8(a)(2). Over time, 8(a)(2) may be destroyed by such initiatives whose ostensible aim is keeping U.S.-based production competitive.

A second question concerns how unions can safely abandon the old "job control unionism" in the absence of strong legal protections (codetermination laws, statutorily mandated works councils, and so forth) or a major labor or social democratic political party providing a legislative voice for organized labor. Eaton and Grattan in particular raise this question.

The third "context" issue is the attitude of workers. Both Grattan and Lazes and Savage address this issue in an explicit and analytical way; Downs, Sheahan, Ngai, and Parker and Slaughter also raise the issue either implicitly or less systematically. Lazes and Savage use polling data to show that U.S. workers overwhelmingly desire cooperative, or nonadversarial, relations with their employers. Grattan uses the same polls to argue that ambivalent and even perhaps somewhat contradictory attitudes prevail. Critics like Downs and Parker and Slaughter believe that workers desire a strong militant collective instrument to confront employers adversarially; they don't explicitly address polls showing more accommodative attitudes. Sheahan and Ngai implicitly project a very pragmatic consciousness of workers: looking for more say and job security, and not being particularly ideologically constrained in their thinking about how to attain them.

Beyond the contextual issues are equally important questions concerning the programs themselves. One is motivation, both on the management and the union side. Grattan, Downs, Sheahan, Ngai, Suntrup and Barnum, Lazes and Savage, and Parker and Slaughter all address questions of motivation. In the private sector, it is almost platitudinous to note that the overall goal of virtually everything undertaken by the company is higher profits, either short term or long term. Yet more specific, individual motivation by management for particular undertakings is usually considerably more complicated. Workplace innovations may be undertaken out of a desire to be in on "the latest innovation," a desire for immediate improvements in productivity or product quality, a desire for less union opposition to planned change, a desire for better communications, a desire to avoid unionization, a desire to improve morale, or for a whole host of other reasons. All of these and more are undoubtedly motivations of individual managers in individual situations.

Grattan sees the general trend of management motivation as being an effort to improve productivity. Suntrup and Barnum see an almost utopian motivation in the most recent federal government leadership. Downs and Parker and Slaughter see antiunion motivation and the desire for control as uppermost. Sheahan, Ngai, and Lazes and Savage see a desire to improve organizational performance in the face of growing competition as the main management goal.

Like the workers' attitude question, this one is fraught with ambiguous and contradictory evidence. Every single motivating factor mentioned has undoubtedly played a role in individual instances. My own reading suggests to me that the *main* goal of management in most workplace reorganization innovations that utilize employee involvement or union-management partnerships is to convince workers to consider their well-being and the well-being of their employer as synonymous, or at least closely intertwined. Provision of a more comfortable working environment (early programs), fear of losing one's job (later programs), contingent compensation tied to the organization's performance, social pressure on "laggards" through team structures, provision of detailed information on the firm's performance, and other means promote this goal: to get the workers to identify with the welfare of their employer to such a degree that they harness all their energies toward achieving the employer's organizational goals. Whether this interpretation is right or wrong, an understanding of management's motivation is crucial to a full understanding of recent workplace innovations.

Union goals likewise need to be studied and scrutinized carefully. Grattan addresses union goals from the viewpoint of the democratization of the workplace. Sheahan lists ten comprehensive union goals in union-management partnerships. Other authors list a number of traditional and new goals for unions. In particular, Lazes and Savage note new goals centering on the creation of new jobs through adroit management of the firm. All goals mentioned have clearly played a role in individual instances. My own interpretation, as noted earlier in this introduction, is that the *main* goal of unions shifted from earlier programs to later ones. From democracy, human dignity, and the like, the emphasis shifted to job security for the workers and organizational survival and security for the union.

An additional major question raised by the readings is the degree to which workplace experimentation inherently involves the decentralization of collective bargaining and work site practices and, consequently, how unions can devolve to "enterprise unions" which are incapable of protecting standards across company or plant lines. Michael Piore has expressed the dilemma well:

> The basic problem is "company unionism" even "plant unionism." The reality of economic life is that individual companies and, these days, the component productive units within large companies, are in competition with each other for business. The new model pulls the workers and management of a single unit into collaboration with each other in the competition and, thus, pits them against other productive units, posing a major threat to the solidarity of the union, whose membership spans numerous productive units, as an organization. Competitive pressure was, of course, also present in the old model, but it was contained by the rule structure: the rules were designed to insure a certain uniformity among practices across an industry, and they were relatively easy to police. The problem is to find some mechanisms for controlling competition in the new model. (Piore 1991, 399–400)

In this volume, Eaton raises this issue as a critical one for unions to consider. It is also at the heart of Downs's and of Parker and Slaughter's critiques of union-management partnerships. Sheahan likewise addresses the topic. The issue could hardly be more fundamental: how can the labor movement's traditional goal of "taking wages and conditions out of competition" be maintained by unions altering both at a very decentralized level in an effort to improve the employer's economic performance? Or should this traditional goal be abandoned?

Proponents of the new union-management partnerships need to pay very close attention to how solidarity (which Jack Metzgar has called the "non-negotiable moral minimum" of unionism) can be maintained under their proposals. This issue is too complicated to enter into here, but it is worth noting that previous major historical examples of unions devoting themselves to employer competitiveness have been confined to skilled craft unions operating in localized markets (for example, the construction trades), unions operating in domestically highly unionized but extremely competitive industries with relatively low wages and much foreign competition (for example, the garment industry), or isolated examples in other industries such as gainsharing plans like the Scanlon Plan or various worker buyout Employee Stock Ownership Plans (ESOP). The building trades unions had other methods of taking wages and conditions out of competition: apprenticeships and total organization of the relevant workforce. The garment industry unions have found themselves unable to take wages and conditions out of competition, so they have historically helped their own employers individually, but the strategy was a very defensive one adapted to a position of relative powerlessness. It has not been able to win either high wages or job security for workers employed in this industry.

Some answers have been put forward to this question. For example, perhaps wage competition can be controlled by as much centralized or patterned bargaining as possible. However, contingent forms of pay as advocated for the new workplace would undercut such wage uniformity. The stickier question of working conditions may be addressed by efforts to keep the competition limited to ways to work smarter, not work harder or more dangerously. Perhaps, although this begs the question of how unions will actually be able to keep the competitive pressures channeled in only this way. Lacking truly centralized bargaining, or even strongly patterned bargaining anymore in most industries, U.S. unions also lack centralized political and legislative regulation of employer behavior. This makes the decentralized "enterprise unionism" dilemma especially acute.

Of course, alternative methods to address the same dilemma must also be carefully assessed. Can a "solidarity" alternative based on militancy and internationalism actually work? Most industrial relations scholars don't even consider such an alternative realistic enough to be worth consideration. Alternatives based on a traditional left program involving class solidarity and truly international union alliances need to address the same global competitive pressures as do the programs based on union-management partnerships.

A final issue raised by these chapters is how unions must reorganize themselves internally to deal effectively with the workplace of the future. Lazes and Savage devote much of their chapter to discussion of the many ways unions must transform themselves if they are to carry out the authors' program. At the opposite end of the debate, both Downs and Parker and Slaughter present their prescriptions for union reorganization and reorientation. Sheahan and Ngai offer glimpses of unions operating in new programs. Eaton briefly notes some new models of unionism that writers have begun to develop.

The varying views put forward grow out of the differences of opinion expressed earlier on fundamental issues of union purpose and function. The one thing all these authors seem to agree on is that unions need to change the way they have functioned in the past. And some items, like greater mobilization of the membership and more internal democratic involvement, seem to be on everyone's agenda.

BIBLIOGRAPHY

Adams, Roy J. 1995. *Industrial Relations Under Liberal Democracy.* Columbia: University of South Carolina Press.
AFL-CIO Committee on the Evolution of Work. 1983. *The Future of Work.* Wash-

ington, D.C.: American Federation of Labor-Congress of Industrial Organizations.

———. 1985. *The Changing Situation of Workers and Their Unions*. Washington, D.C.: American Federation of Labor-Congress of Industrial Organizations.

———. 1994. *The New American Workplace: A Labor Perspective*. Washington, D.C.: American Federation of Labor-Congress of Industrial Organizations.

AFL-CIO Human Resources Development Institute. 1994. *Changing Work: A Union Guide to Workplace Change*. Washington, D.C.: American Federation of Labor-Congress of Industrial Organizations.

AFL-CIO News. 1984. " 'Worklife' Plans Given Mixed Reviews." 28 January, 6.

Alexander, Kenneth D. 1987. "The Worker, the Union, and the Democratic Workplace." *American Journal of Economics and Sociology* 46: 387–97.

Appelbaum, Eileen, and Rosemary Batt. 1994. *The New American Workplace: Transforming Work Systems in the United States*. Ithaca, N.Y.: ILR Press.

Babson, Steve. 1995. *Lean Work: Empowerment and Exploitation in the Global Auto Industry*. Detroit: Wayne State University Press.

Banks, Andy, and Jack Metzgar. 1989. "Participating in Management: Union Organizing on a New Terrain." *Labor Research Review* 14 (Fall): 5–55.

Bluestone, Barry, and Irving Bluestone. 1992. *Negotiating the Future: A Labor Perspective on American Business*. New York: Basic Books.

Bluestone, Barry, and Bennett Harrison. 1982. *The Deindustrialization of America: Plant Closings, Community Abandonment, and the Dismantling of Basic Industry*. New York: Basic Books.

Braverman, Harry. 1974. *Labor and Monopoly Capital: The Degradation of Work in the Twentieth Century*. New York: Monthly Review Press.

CAW-Canada Research Group in CAMI. 1993. *The CAMI Report: Lean Production in a Unionized Auto Plant*. Willowdale, Ont.: Canadian Auto Workers.

Clawson, Dan. 1980. *Bureaucracy and the Labor Process: The Transformation of U.S. Industry, 1860–1920*. New York: Monthly Review Press.

Cohen-Rosenthal, Edward, and Cynthia E. Burton. 1993. *Mutual Gains: A Guide to Union-Management Cooperation*. Ithaca, N.Y.: ILR Press.

Cooke, William N. 1990. *Labor-Management Cooperation: New Partnerships, or Going in Circles?* Kalamazoo, Mich.: W. E. Upjohn Institute for Employment Research.

Craypo, Charles. 1990. "The Decline in Union Bargaining Power." In *U.S. Labor Relations, 1945–1989: Accommodation and Conflict,* ed. Bruce Nissen. New York: Garland Publishing.

Craypo, Charles, and Bruce Nissen, eds. 1993. *Grand Designs: The Impact of Corporate Strategies on Workers, Unions, and Communities*. Ithaca, N.Y.: ILR Press.

Donohue, Thomas. 1982. "Labor Looks at Quality of Worklife Programs." Paper read at Labor Relations Research Center of the University of Massachusetts at Amherst, Jan. 7. Reprinted in U.S. Department of Labor Bureau of Labor-Management Relations and Cooperative Programs. 1984. *Labor-Management Cooperation: Perspectives from the Labor Movement*. Washington, D.C.

Eaton, Adrienne. 1995. "New Production Techniques, Employee Involvement and Unions." *Labor Studies Journal* 20, no. 3 (Fall): 19–41.

Eaton, Adrienne, and Paula Voos. 1992. "Unions and Contemporary Innovations in Work Organization, Compensation, and Employee Participation." In

31

Unions and Economic Competitiveness, ed. Lawrence Mishel and Paula B. Voos. Armonk, N.Y.: M.E. Sharpe.

Edwards, Richard. 1979. *Contested Terrain: The Transformation of the Workplace in the Twentieth Century.* New York: Basic Books.

Freeman, Richard. 1992. "Is Declining Unionization in the U.S. Good, Bad, or Irrelevant?" In *Unions and Economic Competitiveness,* ed. Lawrence Mishel and Paula B. Voos. Armonk, N.Y.: M.E. Sharpe.

Glyn, Andrew, et al. 1990. "The Rise and Fall of the Golden Age." In *The Golden Age of Capitalism: Reinterpreting the Postwar Experience,* ed. Stephen A. Marglin and Juliet Schor. Oxford: Clarendon Press.

Goldfield, Michael. 1987. *The Decline of Organized Labor in the United States.* Chicago: University of Chicago Press.

Graham, Laurie. 1995. *On the Line at Subaru-Isuzu: The Japanese Model and the American Worker.* Ithaca, N.Y.: ILR Press.

Grenier, Guillermo J. 1988. *Inhuman Relations: Quality Circles and Anti-Unionism in American Industry.* Philadelphia: Temple University Press.

Hammer, Michael, and James Champy. 1993. *Reengineering the Corporation: A Manifesto for Business Revolution.* New York: Harper Business.

Harrison, Bennett, and Barry Bluestone. 1988. *The Great U-Turn: Corporate Restructuring and the Polarizing of America.* New York: Basic Books.

Heckscher, Charles C. 1988. *The New Unionism: Employee Involvement in the Changing Corporation.* New York: Basic Books.

Kelley, Maryellen R., and Bennett Harrison. 1992. "Unions, Technology, and Labor-Management Cooperation." In *Unions and Economic Competitiveness,* ed. Lawrence Mishel and Paula B. Voos. Armonk, N.Y.: M.E. Sharpe.

Klein, Janice A., and David Wanger. 1985. "The Legal Setting for the Emergence of the Union Avoidance Strategy." In *Challenges and Choices Facing American Labor,* ed. Thomas A. Kochan. Cambridge, Mass.: MIT Press.

Klingel, Sally, and Ann Martin. 1988. *A Fighting Chance: New Strategies to Save Jobs and Reduce Costs.* Ithaca, N.Y.: ILR Press.

Knauss, Keith, and Michael Matuszak. 1994. "An Anti-Union Corporate Culture and Quality Improvement Programs." *Labor Studies Journal* 19, no. 3 (Fall): 21–39.

Kochan, Thomas, Harry Katz, and Robert McKersie. 1986. *The Transformation of American Industrial Relations.* New York: Basic Books.

———. 1994. *The Transformation of American Industrial Relations.* 1986; rpt. with new introduction. Ithaca, N.Y.: ILR Press.

Kochan, Thomas, Harry C. Katz, and Nancy R. Mower. 1984. *Worker Participation and American Unions: Threat or Opportunity?* Kalamazoo, Mich.: W.E. Upjohn Institute for Employment Research.

Lever-Tracy, C. 1990. "Fordism Transformed? Employee Involvement and Workplace Industrial Relations at Ford." *Journal of Industrial Relations* 32 (June): 179–96.

Marshall, Ray. 1992. "Work Organization, Unions, and Economic Performance." In *Unions and Economic Competitiveness,* ed. Lawrence Mishel and Paula B. Voos. Armonk, N.Y.: M.E. Sharpe.

Moody, Kim. 1988. *An Injury to All.* New York: Verso.

Nadworny, Milton. 1955. *Scientific Management and the Unions, 1900–1932.* Cambridge, Mass.: Harvard University Press.

Nelson, Daniel. 1975. *Managers and Workers: Origins of the New Factory System in the United States, 1880–1920.* Madison: University of Wisconsin Press.

Parker, Mike. 1985. *Inside the Circle: A Union Guide to QWL.* Boston: South End Press.

Parker, Mike, and Jane Slaughter. 1988. *Choosing Sides: Unions and the Team Concept.* Boston: South End Press.

———. 1992. *A Union Strategy Guide for Labor-Management Participation Programs.* Detroit: Labor Notes.

———. 1994. *Working Smart: A Union Guide to Participation Programs and Reengineering.* Detroit: Labor Notes.

Piore, Michael. 1991. "The Future of Unions." In *The State of the Unions,* ed. George Strauss, Daniel G. Gallagher, and Jack Fiorito. Madison, Wisc.: Industrial Relations Research Association.

Piore, Michael J., and Charles F. Sabel. 1984. *The Second Industrial Divide: Possibilities for Prosperity.* New York: Basic Books.

Rinehart, James. 1984. "Appropriating Workers' Knowledge: Quality Control Circles at a General Motors Plant." *Studies in Political Economy* 14 (Summer): 75–97.

Rosow, Jerome, ed. 1986. *Teamwork.* New York: Pergamon Press.

Special Task Force to the Secretary of Health, Education, and Welfare. 1973. *Work in America.* Cambridge, Mass.: MIT Press.

Taylor, Samuel. 1947. *Scientific Management.* New York: Harper and Row.

Uchitelle, Louis. 1993. "Union Leaders Fight for a Place in the President's Workplace of the Future." *New York Times,* 8 August, 32.

U.S. Department of Labor. 1984. Bureau of Labor-Management Relations and Cooperative Programs. *Labor-Management Cooperation: Perspectives from the Labor Movement.* Washington, D.C.: U.S. Department of Labor.

———. 1994. Office of the American Workplace. *Road to High-Performance Workplaces.* Washington, D.C.: U.S. Department of Labor.

Verma, Anil, and Robert B. McKersie. 1987. "Employee Involvement: The Implications of Noninvolvement by Unions." *Industrial and Labor Relations Review* 40, no. 4 (July): 556–68.

Wells, Donald M. 1987. *Empty Promises: Quality of Working Life Programs and the Labor Movement.* New York: Monthly Review Press.

———. 1991. "What Kind of Unionism is Consistent with the New Model of Human Resource Management?" Kingston, Ont.: Queen's University at Kingston School of Industrial Relations.

Whyte, William F., et al. 1983. *Worker Participation and Ownership.* Ithaca, N.Y.: ILR Press.

II

THE AFL-CIO
ON
WORKPLACE
REORGANIZATION

2

THE NEW AMERICAN WORKPLACE: A LABOR PERSPECTIVE

AFL-CIO COMMITTEE ON THE EVOLUTION OF WORK (1994)

The system of work organization that has been dominant in the United States for the better part of this century does not respect basic worker rights, recognize worker potential, and in consequence does not satisfy basic worker needs. Workers have formed unions to change that system through their collective power.

Unions have sought as a first priority to take wages and working conditions out of competition and negotiate labor standards that temper the market with human values. But that has never been the limit of the labor movement's agenda for workplace change. The labor movement also has sought, since our earliest days, to improve the quality of worklife, to enhance the opportunities for workers to develop their skills and participate in the workplace, and to create industrial democracy—long before these approaches become fashionable. But unions have largely been kept outside of the management process by an environment and legal framework in which it has been deemed to be management's sole prerogative to decide what work is done, when, how, where, and by whom.

Over the past decade, however, an increasing number of employers have concluded that this system of work organization no longer serves their needs and have been open to joining with the unions representing their workers to create partnerships to transform the work system. These partnerships have succeeded in creating new work systems which alter in the most basic was the manner in which work is organized, businesses are managed, and labor and management treat each other.

By restructuring jobs and work processes, these new systems fundamentally redesign the role and responsibilities of workers and managers so as to provide new levels of *individual worker participation* in the workplace. At the same time, these new partnerships restructure decision-making processes from the shop floor to corporate headquarters so as to enhance *collective worker representation*.

In the industries and workplaces in which circumstances have permitted shifting to these new systems of work organization, the change has served to increase worker opportunities, to enhance job satisfaction and to bring greater democracy to the workplace. At the same time, the new work systems have demonstrated their capacity to improve the quality, and reduce the cost, of the goods and services being produced. The new systems thus have succeeded in achieving work organizations which at one and the same time are more democratic and more productive. Therein lies the source of their power and their legitimacy.

The inherent obstacles to any such fundamental change in work organization and labor-management relations are formidable. As a result, the pace of change has been slow. Despite all the talk about the workplace of the future, the truth is that the great majority of workers continue to labor in traditional work systems in which they are expected to do what they are told, and only what they are told.

Left to its own devices, management is most likely to continue to adhere to the old ways of organizing work or to pursue work reorganizations which leave the underlying power relationships unchanged and which offer the appearance, but not the substance, or genuine worker involvement. It is unlikely in the extreme that such management-led programs of employee involvement or "empowerment" can sustain themselves over the long term. It is certain that such systems cannot meet the full range of needs of working men and women.

It is thus incumbent upon unions to take the initiative in stimulating, sustaining and institutionalizing a new system of work organization based upon full and equal labor-management partnerships. Such a system presupposes, of course, partners prepared to deal with each other as equals in an atmosphere of mutual recognition and respect. For unions, offering such recognition and respect has never been difficult; finding employers willing to reciprocate has been the rub. The time has come for labor and management to surmount past enmities and forge the kind of partnerships which can generate more productive, democratic and humane systems of work.

Partnerships formed along these lines will not, as some would have it, substitute "cooperation" for "adversarialism" in labor-management relations. It is the nature of things that workers and the employers for whom they work do have some conflicting as well as common interests. But the fact that such conflicts do, will and must exist does not mean that labor-management relations must be antagonistic. In the partnerships we envision, such conflicts of interest can be worked out in an atmosphere of mutual respect, trust and good will.

For many labor leaders, entering into new partnerships and designing new work systems is a venture into uncharted terrain. The AFL-CIO can play an important role in bringing together from across industries and across countries the experiences and insights of trade unionists who have been involved in restructuring work systems. And the Federation should help unions—and employers—identify paths to success so that the labor movement can become more and more active in spreading the new model of work organization.

In the sections of this report that follow, we describe the old system of work organization and its multiple failures and outline the role unions have played historically in seeking to change that system. We then articulate in detail our vision of a model work system and the type of labor-management partnerships required to create and sustain such systems. We also discuss the obstacles to such change and the role that labor unions and the AFL-CIO can play in stimulating new systems of work organization.

THE DOMINANT SYSTEM OF WORK ORGANIZATION

From factories to offices, from the largest government agencies to the smallest of businesses, and from the most complex and technical professions to those jobs considered to be the least skilled, for most of this century work in the United States has been organized around four core principles.

First, and most fundamentally, the basic premise of the dominant system of work organization is that the tasks of thinking, planning and decision making are best done by an elite corps of thinkers, planners, and deciders. This corps goes by a variety of names: owners, executives, managers, industrial engineers, policy planners, etc. Some are directly employed by the enterprise using their services; others are outside consultants retained because the enterprise has not developed the skills of its own employees. But regardless of label, their fundamental role is to centralize knowledge about, and control over, the workplace. Frederick Winslow Taylor, who is generally regarded as the father of this system of work organization, put it this way:

The managers assume . . . the burden of gathering together all of the traditional knowledge which in the past has been processed by the workmen and then of classifying, tabulating, and reducing this knowledge to rules, laws and formulae. . . . All possible brain work should be removed from the shop and centered in the planning and laying-out department.

From this starting premise it follows, second, that the role of the individual worker is to perform assigned tasks in an assigned manner. This is accomplished in the archetypal work organization through a high degree of specialization and division of labor. Each worker is given a small, fixed task to be repetitively performed. The worker requires and develops great expertise in that task, rather than broader knowledge or more general skills. In Taylor's words:

The most prominent single element in modern scientific management is the task idea. The work of every workman is fully planned out by the management . . . and each man receives in most cases complete written instructions, describing in detail the task which he is to accomplish, as well as the means to be used in doing the work. This task specifies not only what is to be done, but how it is to be done and the exact time allowed for doing it.

Third, this work organization requires a hierarchical, regimented environment in which layers of management are created to assure that the decisions of the thinkers and planners are correctly executed. Through this chain of command decisions are communicated to workers who are instructed in what they are expected to do and then are closely monitored to make sure that the workers do as they are told. When questions or problems arise, those issues are carried up the chain of command to the appropriate level of supervision for a decision. The model is, in essence, the military model of command and control.

Fourth and finally, in this dominant method of work organization workers are seen by management and owners as merely another "input" into the production process—a disposable commodity like any other production input. The employer's aim is to get the maximum output from the worker at the lowest possible cost.

Because this dominant system of work organization is, by now, so well entrenched, it is sometimes assumed to be inherent in the very nature of things. It is useful to recall, therefore, that there was a time in our history when workers were extensively trained in their crafts and were expected to—and did, in fact—exercise judgment, discretion, and initiative on the job. Indeed, the earliest forms of trade unionism in this country were those which sought to protect the interest of craft workers and their crafts.

In a handful of industries—most notably the unionized sector of the construction industry—the craft system remains a strong and vital form of work organization. That system depends upon apprenticeship programs which develop highly skilled craft workers. Those workers acquire a thorough understanding of the total operation, work processes and work organization and then apply their craft skills to the job at hand independently, with minimal direction and only distant and intermittent managerial control. Similar apprenticeship programs have been successfully implemented in various industrial settings to produce skilled workers for those industries. But in the main the current system of work organization is, as Professors Ray Marshall and Marc Tucker put it, designed to "reduc[e] control that skilled workers had over production and transfer . . . that control to management."

This work system is, of course, most commonly associated with the assembly line and mass production. But these same principles have in fact formed the basis for work organization in most of our industries.

Banks and insurance companies, for example, have created what amounts to paper assembly lines in which an application, a payment, or a claim is passed from station to station so that workers in each area can successively perform a quite limited function until the transaction is fully processed. This mode of operation assures that thinking is centralized, work is specialized, and control is all-encompassing.

Most government agencies have adopted a similar approach. Any citizen who has ever gone to apply for a driver's license has experienced first-hand the traditional work system as the individual goes from station to station in what feels like a never-ending series of small steps forward.

That quintessential modern American institution—the fast-food restaurant—provides another example. The very point of the work system is to assure that each outlet throughout the country produces standardized results by giving each worker a narrowly defined task to be repetitively performed in a manner decreed by management.

Even employers which offer professional services—and which cannot take away all discretion from their professional employees—nonetheless have often adopted structures which maximize centralized control. School teachers, for example, report to department heads who report to principals who report to assistant superintendents and so on; somewhere up the chain of command decisions are made as to what will be taught with what materials at what times and by whom.

There can be no doubt, then, that what we have called the dominant system of work organization is deeply ingrained in American society.

THE SYSTEM'S IMPACT ON WORKERS AND THEIR EFFORTS AT REFORM

By reason of its premises, the dominant American model of work organization does not meet the needs of working men and women.

To begin with, that model drives down wages and working conditions by requiring workers to compete with each other for jobs. Those who are most desperate, and thus least demanding, effectively establish the labor standards for all. Those "market" standards do not necessarily include decent wages and benefits, safe and healthful workplaces, job security, protection of worker rights or humane working conditions.

At the same time, the dominant system of work organization denies workers the sense of satisfaction and fulfillment that work can and should provide. Human beings want a sense of meaning and accomplishment in work—a feeling of a productive job well done. But the dominant system of work organization does not allow workers the opportunity to make a full contribution because it denies workers the freedom to use their capacities and skills fully, let alone to further develop those capacities and skills.

Workers form labor organizations in order to realize the collective power through which these conditions can be changed and the workers' needs advanced. Unions have proceeded to do so on several fronts.

As a first priority, unions have sought to take wages and working conditions out of competition. Unions thus endeavor to negotiate labor standards that reflect human values and that meet working peoples' basic human needs. And unions seek to extend those standards to all competitors in an industry by organizing the workers throughout the industry.

The contributions of the labor movement in this regard are many and profound. The labor movement and the collective bargaining process, for example, established the wage standards which enabled workers to enter the ranks of the middle class. The labor movement, too, created our system of employer-paid health insurance and private pensions. And the labor movement introduced such innovations as protections from discharge without just cause; guarantees of occupational safety and health; and limits on the number of hours workers can be required to work.

As important as these advances have been, this has never been the limit of the labor movement's agenda for workplace change. For example, unions have always sought to secure for the workers they represent opportunities for advancement and growth. Thus, unions have pressed for training programs designed not merely to enable workers to do their existing jobs better but to develop skills and abilities so that they can handle new and more challenging jobs. Indeed, in many industries unions have negotiated for joint control over—as well as adequate funding for—such training programs. Unions have resisted efforts at deskilling work. And unions have negotiated for promotional systems and lines of progression which afford workers the opportunity to advance to more skilled, more responsible jobs over the course of their careers based on their seniority.

More generally, from its earliest days, the labor movement has sought to improve the quality of worklife, enhance the opportunities for workers to participate in the workplace, and to create industrial democracy. But unions have been largely frustrated in their efforts to achieve these ends by a system that assumes that workers have no capacity for responsible decision making. Thus, management has maintained that workers, through their unions, have no business "meddling" in any decisions that go beyond the scope of wages, hours, and working conditions.

Management has been fortified in its position by the framework of our labor laws. The National Labor Relations Act generally does not extend to workers who exercise supervisory responsibility or decision making authority. Moreover, the NLRA requires bargaining only with respect to "wages, hours, and other terms and conditions of employment"—a phrase which the Supreme Court has narrowly interpreted to exclude a range of issues of critical importance to workers.

It is not surprising, then, that the typical collective bargaining agreement, at the employer's insistence, contains a "management's rights clause" which reserves to management a set of specific prerogatives—including generally the prerogative to determine the type of work to be performed and the "methods, manner processes and means" of performance—and also reserves to management a residual right to control all matters not specifically covered by the contract. To protect workers in this framework, unions must negotiate specific contractual provisions to restrict what would otherwise be a management prerogative under the management rights clause. As problems or abuses are uncovered, or new needs articulated, provisions are, of necessity, added to the contract. Over time, agreements can grow to hundreds of pages with each new provision designed to provide workers with protection in response to some management action.

Through this process, unions have succeeded to a large extent in humanizing the traditional system of organizing work and, through a series of contractual provisions, in exercising joint control over a range of workplace issues. But in most cases unions have been unable to displace management's authority to dictate the system of work organization, and thus the traditional system has remained largely intact.

The Dominant System of Work Organization under Challenge

The prevailing system of work organization, to repeat, has never fully served the interests of workers. If anything, from the perspective of workers, its failings have grown more acute over time. As unions have succeeded in improving labor standards so that workers can enjoy decent wages and working conditions—and as workers have seen quality sacrificed to the bottom line profits—the demand of workers for more responsibility and opportunity to contribute has grown more insistent.

For many years, the prevailing work system—as modified through the

43

contributions of the labor movement—did meet the needs of employers. But that work system always has been plagued by inefficiencies. Its operation requires a large number of "indirect workers"—consultants, planners, thinkers, decision makers, schedulers, supervisors, managers, inspectors and the like—who add substantially to the cost of the product or service. The hierarchical, bureaucratic structure of the traditional work system is, moreover, incapable of responding quickly to new needs or desires in the marketplace. And by setting rigid norms of standardized performance, the traditional work system has always had the perverse effect of stifling worker initiative and discretionary effort.

The adverse effects on cost and quality of these inherent limitations are now being felt by owners and managers.

For the private sector, the failings of the traditional system of work organization have contributed to the much-discussed competitiveness crisis. In a world in which technology and capital are mobile, multi-national corporations have discovered that they can produce standardized goods and even some services cheaper by transferring the dominant work system—which does not, after all, require large numbers of highly skilled workers—to the newly industrializing nations. Businesses operating in this country cannot compete on the basis of price with goods produced by exploiting the cheap labor available in those countries (although too many American employers have made a misguided, and ultimately self-defeating effort to drive down labor costs in an effort to meet the competition of these nations). At the same time, many American employers have discovered that they suffer a substantial disadvantage when competing with the high quality goods and services produced in advanced industrialized nations which have implemented more modern systems to work organization.

The public sector faces analogous pressures. The traditional work system too often fails to produce services of the quality or quantity demanded by the public. The refusal of taxpayers to provide the resources needed to fund the services governments are created to provide causes further deterioration in the quality of such services. The effort of some public employers to respond to the resulting fiscal crisis by "privatizing" or contracting out the work of government to exploit cheap labor only serves to exacerbate the situation.

DEFINING A NEW MODEL OF WORK ORGANIZATION

Efforts to reform the traditional system of work organization are almost as old as the system itself. But, until recently, those efforts for the most part have not addressed the fundamentals of the problem and consequently have failed to take root.

By and large, "work reform" has amounted to little more than attempts to make workers "feel good" and work harder. Such reforms have come and gone with little impact and less value.

In the 1970s a number of unions sought to go further through negotiated quality of worklife programs. These QWL programs ultimately proved disappointing for workers and employers alike. But their failure highlighted the necessity of more fundamental change. The conjunction of these experiences and the crisis in the traditional system of work organizations served to move a number of employers to join with their unions to alter in the most basic ways the manner in which work is organized, businesses are managed, and labor and management deal with each other.

These new work systems have received greatest attention in the industrial sector. There such systems have helped save parts of the automotive and steel industries, and have improved the performance of major manufacturers such as Xerox and Corning Glass. Examples of new approaches to work organization can also be found in a variety of service industries and in a number of public agencies as well. Indeed the federal government is currently embarked on perhaps the largest experiment to create a new partnership as part of its effort to "reinvent" government.

From all of these experiences and experiments, it is possible to discern five principles which together define a model for a new system of work organization.

• First, the model begins by rejecting the traditional dichotomy between thinking and doing, conception and execution. Workers—the individuals who actually do what it is the organization is doing—are in the best position to decide how their work can most efficiently and effectively be accomplished. Such decisions are never final but should be constantly revisited through an ongoing process in which change is the only constant. This process requires a fundamental redistribution of decision-making authority from management to teams of workers. These workers must not only be given such decision-making authority but also must be afforded the opportunity to develop and refine analytic and problem-solving skills so that they will be able to make the best possible work decisions.

• Second, in the new model, jobs are redesigned to include a greater variety of skills and tasks and, more importantly, greater responsibility for the ultimate output of the organization. Workers are organized into work groups (or teams); the workers learn not merely a particular task but an understanding of the overall process of producing a good or service and often they are trained to perform the various functions required for that process. Moreover, workers are given the authority, and the training, to exercise discretion, judgment and creativity on the job. Workers' ingenuity is viewed as a key to success; workers are free to do the right thing, rather than being compelled to do the prescribed thing.

• Third, this new model of work organization substitutes for the traditional, multi-layered, hierarchy a flatter management structure. At the same time, the role of the manager is transformed since the aim of the system is no longer to assure that workers do prescribed tasks, in prescribed manners, for prescribed intervals. In this less authoritarian work culture, the aim is to enable workers to be self-managers who are responsible for their own performance, and the work teams are often self-managed with responsibility for scheduling work, ordering materials, hiring workers and the like. The foreman is replaced by a team leader; the role is to lead rather than mandate.

• Fourth, the new model goes beyond the workplace level to insist that workers, through their unions, are entitled to a decision-making role at all levels of the enterprise. Just as workers understand best how the work should be organized, workers—through their representatives—have expertise to contribute to strategic decisions as well including, for example, about what new technologies should be acquired or about what changes to make in products or services. Moreover, as stakeholders in the enterprise, workers have a vital interest in the strategic decisions which ultimately determine how much work will be done, where and by whom. Because workers have long-term ties to their jobs, they bring a long-term perspective and can be counted on to promote policies designed to insure that businesses have long-term futures and can provide long-term employment at decent wages. Thus, in this new model such strategic decisions are to be jointly made by workers—acting through their unions—and the other stakeholders.

• Fifth and finally, the new model of work organization calls for the rewards realized from transforming the work organization to be distributed on equitable terms agreed upon through negotiations between labor and management. This means, in the first instance, a negotiated agreement to protect income and employment security to the maximum extent possible. Of equal importance it means a negotiated agreement to compensate workers fairly for their enhanced contribution to the success of the organization. This may be achieved through increases in base wages or, in other cases, through agreements providing for some form of supplementary contingent compensation (such as gain sharing, profit sharing, stock ownership or the like). What is most important is that the worker's share is not set as an act of grace by managers and owners but is the product of a negotiated agreement between the employer and the union representing the workers.

These five principles form an integrated whole—a vision of a new system of work organization. They combine *individual participation* through restructured work processes and redesigned jobs, with *collective representation,* through restructured decision-making processes from the shop floor to corporate headquarters. The aim of this approach is to achieve work organizations which at one and the same are more productive *and* more democratic. Therein lies the source of its legitimacy and its power.

Of course, in the real world the model we have outlined, and the principles we have articulated, must be adapted and applied to the specifics of particular industries and particular companies. There is no one right approach to redistributing decision-making authority, redesigning jobs, or to achieving any of the other principles we have outlined. Indeed, an approach that works well in one industry or one enterprise may be ill-suited for other industries or enterprises. One of the geniuses of the collective bargaining system is precisely its ability to find particular solutions in response to the needs and desires of a group of workers and an employer in a specific industry and market. Thus, in the real world no two applications of the model we have drawn is—or can be—precisely the same.

It is also true that changing the system of work organization is, of necessity, an evolutionary process. Different employers and unions always will be at differing stages in the process of change. And even the most advanced work systems, like any system designed by mere mortals, will fall short of the ideal and can be expected to evolve further over time.

Thus, the model we have outlined is just that—a model—and not a description of any single work organization. Nonetheless, this model needs to be carefully distinguished from alternatives that are much discussed—with much hype—today.

Many employers continue to pursue variations on the old theme of making workers "feel good" in order to make them work harder. Other employers are bent on "involving" employer-selected groups of workers, as "teams" (or committees or quality circles) in decisions by management. Still other employers are enamored of top-down efforts to "empower" workers to achieve ends that management sets for those workers.

To a greater or lesser extent, such programs may generate more individual worker participation than exists in traditional work organizations. But these "feel-good" programs and these "involvement" or "empowerment" programs which emanate from management and which stop at the task level cannot, by definition, provide workers with any real power over their working lives. Rather, these systems subordinate workers to management in essentially the time-tested ways that have proved wanting. At bottom, then, these programs are a mirage: they offer the appearance, but not the substance, of genuine worker involvement.

More than forty years ago Peter Drucker recognized that:

> Management with its political authority over the enterprise can neither be avoided nor be transformed, no matter what political, economic, or legal arrangements are tried. At the same time, this governmental authority can never put the welfare of its subjects first; it cannot be legitimate.

. . . The only way to make the government of the enterprise legitimate is through a counter power which represents the members against the government while at the same time itself forming a part of this government. The *union* is thus the institutional expression of the basic political tension of the enterprise.

For the reasons Drucker articulated, it is unlikely in the extreme that management-led programs of employee involvement or "empowerment" can sustain themselves over the long term. It is certain that such systems cannot meet the needs of working men and women.

TOWARDS A NEW LABOR-MANAGEMENT PARTNERSHIP

The new systems of work organization require, as a first requisite, that workers be represented by free and independent labor unions which they control. The very presence of such a union fundamentally changes the nature of the workplace and the relationship between the individual worker and the employer. Trade union representation removes fear from the workplace and assures workers the protection that is essential if they are to feel free to express their views and to fully participate in workplace decisions. And such unions provide the vehicle through which workers can be represented with respect to decisions that affect their work lives.

What President Clinton said about the federal sector in creating his National Partnership Council is equally true of all sectors: "the involvement by federal government employees and their unions is essential . . . Only by changing the nature of Federal Labor-Management relations will it be possible to design and implement comprehensive change."

The specifics of the partnership required to affect workplace change will, of course, vary from case to case and will, no doubt, evolve over time. Nonetheless, some general guidelines can be articulated to define the kind of partnerships which the labor movement must seek to make the new model of work organization a reality.

First, we seek partnerships based on mutual recognition and respect. Most employers have never come to terms with the legitimacy—let alone the necessity—of work organization or trade union representation; many employers actively seek to oust unions from "their" workplaces. A partnership requires management to accept and respect the union's right to represent the right of workers in units already organized and equally to accept and respect the right of workers in unorganized units to join a union. An employer who extends one hand to the union while at the same time using the other hand to do everything possible to prevent the organization of other employees of the enterprise—as so many employers do—lacks a full commitment to partnership.

Second, and in accordance with the concept of recognition and respect, the partnerships we seek must be based on the collective bargaining relationship. Changes in work organizations must be mutually agreed to—and not unilaterally imposed—and must be structured so as to assure the union's ability to bargain collectively on behalf of the workers it represents on an ongoing basis. The union must likewise be recognized as the representative of the workers in the process of implementing agreed-upon changes and such changes cannot become an occasion for undermining worker support of their union.

Third, the partnerships must be founded on the principle of equality. In concrete terms, this means that unions and management must have an equal role in the development and implementation of new work systems, including equal representation and control over any bodies created as part of the work reorganization. Similarly, unions and management must have equal access to any information relevant to the issues they are jointly addressing.

Fourth, the partnerships must be dedicated to advancing certain agreed-upon goals reflecting the parties' mutual interests. Partnerships will not succeed if management's ultimate aim is to speed up work or to eliminate workers' jobs. Rather, successful partnerships must be dedicated to achieving both more productive and more democratic and humane workplaces.

Partnerships formed along these lines will not, as some would have it, substitute "cooperation" for "adversarialism" in labor-management relations. It is the nature of things that workers and the employers for which they work do have some conflicting as well as common interests. That is most obviously true with respect to distributive issues: workers want as large a share of the economic pie as possible consistent with the need of the firm to attract and retain capital while capital wants as large a share of the pie as possible consistent with the need of the firm to attract and retain labor. A labor organization that fails to recognize the divergent interests of workers and employers is not worthy of the name.

To be sure, the conflicts between organized labor, as the representative of workers, and management, as the representative of capital, can be more apparent than real. Numerous recent examples exist in which labor and management have been able to resolve disagreements in ways that redound to the mutual gain of all. But at other times, the conflicts are quite real and unions cannot give ground on worker interests for some abstract notion of "cooperation" as an end in itself.

The fact that such conflicts do, will and must exist does not mean, however, that labor-management relations must be *antagonistic*. In the partnerships we envision, such conflicts of interest can be worked out in an atmosphere of mutual respect, trust and good will.

THE OBSTACLES TO CHANGE

The obstacles to change of such a fundamental nature are many and complex. Change is always threatening and resistance to change deep-seated; it is one part of human nature to fear the unknown. This is especially true of change of the magnitude required to create a system of work organization and labor-management relations that is different in kind from its predecessor.

Workers and supervisors alike understandably fear that they will not be able to meet the demands of the new work system. Supervisors are accustomed to giving, or at least conveying, orders and workers to complying; both have concerns about how they will adapt to a world in which workers are expected to think and supervisors to lead.

Executives and owners have at least equal concerns. In the new system of work organization, management must give up much of the authoritarian control it now exercises. That hardly comes easily and cannot come without anxiety.

At the same time, American management is accustomed to being judged in the capital markets by short-term results, and to focusing on financial transactions which yield an immediate return. Yet the road to the new workplace requires investments to strengthen and develop the workforce and the company—investments which offer a payback over the long term.

For union leaders, too, change can be threatening. Many unions have been accustomed, of necessity, to rally workers in response—and often in opposition—to decisions made by management. A new work system will require union leaders to assume new and quite different roles and responsibilities for which they have not always been well prepared.

Adding to the difficulty is the distrust between labor and management which is endemic to the old system. The traditional system of work organization is built on mutual distrust; that is why it relies on a hierarchical command-and-control regime. The new system, in contrast, can function effectively only if those deep suspicions are dispelled and replaced by mutual respect.

It is not surprising, then, that the pace of change has been slow. Despite all the talk of the workplace of the future in the academy, the press, and the halls of government, the fact is that new work systems are exceedingly rare. The overwhelming majority of workplaces are still operated along traditional lines and likely will continue that way for a very long time. The vast majority of American workers are still expected to check their brains—and their rights—at the door to their workplace and to do only as they are told while on the job.

Moreover, huge numbers of American workers continue to be treated or forced to live in ways that defy basic standards of decency. For example, there are today over 14 million full-time, year-round workers—one fifth of all such workers—whose earnings are below the poverty level for a family of four. There are 17 million full-time workers who lack health insurance and 39 million full-time workers without pension coverage.

And each year, at least 60,000 workers die from occupational injuries or diseases, another 60,000 workers are permanently disabled, 6,000,000 workers are injured in occupational accidents and upwards of 25,000,000 workers are exposed to toxic chemicals in their workplaces.

In a report issued in 1990, the Commission on the Skills of the American Workforce, chaired by former Secretaries of Labor William Brock and Ray Marshall, found that less than 5% of all employers have created what the Commission termed a "high performance work organization." The non-partisan Work in America Institute estimates that the figure is even lower, and that such organizations as exist are concentrated in Fortune 1000 Companies. Furthermore, according to the Institute, there is not a single large company in the United States which has been able to institutionalize its own best practices throughout its own organization.

Everything we know, then, shows that resistance to change is embedded in the culture of virtually every workplace.

THE ROLE OF ORGANIZED LABOR IN DRIVING
TOWARDS WORKPLACE CHANGE

If the 1980s taught one lesson, it is that the task of management is too important to be left to owners and their managers. Owners come and go with changes in stock prices; their interest is to make money now, come what may. But the national interest lies in building strong and stable enterprises, not in short-run efforts to titillate the stock market watchers.

We also have learned that the first victims of poor management are not the managers themselves nor those who hire the managers and provide the capital. Rather the victims are first and foremost workers who do not enjoy the benefit of golden (or even tin) parachutes to cushion their fall. Workers invest themselves in their jobs, their employers and their industries.

We know, too, that the whole course of human history teaches that power is rarely freely surrendered by those who enjoy it. Left to its own devices, management is most likely to continue to adhere to the old ways and, when confronting a crisis, to seek low-wage solutions or to propose work reorganizations which leave the underlying power relationships unchanged.

All of this requires unions to take the initiative in pushing towards our vision of a new model of work organization based upon equal partnerships. Although unions have, in the past, found it necessary to agree to management's demand that certain of its prerogatives remain inviolate, the fact remains that, as Neil Chamberlain observed more than forty-five years ago in his book, *The Union Challenge to Management Control:*

It is difficult to reach any conclusion but that union officials . . . have generally adopted a flexible and evolutionary approach to the question [of management rights] with the consequence that into any statements acknowledging and accepting the existence of managerial prerogatives must be read the addendum "as of this moment."

The moment has come for unions to insist upon the right of workers to participate in shaping the work system under which they labor and to participate in the decisions that affect their working lives.

Unions have an equally important role to play in assuring that workplace change plants strong roots. Unions provide a check on managers and owners who waver in their commitment to the new work order or who seek to revert to old ways. Unions assure continuity, especially in the face of management turnover. And union-represented workers will have more confidence in and commitment to new work systems developed jointly with their union. As Professors Eaton and Voos have put it, "[i]ronically, it is precisely because unionized workers can say 'no' as a group that they can also collectively say 'yes' to such efforts. This potentially provides participative and cooperative programs with a greater degree of legitimacy."

Perhaps most important of all, the new work systems require unions to embrace an expanded agenda and to assume an expanded role as the representative of workers in the full range of management decisions in which those workers are interested. In a variety of forums, at various levels within the enterprise and the industry in which the enterprise is located, unions must represent these workers not only with respect to their terms and conditions of employment but also with respect to the strategic decisions that shape their working lives. As Professors Kochan and Wever have written, in the workplace of the future unions must make sure that "worker interests are adequately taken into account in the economic and political choices that shape employment practices. . . . The absence of a strong labor voice in these choices creates a vacuum that allows employers to focus on other, more powerful constraints while worker interests become merely residual considerations."

THE ROLE OF THE AFL-CIO

For many labor leaders, entering into new partnerships and designing new work systems is a venture into uncharted terrain. They must learn a new lingo, new concepts, and sometimes new skills. More importantly, they must find ways to separate wheat from chaff, programs of substance that hold the promise of advancing workers' interests from programs that are without real value but are slickly packaged and peddled by hustlers.

In this area, we in the AFL-CIO have, regrettably, been insufficiently attentive to the needs of trade union leaders who are on the firing lines.

Not enough has been done to provide them with useful information, instruction or assistance. The result has been that outside of national bargaining relationships, unions have often not been well enough prepared to respond to management's proposals, let alone to take the initiative in seeking the reorganization of work.

A number of national unions have formulated policy statements and training materials for their locals. Others are in the process of doing so and of developing training programs for union negotiators. The AFL-CIO can play an important role in bringing together from across industries and even across countries the experiences and insights of trade unionists who have been involved in restructuring work systems. The Federation should become a resource to which unions can turn for information about what has been tried—successfully and unsuccessfully—in this area. The Federation should take the initiative in convening conferences and seminars for trade unionists to share their experiences, to teach and learn from each other. Most important, the Federation should help unions identify paths to success so that the labor movement can become more and more active in pushing our vision of a new model of work organization.

Conclusion: The Nation at a Crossroad

Many employers today proceed as if reducing what is paid to workers for the goods and services they produce is the way to economic prosperity. The result is that since 1979, the real average weekly earnings of non-supervisory workers have declined by more than 20%, and the number of full-time workers earning below the poverty level has increased by 35%. The number of workers without health insurance or pension coverage likewise has grown. And the number of contingent workers—workers who generally lack any permanent attachment to an employer but who work on a temporary or contract basis—has increased by upwards of 33%.

This low-wage strategy leads inevitably to a continuing degradation of the standard of living of the average working person and to greater levels of inequality. Social unrest and political instability are all but certain to follow.

In contrast, many other industrialized nations are pursuing a labor policy premised on the proposition that prosperity is best achieved when highly-skilled workers produce high quality goods and services for which they are well paid. That approach holds the promise of greater equity and an improving worker standard of living.

The new model of work organization which we have described is one component of this "high-skill, high-wage" approach. The benefits of that model should neither be overstated nor overlooked. New systems of work organization cannot substitute for sound macro-economic policies, sound industrial policy, fair and balanced trade policies, or the other essential determinants of economic health. But within the context of a strong national program for economic renewal, labor-management partnerships which transform work organization can make an important contribution.

The time has thus come for our government to provide a legal framework and a climate which encourage partnerships between labor and management based on mutual recognition and respect which will improve the lives of workers and increase the level and quality of production. The time likewise has come for American management to abandon its quest for a union-free environment and to recognize the right of workers to representation through unions of their own choosing. And the time has come for labor and management to surmount past enmities and to forge the kind of partnerships which can generate more productive, humane and democratic systems of work organization.

III

OVERVIEW
AND
CONTEXT

3

THE NEW AMERICAN WORKPLACE: BIG DEAL OR TOO LITTLE, TOO LATE?

ADRIENNE E. EATON

Introduction

In the spring of 1994, a Rutgers labor center librarian mentioned to me that a student had asked him for a copy of the new AFL-CIO report on "cooperative programs"; did I know anything about it? "Sure," I replied, "it's very exciting, very important. Our library should definitely have a copy." A few days later I took one of the several copies of *The New American Workplace* I had received in the mail and handed it to the librarian. His disappointment was palpable; "Is this it? I was expecting something much bigger."[1]

In the course of writing this paper, I've thought about this comment several times. In the librarian's sense of "big" as in size, it's not a very "big" document. In a different sense of "big" as in "important," however, it is indeed big. I seek in this essay to "evaluate" *The New American Workplace* (NAW) report in a number of ways. First, I will discuss two ways in which the report is important, with a particular emphasis on the events the report has set in motion or at least supported. Second, I will compare the AFL-CIO's position on new work systems and workplace change with that of other labor federations, looking for similarities and differences; strengths and weaknesses. Finally, and emerging in part from the comparisons, I will raise a number of issues that are not discussed in the report but provide essential context to it.

IMPORTANCE AND IMPLEMENTATION

One way in which the report is "big" is common knowledge among even casual observers of the U.S. labor movement; that is, it reflects at long last a degree of agreement among the international union affiliates as to how to approach workplace change.[2] The U.S. labor movement has long been and is, in fact and in many ways, still divided over appropriate reactions to workplace change.

Ten years ago this division was evident in the range of opinions issued by national unions or their leaders (U.S. Department of Labor 1984; see also Wever 1995, 214, on earlier efforts by the Committee on the Evolution of Work (CEW) to issue a report on these issues). National union policies now appear to have reached a degree of convergence with much less outright opposition to programs (Szapiro 1996); this convergence makes the NAW report possible. At the same time, considerable opposition remains within the leadership of each national union (see for example Keefe and Boroff 1994, 332, 338, on CWA). Diversity of opinion is almost certainly even greater at the local level.

A second and perhaps more consequential measure of the report's importance is its implementation. Unlike the earlier Committee on the Evolution of Work report issued in 1985, the NAW report does not emphasize action steps. Yet it doesn't ignore action either. The report identifies four roles for the federation (15) all of which serve the goal of diffusing union experience with workplace change: bringing together trade unionists to share "experiences and insights"; serving as a resource for information about successful and unsuccessful cases; "convening conferences and seminars"; and helping to "identify paths to success."

Several constituent units of the AFL-CIO have taken (or been assigned) responsibility for implementation. Not surprisingly, given the emphasis on the need for education, the George Meany Center has had a major role thus far (for a full description of the organizations mentioned in this essay, see the glossary below). The center now regularly offers courses on new forms of work organization, employee involvement and total quality management, though this development was already under way at the time the report was issued. In addition, the Meany Center and a four-union consortium (Amalgamated Clothing and Textile Workers, Communications Workers of American, United Automobile Workers, United Steelworkers) developed and conducted a four-week in-depth course on workplace change for union staffers in 1995 under a grant from the U.S. Department of Labor. That project is now being extended to a wider range of unions. Meany Center staff have also been involved in a series of meetings of representatives of the University and College Labor Education Association (UCLEA) Worker Participation Task Force (a long-standing institution of which the author is current chair), the Industrial Union Department's (IUD) Technology Working Group, the AFL-CIO Education and Research Departments, Human Resource Development Institute (HRDI), and the Work and Technology Institute (WTI), the purpose of which has been to craft a national educational strategy to support workplace change and new work systems that *build unions* (Baugh 1995).

The other institutions just listed have similarly been increasing their efforts in this area. In late 1994, HRDI issued an extensive guide for unions dealing with new work systems entitled "Changing Work: A Union Guide to Workplace Change," a project that emerged directly out of the NAW report (Baugh 1994). The guide presents an overview of the changes taking place in work, the forces driving that change, and lots of specific ideas and "tools" for local unions confronting change.

IUD and WTI staff have also begun cooperating on a number of related projects including one that will identify national policies on and structures for aiding locals to deal with new work systems. WTI staff have assembled six case studies of both failed and successful union involvement in work reorganization and new labor relations (Kaminsky et al. 1996). The case studies will be used in, among other things, the Meany Center curriculum. The IUD's Technology Working Group has continued to be a productive forum for networking on these issues, particularly for manufacturing sector unions; WTI recently organized a counterpart for the service sector.

Most recently, the new leadership at the AFL-CIO announced plans for the creation of a Center for Workplace Democracy within a new Corporate Affairs Department. While the center will be important in giving the goals of the NAW an institutional home in the federation, its success will depend on striking an appropriate balance between the ongoing but relatively decentralized activities described above and centralized coordination and support. In this, the AFL-CIO is a johnny-come-lately to the question of federation policy and structures for dealing with new work systems. Indeed, the AFL-CIO's efforts may best be evaluated in comparison with other labor federations in developed industrial countries. It is to that comparison that we now turn.

INTERNATIONAL COMPARISONS

It is clear that national labor movements, probably throughout the world but certainly in the developed industrial world, are confronting many of the same problems related to technological change and work reorganization, a fact to which the NAW report alludes.[3] While there are many similarities in the issues, there appear to be some important differences in the reactions of various national labor movements. Placing the AFL-CIO document in this broader context should improve any attempt to evaluate it.

The countries described below were not randomly selected. I chose the two English-speaking countries in part because I knew I would be able to read the policy statements from the respective federations and partly because there are some similarities (although many differences) in the respective industrial relations systems. Canada is omitted because the peak federations there have, as of yet, issued no policy statements on these issues.[4] I chose Sweden and Denmark because of the common wisdom that the Scandinavian countries are light-years ahead of most others in creating humane work (and left out Norway because of space limitations). I chose Germany because of its advanced forms of union and worker involvement in decision making and the impression that its labor movement is relatively strong and operating in a relatively strong economy.

In each case I have attempted, given the information available, to describe both the context and history of the labor movement's reaction to workplace change at the macro level, as well as current policy. I have tried to highlight differences and similarities across cases with attention in particular to a policy's treatment (or lack thereof) of Taylorism, contingent or casual work, women and minorities, safety and health, the environment, and training and skill formation.

Britain. The British labor movement has been struggling with appropriate policies vis-à-vis workplace change for several decades. The "modern era" of experimentation with post-Taylorist forms of work actually began in Britain in the 1950s. Throughout the 1960s and 70s, change in the organization of work came through productivity bargaining but had more to do with increasing efficiency by breaking down craft lines than increasing worker autonomy or participation (Batstone 1989, 101). At roughly the same time, the trade unions began to develop a program to increase industrial democracy principally in the form of worker representatives on boards of directors. While labor's interest in this form of participation waned, in the 1980s British employers began to push for forms of employee involvement similar to those then being tried in the United States.

In 1989, Batstone reported that the "approach of the unions to job redesign and new forms of employee involvement has been somewhat ambivalent." On the one hand, like their counterparts in the United States, they were suspicious of management motives and concerned about the potential to undermine unions. On the other hand, if participative programs were "not used in this way, and as long as members receive[d] adequate compensation, unions [were] generally prepared to accept these changes." Batstone also notes that labor identified the need for improved representation at strategic levels of decision making (108).

The Trades Union Congress (TUC), the British equivalent to the AFL-CIO, published a policy document on workplace change in 1994. The document, entitled "Human Resource Management: A Trade Union Response" is longer and somewhat broader than the NAW but is reactive to management initiatives rather than proactive in putting forth a labor vision.[5] In this respect, the NAW report is a superior document. With a few exceptions throughout the almost fifty-page document, there is little mention of what workers want out of their work; there is no mention let alone critique of Taylorism. However, if Batstone's observation regarding the incomplete Taylorization of work in Britain still holds, it makes sense that the labor movement would be more defensive of work systems that already provide autonomy and control. This defensiveness is also not surprising given the decline in unionization and the precarious state of the labor movement in the British economy and political system.

Besides the general tone of the document, there are several other interesting differences. Health and safety concerns are linked to work organization in the TUC document but, consistent with the overall tone, it is the dangers and decline in standards that are the focus. While problems such as increased hazards resulting from the increased production and peer pressures that may accompany teamwork should not be underestimated, there is no mention of the potential of improving health through forms of work organization that provide autonomy and control. This linkage between work organization and health is an important theme in the Scandinavian "work environment" tradition (see for example Karasek and Theorell 1990).

In addition, an entire section is devoted to equal opportunity and diversity issues. Particularly interesting are the concerns raised around possible discrimination in new pay schemes and team work. The potential for women and minorities to be disadvantaged in team work has been ignored in much, though not all (see for example Gottfried and Graham 1993), of the academic literature in the United States as well as the union commentary. Relatedly, the "increased casualisation" of the workforce, including temporary, part-time, and homework (30), is at least briefly mentioned.

Finally, the area of training and development receives a great deal of attention. Here, the TUC articulates both a union and worker vision of good training and development policies and programs.

In sum, the British labor movement resembles the United States in its fundamental ambivalence toward workplace change but also in its definition of what the threats and opportunities are. As the TUC report indicates, the issues remain "highly contentious" (48). Finally, in fairness to the TUC, the conclusion makes clear that this report is "the beginning of a process rather than the end." In particular and as with the NAW report, courses and further "briefings" were to emerge out the report.

61

Australia. The Australian Council of Trades Union (ACTU) has been at the center of workplace change efforts since 1983 when it reached an agreement (accord) with the newly elected Australian Labor Party to reorganize the industrial relations system (Matthews 1994). The full scope of this reorganization is beyond the scope of this essay. Among other things, the accord loosened a system based on centralized, arbitrated industry-wide wage settlements and pushed collective bargaining down to the enterprise level.[6] This enabled and encouraged a simultaneous increase in the scope of bargaining including over the organization of work. Further, ACTU has taken a strongly proactive view of its role in work restructuring, advocating leadership by the labor movement in humanizing work.

ACTU's visions of appropriate work organization can be found in a document (1991b) that places work reorganization into the broader context of skill development, education reform, and labor market policy: "Work organization in the future must overturn the Taylorist approaches of the past. Workers must be provided with greater scope for individual initiative, judgement and responsibility for quality outcomes. The nature of management and supervision must change from an emphasis on control and direction to one which co-ordinates and develops the skills and potential of all employees" (204).

A second document (n.d.) summarizes an in-depth review of workplace change efforts and identifies future needs. Despite differences in context, Australia and the United States have many issues in common. The report notes, as does the NAW, that "the best results are where a union is strong and active, and management has a commitment to change" (1). Similarly, the report identifies a need for education, training, materials, and resources to help union representatives, particularly at the enterprise level. On the down side, the report notes a tendency for management to "achieve what they couldn't obtain in normal negotiations" through joint processes (3) and that "with a few exceptions . . . consultants were not seen in a very good light by most unions" (6), both commonplaces in the U.S. scene as well.

The report indicates that the new, joint activities had "considerably increased workload[s] for union [representatives]," a difficulty also being encountered in the United States. On the plus side, ACTU finds that joint activities are "generat[ing] new, and more union activists" (4). Further, the results demonstrate "far more involvement with the members in the workplace" and "an increase in both the number and ability of shop stewards" (6). Both of these comments identify the possibility for workplace change programs to be union-building, something that is underemphasized in the NAW. It should be kept in mind, however, that because of the centralized nature of the labor relations system in Australia, unions have been quite underdeveloped at the workplace in the past.

One of the reasons given for the strengthening of the shop steward system was a huge increase in training. Indeed, the report identifies a growing number of "awards" (contracts) with provisions for steward training. Interestingly, the sense was that union representatives overall were far better prepared than management to deal with workplace change, and many top union officials suggested that more joint training was needed "to get managements up to the level of their shop stewards" (6). This is a clear difference with the American scene where there appears to be a great deal of joint training, of varying quality, but little union-only training. The Australian report further notes that government funding of workplace change specialists has been extremely helpful.

The report concludes with a series of suggestions for ACTU. Several of these relate to diffusion within the labor movement and parallel those in the AFL-CIO report: holding regular regional or local meetings and seminars where unionists could share experiences; publication of a newsletter presenting case studies; and more training on work redesign for staff representatives, stewards, and workplace change advisors. Others perhaps should have been included in the NAW: briefing consultants on labor strategy and policy; creating a list of acceptable consultants and guidelines for their work; and seeking a "higher public profile through the media about . . . the very positive role played by the union movement [in workplace change]" (8).

One last point is worth noting. ACTU's stance toward workplace change includes a special statement dealing with women workers. The "Workplace Change and Women Policy" (1991) essentially recognizes the need to address job segregation and related pay equity issues when work is reorganized. It notes the need to take into account women's family responsibilities and pattern of part-time work as well as the importance of ensuring women's involvement in work redesign.

Germany. As in the other cases, the German labor movement's approach to workplace change reflects that country's industrial relations system and institutions. The German system has long featured worker representation at the strategic level through elected representatives to boards of directors and at the enterprise level through works councils. Unions achieve protections for workers primarily through centralized industry-wide collective bargaining and through legislation. The majority of worker representatives to works councils are union members, but their role is not as "union representatives" per se.

The German labor movement's interest in reforming Taylorist work systems is longstanding, though perhaps not as long or as deep as the Swedes' (or other Scandinavian labor movements). One of the earliest institutional expressions of this interest was the German Trade Unions Federation's (DGB) support for the 1974 passage of the Humanization of Work (HOW) Program, a government-funded organization that supported research, pilot projects, and dissemination of information about new work

63

systems. As early as 1977, however, the DGB criticized HOW for being more interested in employer-initiated "rationalization" schemes and insufficiently attentive to union concerns such as skill development and worker autonomy and control (International Institute for Labour Studies 1977).

While labor was able to obtain more influence within the HOW and to shape the criteria used to evaluate projects, observers appear to disagree on the importance of HOW as a vehicle for union impact on work organization. Düll (1989, 200), for instance, argues that the HOW program provides no direct input for the labor movement into work organization decisions. Wever (1995, 66), on the other hand, notes that unions have applied for and received funding from the program and that HOW projects have been key to implementing labor's upskilling strategy (more on which below). In any case, in 1990 HOW was transmuted into a much broader "work and technology" program (Altmann 1992, 364).

Different pictures are also offered regarding the role of works councils in work reorganization.[7] While works councils have the legal right to veto work reorganization under certain circumstances, some observers argue that, in practice, they have exercised little influence (Düll 1989; Levie and Sandberg 1991). This view is disputed by Wever's descriptions of cases of intense involvement by works councils in work reorganization including some supported, politically and technically, by unions (1995, 77–89). The DGB itself, as well as its member unions, provides training and consulting assistance to works councils around new technology and work organization issues (Wever 1995, 104).

Observers of the German scene argue that DGB policy in this area is largely reflective of the most important affiliate, the metalworker's union, IG Metall.[8] IG Metall addressed its vision of work organization in a 1984 document focused on the implications of technological change: "Alternative work organization . . . must be pursued in order to reverse existing forms of the extreme division of labor and hierarchization of work and to reduce health strain and stress" (8). The emphasis in the report is on action: "The goal is a mass movement—Work and Technology for People" (9). A limited number of specific issues receive detailed attention including training policy, healthy work, and computerized monitoring and control. The report addresses the concerns of women and foreign workers briefly, arguing that these groups tend to be underserved by employer retraining initiatives. Finally, the report criticizes the government's technology policy for being underfocused on worker concerns and contends that the HOW program is too small and "detached" from other technology programs.

More recently, German unions have found themselves, like their counterparts elsewhere, reacting to various management-initiated programs. Mueller-Jentsch and Sperling (1995) suggest that the unions were initially "sceptical and disapproving" and "argued that quality circles were primarily motivated by plans for further rationalization and work intensification and . . . aimed at evading and undermining works councils' rights of participation" (19). (Observers of the American scene will recognize these concerns as virtually identical to those of U.S. unions, substituting "union" for "works council.") However, German works councils have been aggressive in negotiating "the arrangements for the introduction and implementation of quality circles" in a way that protects both worker and council rights (Mueller and Sperling 1995, 19). German companies, like their counterparts elsewhere, have lately moved on to total quality management and forms of "team work." At least in regards to the latter, IG Metall has backed off somewhat from initial skepticism (Mueller-Jentsch and Sperling 1995, 21). All of these workplace issues are placing pressures on German's centralized collective bargaining institutions.

Comparisons between the 1984 IG Metall document and the NAW are difficult. Most obviously, the document dates from a different time period than the others reviewed here. Further, IG Metall is neither a true peak federation nor an industrial union; its concerns are focused on a sector or set of related industries. Like the others, it is a reflection of the context in which it was written. As such, its focus is on the effects of technological change on employment and working conditions. On the other hand, it does critique Taylorism, though not by name. Interestingly, Jürgens (1995, 296) indicates that the dominant approach to reforming Taylorism in Germany in the 1980s was a supply-side approach: "a new model emerged which aimed at the increased employment of skilled workers—*Facharbeiter*—in direct production tasks." The expectation was that if sufficient numbers of young people went through apprenticeship programs and then to work in manufacturing, employers would be stimulated to raise the level of automation and of "high technology work structures" to make use of their talents (and pay for their high wages). Jürgens's account suggests that this strategy has not worked out so well in practice.[9]

Finally, it appears that while work reorganization and new forms of direct participation are important issues, the German labor movement, particularly at the higher levels, has been focused on other matters. These include the *Facharbeiter* strategy discussed above but also the continuing battles over the length of the work week, and perhaps more important, the integration of the East and integration with Europe. In particular, labor has been focused on the extension of the institutions of codetermination into the East and, eventually, the rest of Europe. Internally, there appears to be a consensus that those institutions remain sound.

Sweden. Like the Germans, the Swedish labor movement has historically relied on centralized bargaining and legislation as its chief strategies for protecting workers. These approaches are also evident in the Swedish trade unions' approach to questions of workplace democracy and work organization. The first wave of activity and interest in workplace change in Sweden dates to the mid to late 1960s (Rehnström and Gustavsen 1989; Cole 1989). It began with the enthusiastic embrace, at least in theory if not practice, by representatives of labor and management of the sociotechnical systems approach emerging out of Britain via Norway. Labor's interest in work organization was piqued by growing signals of union member discontent with the organization of work, particularly in the form of a wildcat strike in an iron mine in 1969 (Cole 1989, 256–57). In 1971, the primary blue-collar labor federation, the Swedish Confederation of Trade Unions (LO), committed itself to pursuing worker participation at all levels of management (258). This included demands for new forms of work organization based in critiques of Taylorism and cautious interest in autonomous work groups (Sandberg et al. 1992, 75–76; Cole 1989, 259).

Joint labor-management interest eventually became institutionalized in a number of organizations and projects. The URAF (Development Council for Cooperation Issues Working Group for Research) was a joint organization of the Swedish Employers Association (SAF) and two major union federations, the Swedish Trade Union Confederaton (LO) and the Swedish Confederation of Professional Employees (TCO); its focus was on the development and evaluation of experiments in workplace democracy, typically involving autonomous work groups. A second joint organization, the Delegation Programs, focused its efforts in the broadly defined Swedish public sector (Rehnström and Gustavsen 1989, 90–91; Cole 1989, 263). A third set of experiments were initiated unilaterally by management under the guidance of the SAF's technical department ("New Factories project") (Rehnström and Gustavsen 1989, 91; Cole 1989, 257; Sandberg et al. 1992, 65–71).

The URAF and the Delegation Programs ended in the mid-1970s as both parties shifted directions. The SAF focused its efforts on increasing productivity and efficiency through the New Factories projects and resisted labor's demand for new forms of direct and indirect participation (Sandberg et al. 1992, 60). The labor movement in turn directed its resources toward legislation requiring participation at all levels. This goal was achieved in 1976 with the passage, despite employer opposition, of the Codetermination Act or Medbestammandelagen (MBL). The law required management to negotiate over most managerial decisions, including decisions over work organization. In turn, the act was intended to be implemented through central and local codetermination agreements by labor and management that would specify the procedures through which unions and workers would participate in decisions.

By 1982, the primary actors in the private sector, the SAF, LO, and PTK (the private sector salaried workers' federation) reached an "Agreement on Efficiency and Participation," still in effect today. As its title indicates, its focus is on the goals of each party: "efficiency" for the employer, and good, secure jobs for workers. Emphasis is placed on processes for reaching those goals, including the rights of workers to participate in planning and designing work and rights to information. Interestingly, the agreement includes a call "for companies to finance the union selection and training of internal and external 'employee consultants' to advance union participation in evaluating the company's financial and economic situation" (Cole 1989, 259–60). As planned, similar agreements were subsequently developed first at the branch and then the local level (Sandberg et al. 1992, 54). Unfortunately, research on the experience of several local unions in Sweden in reorganizing work (Levie and Sandberg 1991; Sandberg et al. 1992) as well as Hancké's (1993) description of both the development and the demise of the Volvo Uddevalla plant (where small teams built entire cars) indicate that sufficient resources may not be going to the local level. While this problem likely resulted from the parties' historic reliance on centralized institutions, the ongoing collapse of centralized bargaining in Sweden is no doubt altering relations among local and national union bodies.[10]

In 1991, the LO, through its Committee on Democracy and Participation, again addressed the issue of the broader "meaning" of work (Swedish Trade Union Confederation 1991a). While many things are noteworthy about this report, three stand out. One is a strong emphasis on class differences in noneconomic outcomes of work; the report argues that while centralized collective bargaining and economic policy (now in decline) have reduced income differences, sharp differences between blue- and white-collar workers remain in levels of "freedom, responsibility and authority, a stimulating working life and knowledge" as well as in health (2). These issues at work are then linked to powerlessness, apathy, ill health, and other undesirable outcomes outside of work. Thus, the authors state at one point that "the report is mainly about the meaning of life" broadly. Finally, the report is one of the more self-critical; it makes clear that one obstacle to the reform of work is the many "traditionalists" in the labor movement itself.

It should be noted that despite struggles between labor and management over levels and types of participation, the Swedes built jointly supported institutions committed to work reorganization. In 1976, the Swedish parliament created the Working Life Research Center as a government-funded but labor-management-directed research organization. In addition, the Codetermination Act set up the Work Environment Fund financed through a payroll tax on employers. The fund provides resources to a wide variety of programs, including projects dealing with technological change and work reorganization. A central concern of the efforts to reform work in Sweden has been the impact on worker health.

What lessons are there in the Swedish case for the American labor movement? First it is clear that the labor movement has long had a deep interest in broader participation in management decision making. While wildcat strikes (Lordstown in the U.S. context) sparked interest in work reorganization in both countries, that interest did not become widespread in the U.S. labor movement until recently. However, at the time when the Swedes began articulating demands in this area, the institution of collective bargaining was considerably narrower in scope, although more centralized then in the United States. Thus, some of the demands for negotiation rights and access to information were for things that U.S. unions already enjoyed. Clearly, however, both the demands and the rights won went far beyond those in the United States. At the same, the tension in Sweden among the different levels and forms of participation has some U.S. parallels.

One noteworthy difference in the Swedish institutional context is the centralization on the employer side. In fact, Cole argues that the lack of central employer institutions largely explains the lag in what he terms "small group activity" in the United States. Though labor and management in Sweden have substantial differences in opinion about appropriate forms of work and degrees of participation, the existence of an organized employer federation made possible the creation of joint institutions and successful extraction of governmental resources to support research and development work. The lack of institutions for interemployer cooperation and resultant heightened competition in the United States might well be added to NAW's list of "obstacles to change."

Denmark. The Danish industrial relations system resembles the Swedish system particularly in the centralization of collective bargaining through peak federations or associations. Similarly, the Danish Confederation of Trade Unions (LO) maintains a close relationship with the Social Democratic party, and many gains for workers are achieved through legislation. At the firm level, Danish law (since 1973) calls for employee representation on company boards of directors and (since 1947), joint "cooperation committees" with equal representation from management and workers. Cooperation committees "have the right to exercise co-determination in formulating principles which govern the organization of local work" (IDE International Research Group 1981, 74). As with the other Scandinavian countries, experiments in work reorganization, including "semi-autonomous work groups," have been ongoing for over two decades.

In 1991, the Danish LO adopted a strategy around work reorganization entitled, in English, "Work and Development." The LO's approach is not a policy as such but rather a set of principles. The overall "strategy" emphasizes a simultaneous improvement in jobs, product quality, and the environment. As such, it is probably the broadest vision of those reviewed here, with changes in work embedded in wider social concerns and the labor movement positioned as a defender of those concerns. The "vision" articulated includes the following objectives: "to increase the respect paid to the individual; to create better conditions in which protection of the environment, contents of work, pay, quality and good service are at the centre; to provide meaningful work for all; to enable people to develop their own resources while at the same time respecting the interests of the community; to create the type of democracy in which everyone would want to participate" (Danish Confederation of Trade Unions, 8).

The LO makes an explicit distinction between its vision, with its broader focus on democracy and the environment, and what the Danish, like the British, call human resource management. Human resource management, they argue, is focused exclusively on linking human resources and competitiveness.

The concept includes ten areas for "action," some more interesting than others: developing a personnel policy, new leadership roles, organization of work, offensive cooperation, pride in product and quality, active seats on the board of directors, development and training, increased value in the job, personal development, and the working environment and the external environment. Two themes running through most of these areas are increased participation in decision making and the need to improve the intrinsic rewards of work. The term "offensive cooperation" is intriguing but not fully defined. Perhaps the most unique thing about the Danes position is its constant emphasis on a healthy environment. Finally, the Work and Development report references a "Tool Kit," a set of information materials and analytical tools to be used at workplaces to develop a personnel policy (16).

What the NAW Doesn't Say

A quick review makes clear that relative to other federation policies, the NAW is strong on its critique of Taylorism and the need for labor-management partnerships and weak on related issues such as training and skill formation, safety and health and the environment, and the position of underrepresented groups including women, minorities, and contingent or casual workers. This last group presents a particular challenge for U.S. unions and their current representational strategies as well as for labor movements throughout the world. Indeed, it could be argued that there are a number of alternative "new American workplaces" not discussed in the AFL-CIO document: workplaces to which workers have no permanent attachment or in which workers work only part-time; workers' homes; or, most troubling, no workplace whatsoever.[11] The growth in all of these types of work, as well as in "nonwork" are well-documented. While these issues were clearly beyond the scope of the CEW's efforts, they constitute an important context for the other workplace envisioned in the report, particularly if they are viewed as alternatives by employers (Schurman and Eaton 1996).

Beyond these gaps, the comparisons raise a couple of additional, interrelated issues. One tension common to all the cases concerns the relationship between indirect and often centralized forms of worker participation (for example, collective bargaining) and direct, usually local forms. As one worker participation scholar observes, "In principle . . . participation in various forms and on various levels of the company is complementary. In practice, there has often been strong union infighting over the priorities they should assign to the different forms of participation" (Cole 1989, 261). Clearly, the NAW addresses both strategic or corporate level participation in the form of labor-management "partnerships" and the workplace level in the form of local union and worker participation in work reorganization as well as new forms of work that increase decision-making opportunities; these are explicitly viewed as two sides of the same coin. In practice, unions in the United States have tended to prefer traditional collective bargaining and newer partnerships (indirect participation) over direct participation by members (Schurman and Eaton 1996).

Indeed, direct participation appears to challenge the practice of collective bargaining, or at least centralized bargaining, throughout the developed world and especially in the United States, where it remains the central institution through which unions represent their members. Most of the well-publicized experiments in both work reorganization and labor-management partnerships in the United States are in industries with centralized bargaining relationships, particularly auto, telecommunications, and steel. Yet, as Harry Katz suggests, experimentation with new forms of work pushes the focus if not the actual practice of collective bargaining to lower and lower levels of organization (1993). As is clear from the countries reviewed above, decentralization in bargaining is an international phenomena. Since the modern wave of experiments with work reorganization and worker participation began in the United States in the 1970s, it is primarily local unions or local representatives that have negotiated the particulars and had to live with their consequences. Further, participation itself, either offline through participation groups or online through work teams (see Rubinstein, Bennett, and Kochan 1993 for this distinction), provides formal venues for "bargaining" between managers and workers at the lowest level.

The difficulties in providing resources to those levels and allowing them autonomy while still preserving solidarity and unity as well as the ability to set corporate or industry-wide standards constituted a central challenge to U.S. unions. This challenge is basically ignored in the NAW report. U.S. unions are not alone in finding it difficult to shift resources and authority to lower levels. They need to be confident of local leader and member commitment to both workers' and the union's institutional interests. At the same time, many of the new relationships have the potential to drift toward enterprise unionism. This is particularly a problem in the U.S. system, which lacks centralized wage-setting through industry-wide bargaining or government standards. Here the United States must learn from the Australian, German, and Swedish cases while recognizing that their central institutions are also in decline or under challenge.

All of these observations suggest the need for a more fundamental reconsideration of representational strategies and structures. Both the "New American Workplace" envisioned by the AFL-CIO and those other "new" workplaces mentioned above may require alternate models of unionism, or even multiple alternate models. One thing noticeably absent from the NAW report, though its absence is no surprise, is an understanding of the extent to which industrial unionism in the United States has accommodated, indeed shaped itself around the Taylorist organization of work. As one group of Swedes observed, "American industrial unionism has come to presuppose Taylorism" (Sandberg et al. 1992, 227). It is this intimate tie that makes it particularly difficult for U.S. unions to embrace change and that ultimately explains why the NAW was a long time in coming.

While it is beyond the scope of this essay to describe what new forms of unionism might be appropriate, the comparative perspective does suggest a need for a focus outside the firm, perhaps to a more political unionism (see Merrill 1996 for a discussion of the importance of labor's political strategies to its firm and workplace strategies).[12] Indeed, a final observation arising out of the other cases and related to the point about centralized bargaining is the importance of legal rights and of social partnerships with employers and government in supporting change efforts. First, it would appear that legal rights to participation are helpful or even necessary but not sufficient to ensure a union role in workplace change. Second, Labor or Social Democratic parties-in-power are the underpinning of those rights as well as guarantor's of broader labor participation in the economic and political spheres. Indeed, if the labor movements in some countries have had to develop institutions at the workplace level to cope with workplace change, the U.S. labor movement may ultimately need to develop an institutional expression at the highest level to provide the security and support it needs to participate in change.

CONCLUSIONS

What then to conclude about the "New American Workplace"? There is a case to be made for the NAW being a "big deal": it signals a new level of agreement on issues of central importance to the labor movement and it has stimulated a number of resource-building activities. Its strongest point is its description and critique of Taylorism, which is, after all, its focus.

At the same time, there is a case to be made for "too little, too late." The report itself, in what might be the only self-critical portion, confesses that the federation has been "insufficiently attentive to the needs of trade union leaders who are on the firing lines." Much has happened at the local level while the federation has remained silent and withheld resources. Further, in comparison to most of the federation statements reviewed in this paper, it is thin on context and related issues. These problems, however, result largely from the strongly decentralized power structure in the U.S. labor movement, especially in comparison to most of the others discussed in this paper.

In the end, we must also ask what role a federation policy statement really can play. In the European countries, especially Sweden, and in Australia, the statements of the peak federations are crucial because those institutions engage in bargaining with both the state and employer organizations. In that sense, it matters less what the AFL-CIO says. Nonetheless, a national union federation has a role to play in the diffusion of workplace change. It is important that the AFL-CIO, as the most public wing and "voice" of labor in the United States, as a lead institution for some parts of the labor movement and as a holder of resources, address these issues. In particular, it is important that its leaders appear to have thought about what work means to individual workers beyond pay and benefits. The creation of the new Center for Workplace Democracy is a particularly hopeful signal in this regard. In the end, then, the best cliché for the NAW may be "better late than never."

GLOSSARY OF ORGANIZATIONS

GEORGE MEANY CENTER—The labor education arm of the AFL-CIO located in Silver Spring, Maryland. Classes are open to officers, representatives, and staff of AFL-CIO affiliates.

HUMAN RESOURCE DEVELOPMENT INSTITUTE—The employment and training arm of the AFL-CIO, it provides "technical assistance to unions and labor-management partnerships nationwide to help them develop a) high performance workplace systems . . . , b) training programs for workers dislocated due to defense downsizing and workforce cutbacks, and c) customized training programs for young people, workers with disabilities and employees with literacy needs."

INDUSTRIAL UNION DEPARTMENT—One of the trade and industrial departments of the AFL-CIO.

UNIVERSITY AND COLLEGE LABOR EDUCATION ASSOCIATION—The "national organization of universities and colleges with recognized programs in the field of labor education/labor studies which serve workers and their organizations, and . . . the professional faculty and staff engaged in such activity."

72

WORK AND TECHNOLOGY INSTITUTE—A nonprofit (501[c]3) organization dedicated to research and education activities linking workers and the workplace to technology and economic competitiveness. Its current objective is to develop the full potential of the human element as a positive factor in new workplace process technologies and systems, to jointly maximize speed to market, productivity, quality and flexibility along with job security, worker skill, job satisfaction, and standard of living.

NOTES

1. Lest it appear that I'm making fun of librarians, I should describe my own reaction upon receiving a copy, all too indicative of the foibles of academics: I raced through the text to see if I was quoted. In the interest of full disclosure, I should point out that I am quoted, with Paula Voos, on p. 14.

2. I use the term "workplace change" here. At other points I refer to "work reorganization," "new work systems," and "new labor relations." Some terminological clarification is in order. I like to distinguish three strains of "programs" confronting unions: worker participation or employee involvement, which includes programs that seek to involve rank-and-file workers in new areas of decision making; union-management cooperation, union participation in management or labor-management "partnerships," all of which refer to programs involving the union as an institution in new areas of decision making; and work reorganization often involving teams, job rotation, cross-training, and so forth. Each of these creates somewhat different sets of challenges for unions. *The New American Workplace* addresses all three but isn't always explicit in its categorization. For this paper, the phrase "workplace change" refers to all three as well as technological changes closely associated with work reorganization.

3. Apparently there is a discussion taking place in the developing world over whether it is possible to skip Taylorization as a phase of development in the organization of work (Gustavsen and Hethy 1989).

4. The fact that neither the Canadian Labor Congress nor the smaller Canadian Federation of Labor has a policy or document comparable to the NAW likely results from continued internal differences among affiliated member unions similar to those that kept the AFL-CIO from acting earlier. It would appear that many of the Canadian unions have been stronger and more consistent in their opposition to certain forms of workplace change (Katz 1988). This certainly has been the case in auto and paper, for instance. While individual national unions have produced policy documents and guidelines, these are beyond the scope of this essay.

5. The use of the term "human resource management" can lead to some confusion in the U.S. context. The TUC document indicates that the concept includes: "Changes in Communications Methods: . . . company newspapers, reports for employees, video presentations, team briefings, face to face meetings with managements/appraisal, attitude surveys, employee suggestion schemes; Changes in work organization: . . . teamworking, quality circles, customer care training, single

73

status, lean production/just in time; Changes in payment system: . . . performance related pay, profit related pay/profit sharing, share option schemes" (11).

6. Katz (1993) indicates that Australia is the single case where decentralization of bargaining structures has been supported by the labor movement. This appears to be owing to the maintenance of an "incomes" policy (Katz 1993, 7) as well as an active labor market policy or what Matthews (1994, preface) refers to as "national standards (covering employment conditions, wages, and training levels)."

7. It is hard to know how to reconcile these differing views. Wever argues that most critiques of works council effectiveness take as their benchmark "full-fledged codetermination." By that standard, it is not surprising that they might fall short. However, she argues, by U.S. standards they do remarkably well at representing worker interests in firm decision making. In other words, German observers see a glass half-empty and Americans see a glass half-full. It may also be that American observers tend to describe a half-full glass as three-quarters or more full. The Volvo case is a sad warning in this regard (see note 10).

8. Both Lowell Turner (Cornell University) and Kathy Thelen (Northwestern University) made this point in telephone conversations with me. It was borne out by the fact that of several documents the DGB representative sent me the closest thing to a recent policy statement was an IG Metall document.

9. This strategy is reminiscent of Robert Reich's emphasis on upgrading worker skills without giving consideration to policies encouraging employers to create jobs for the newly skilled. Indeed, Reich's vision is borrowed, in part, from the German experience.

10. Hancké argues that, on the one hand, Uddevalla was not an outcome of the various union or joint research institutions committed to work reform while, on the other hand, lack of union support for the experiment above the local level enabled Volvo to close (for its own reasons) the plant. Further, he argues that despite the apparent emphasis in Sweden on participation at higher levels of the corporation, the auto union also failed to engage management on the *strategic* (financial) issues that led to its decision to close the plant. According to Hancké, "In retrospect, it is clear that a large set of issues outside the conventional union realm was simply *never* a part of the landscape the unions were looking at. . . . Even in Sweden, the jewel on the North-West European social-democratic crown, trade unions have traditionally left 'production' issues to management and their recent ventures into these new fields are still burdened by the reflexes and organizational constraints that result from many decades of *active disinterest*" (24–25, emphasis in original).

11. It is interesting to note that the starting place of the Swedish Metal Workers' Union's publication, *Rewarding Work,* begins with an "unconditional demand" for the right to work.

12. For interesting examples of alternative models see Cobble 1991 (occupational unionism for service workers); Heckscher 1988 (associational unionism); Piore 1991 (community unionism); Kochan and Wever 1991 (broad discussion of several problems and solutions); Locke 1992 ("reconstruction of the labor movement along more horizontal lines").

BIBLIOGRAPHY

AFL-CIO Committee on the Evolution of Work. 1994. *The New American Workplace: A Labor Perspective.* Washington, D.C.: American Federation of Labor-Congress of Industrial Organizations.

Altmann, Norbert. 1992. "Unions' Policies Towards New Technologies in the 1980s—An Example from the Metal Industry." In *Technology and Work in German Industry,* ed. Norbert Altmann, Christoph Köhler, and Pamela Meil. London: Routledge.

Australian Council of Trade Unions. 1991a. *Workplace Change and Women Policy.* Melbourne: Australian Council of Trade Unions.

———. 1991b. *Workplace Reform, Skill Development and a High Competence, Educated Workforce Policy.* Melbourne: Australian Council of Trade Unions.

———. n.d. *A Review and Conclusions Regarding Workplace Change.* Melbourne: Australian Council of Trade Unions.

Batstone, Eric. 1989. "New Forms of Work Organization in Great Britain." In *New Forms of Work Organization in Europe,* ed. Peter Grootings, Björn Gustavsen, and Lajos Héthy. New Brunswick, N.J.: Transaction.

Baugh, Robert. 1994. *Changing Work: A Union Guide to Workplace Change.* Washington, D.C.: AFL-CIO Human Resources Development Institute.

———. 1995. *Technology and Work Organization: Lessons Learned, Paths to Choose. A Report on the Experiences and Ideas of AFL-CIO Unions, Members, Staff, and Labor Educators.* Washington, D.C.: AFL-CIO Human Resources Development Institute.

Cobble, Dorothy Sue. 1991. "Organizing the Postindustrial Workforce: Lessons from the History of Waitress Unionism." *Industrial and Labor Relations Review* 44, no. 3 (Apr.): 419–36.

Cole, Robert E. 1989. *Strategies for Learning: Small-Group Activity in American, Japanese, and Swedish Industry.* Berkeley and Los Angeles: University of California Press.

Danish Confederation of Trade Unions (LO). 1995. *Work and Development.* Copenhagen: LO.

Düll, Klaus. 1989. "New Forms of Work Organization: Case Studies from the Federal Republic of Germany, France, and Italy." In *New Forms of Work Organization in Europe,* ed. Peter Grootings, Björn Gustavsen, and Lajos Héthy. New Brunswick, N.J.: Transaction.

Gottfried, Heidi, and Laurie Graham. 1993. "Constructing Difference: The Making of Gendered Subcultures in a Japanese Automobile Assembly Plant." *Sociology: The Journal of the British Sociological Association* 27, no. 4 (Nov.): 611–28.

Gustavsen, Björn, and Lajos Héthy. 1989. "New Forms of Work Organization: An Overview." In *New Forms of Work Organization in Europe,* ed. Peter Grootings, Björn Gustavsen, and Lajos Héthy. New Brunswick, N.J.: Transaction.

Hancké, Bob. 1993. "The Volvo Plant in Uddevalla." John F. Kennedy School of Government, Harvard University.

Heckscher, Charles. 1988. *The New Unionism.* New York: Basic Books.

IG Metall (Industriegewerkschaft Metall für die Bundesrepublik Deutchland).

1984. *Action Program: Work and Technology/ People Must Stay!* Frankfurt: IG Metall.

Industrial Democracy in Europe (IDE) International Research Group. 1981. *European Industrial Relations.* Oxford: Clarendon Press.

International Institute for Labour Studies. 1977. "Implications for Trade Unions of the Trend Towards New Forms of Work Organization." Economic and Sociological Institute of the German Trade Union Confederation, Dec.

Jürgens, Ulrich. 1995. "Lean Production and Co-Determination: The German Experience." In *Lean Work: Empowerment and Exploitation in the Global Auto Industry,* ed. Steve Babson. Detroit: Wayne State University Press.

Kaminsky, Michelle, et al. 1996. *Making Change Happen: Six Cases of Union and Companies Transforming Their Workplaces.* Washington, D.C.: Work and Technology Institute.

Karasek, Robert, and Tores Theorell. 1990. *Healthy Work: Stress, Productivity and the Reconstruction of Work Life.* New York: Basic Books.

Katz, Harry C. 1988. "Policy Debates Over Work Reorganization in North American Unions." In *New Technology and Industrial Relations: International Experiences,* ed. Richard Hyman and Wolfgang Streeck. Oxford: Basil Blackwell.

———. 1993. "The Decentralization of Collective Bargaining: A Literature Review and Comparative Analysis." *Industrial and Labor Relations Review* 47, no. 1 (Oct.): 3–22.

Keefe, Jeffrey, and Karen Boroff. 1994. "Telecommunications Labor-Management Relations After Divestiture." In *Contemporary Collective Bargaining in the Private Sector,* ed. Paola B. Voos. Madison, Wisc.: Industrial Relations Research Association.

Kochan, Thomas A., and Kirsten Wever. 1991. "American Unions and the Future of Worker Representation." In *The State of the Unions,* ed. George Strauss, Daniel G. Gallagher, and Jack Fiorito. Madison, Wisc.: Industrial Relations Research Association.

Levie, Hugo, and Åke Sandberg. 1991. "Trade Unions and Workplace Technical Change in Europe." *Economic and Industrial Democracy* 12, no. 2 (May): 231–58.

Locke, Richard M. 1992. "The Demise of the National Union in Italy: Lessons for Comparative Industrial Relations Theory." *Industrial and Labor Relations Review* 45, no. 2 (Jan.): 229–49.

Matthews, John. 1994. *Catching the Wave: Workplace Reform in Australia.* Ithaca, N.Y.: Cornell ILR Press.

Merrill, Michael. 1996. "Labor Shall Not Be Property: The Horizons of Workers' Control in the United States." *Labor Studies Journal* 21, no. 2 (Summer): 27–50.

Mueller-Jentsch, Walther, and Hans Joachim Sperling. 1995. "Towards a Flexible Triple System? Continuity and Structural Changes in German Industrial Relations." In *German Industrial Relations Under the Impact of Structural Change, Unification and European Integration,* ed. Reiner Hoffman, Otto Jacobi, Berndt Keller, and Manfred Weiss. Dusseldorf: Hans Böckler Stiftung.

Piore, Michael. 1991. "The Future of Unions." In *The State of the Unions,* ed. George Strauss, Daniel G. Gallagher, and Jack Fiorito. Madison, Wisc.: Industrial Relations Research Association.

Rehnström, Kerstin, and Björn Gustavsen. 1989. "The Development of New Forms of Work Organization in Norway and Sweden." In *New Forms of Work Organization in Europe*, ed. Peter Grootings, Björn Gustavsen, and Lajos Héthy. New Brunswick, N.J.: Transactions.

Rubinstein, Saul, Michael Bennett, and Thomas Kochan. 1993. "The Saturn Partnership: Co-Management and the Reinvention of the Local Union." In *Employee Representation: Alternatives and Future Directions*, ed. Bruce E. Kaufman and Morris M. Kleiner. Madison, Wisc.: Industrial Relations Research Association.

Sandberg, Åke, et al. 1992. *Technological Change and Co-Determination in Sweden.* Philadelphia: Temple University Press.

Schurman, Susan, and Adrienne Eaton. 1996. "Labor and Workplace Democracy: Past, Present and Future. Introduction to the Special Issue." *Labor Studies Journal* 21, no. 2 (Summer): 3–26.

Swedish Trade Union Confederation (LO). 1991a. *Work and Fulfillment (Translation of Extracts).* A Report to the 1991 LO Congress Compiled by LO's Committee on Democracy and Participation. Stockholm: LO.

————. 1991b. *Work and Fulfillment: Summary of A Report to the 1991 LO Congress.* Stockholm: LO.

Szapiro, Miriam. 1996. "National Union Supports for New Work Systems and Technological Change," *Labor Studies Journal* 21, no. 2 (Summer): 70–95.

Trades Union Congress (UK). 1994. *Human Resource Management: A Trade Union Response.* Report to the 1994 Congress. London: Trades Union Congress.

U.S. Department of Labor. 1984. Bureau of Labor-Management Relations and Cooperative Programs. *Labor-Management Cooperation: Perspectives from the Labor Movement.* Washington, D.C.: U.S. Government Printing Office.

Wever, Kirsten S. 1995. *Negotiating Competitiveness: Employment Relations and Organizational Innovation in Germany and the United States.* Boston: Harvard Business School Press.

4

WORKER DEMOCRACY AND EMPLOYEE INVOLVEMENT PLANS

JIM GRATTAN

The political, economic, and social elites of the United States champion the nation as one where the principles of democracy and freedom predominate in everyday life. Indeed, the successes of the so-called free-world nations and in particular the United States are in no small way attributed to the existence of these democratic freedoms. But the touting of democratic rights by the economic elites of the United States severely strains credibility. Employers in the United States, asserting the legal primacy of private property rights, have historically insisted on unilaterally structuring both the technical means and the social relations of production. Employees are considered as a factor of production to be completely controlled by a managerial hierarchy. Attempts by workers to intrude upon managerial authority through the exercise of democratic rights in the workplace are regarded as egregious breaches of managerial rights. Any suggestion that economic success is even remotely based on democratic rights for workers is at best a convenient pretense.

But international economic developments since the early 1970s have challenged management domination of control in workplaces. Increasing global competition coupled with rapid technological changes have generated pressures on corporations to employ more highly educated and trained workers and to restructure workplaces effectively and efficiently to use those enhanced skills. A significant part of the restructuring throughout the 1980s and 90s has been the introduction of a variety of employee involvement (EI) plans into workplaces where workers are supposedly permitted to "participate" in management-like decision making. But the potential for any such empowerment of workers must be considered in the context of the longstanding regime of hierarchial control insisted upon and defended by management.

Not only do EI plans represent an encroachment on traditional managerial control, they are also a challenge to the historical prerogatives of labor unions in defining the representation process for workers in dealing with management. These changes in the nature of the economy, the demographics of the workforce, and the structure of workplaces, and the coincidental severe decline in the rate of unionization over the last twenty-five years, have forced the AFL-CIO, the central labor federation in the United States, generally to abandon its traditional position of keeping management at arm's length.

The 1994 Report by the AFL-CIO Committee on the Evolution of Work, *The New American Workplace,* advocates a model of labor-management cooperation that calls for unions to be involved in strategic decision making at all levels of the firm and for significant worker empowerment on the shop floor. But the AFL-CIO report, while defining principles of an EI model (8–9), does little realistically to assess the established labor relations landscape in the United States for its prospects of permitting a worker-empowering form of labor relations. The legal and political environment for labor relations, the nature of current implementations of EI plans or concepts, and the perceptions and actions of both employees and employers regarding EI are critical areas to examine in assessing the potential for EI plans.

The democratic participation of the citizenry of the United States in the polity is grounded in formal, constitutional rights, such as rights of assembly, expression, and voting. While these rights are considered vital for a political democracy, their applicability and legitimacy are confined to the relatively narrow public realm. The United States is a nation where virtually all economic and social activity occurs in the private domain where political rights do not directly apply. However, there is, in addition to its formal extent, an informal and broadly held view concerning the reach of democracy: democratic standards or procedures, such as majority determinations, are generally invoked in almost any social grouping despite the lack of a formal, legal basis. But workers, though members of complex workplace societies, have only sporadically and minimally been able to exercise any semblance of democratic rights within workplaces. The legal or quasi-legal grounding of such rights at the level of the firm is essential for their irrevocable, full exercise.

The battles that workers' organizations have had to wage against employers and various legal and judicial institutions since the beginnings of industrialism in the post–Civil War era to establish workers' "voice" within workplaces amply demonstrate the depth of the opposition to establishing any form of democracy in workplaces. According to employers and the legal community, the rights of private property entitle employers to control workplaces completely; private contracts and laws of contract should govern the dealings among economic entities, including individual workers. Of course, the reality of what employers cynically label as contractual negotiations with an individual is unilateral dictation of terms of employment. To countervail the overwhelming power of an employer over individuals, workers have been forced to form worker organizations despite the virtual certainty of a reaction by employers and state institutions to neutralize, if not suppress, such worker mobilizations.

The state is a formation of the powerful and the elites of a society to preserve and further their interests. The overriding interest of the state and the governing class as a whole is the preservation of the economic, political, and social order even at the expense of infringing on the prerogatives of some of the powerful. World War I, the Great Depression, and World War II were times when the state acted to ensure economic stability by creating labor relations frameworks that moderated employer private property prerogatives by sanctioning modest roles for worker organizations within major industries.

The Great Depression was a time when the mass production of standardized goods in large factories became the normal mode of production. The new, large class of unskilled and semiskilled industrial workers did not have the power of traditional craft workers to assert their interests against powerful employers. That lack of power translated economically into the underconsumption that was a major factor in the severity of the depression. The passage of the National Labor Relations Act (NLRA) in 1935 was a recognition that industrial workers on an individual basis were powerless to affect their terms and conditions of employment and were therefore unable to stimulate an economic recovery.

The NLRA granted to workers covered under the act broad rights to act collectively in forming or choosing labor organizations and to act for their own aid or protection. It also granted workers statutory remedies for employer interference, that is unfair labor practices (UFLPs), with the exercise of those collective rights. However, the collective rights provided under the NLRA were a means to an end—that end being the preservation of the economic order of the United States. The intent of the U.S. Congress in passing the NLRA was not to establish a quasi-constitution that created general political or democratic rights enabling workers to be included in decision making at either the managerial or the shop-floor level. In fact, the NLRA preserves the notion that employment should be contractually based. Any worker rights within the NLRA framework are a result of the dynamics of private contract negotiations between employers and labor organizations. But state institutions continue to limit worker empowerment in private enterprises.

Decisions by the National Labor Relations Board (NLRB), the War Labor Board of World War II, and the courts represent a body of law that has set the permissible limits of worker participation in the workplace. Business decisions that do not directly affect the terms and conditions of employment are set aside as the exclusive domain of management; they are not mandatory subjects for bargaining. Direct worker action at the shop-floor level is restrained by contractual clauses that substitute bureaucratic, multilayered grievance procedures. Furthermore, both worker access to statutorily defined procedures for employer UFLPs and the right to strike are preempted by the same grievance process. Under the NLRA, worker empowerment is, at best, obtained indirectly by negotiating highly detailed shop-floor rules that constrain unilateral management actions, and is probably more accurately characterized as worker protection, not worker empowerment.

By the 1970s, the oligopolies of the U.S. economy began to face concerted competition from the reemerging economies of Japan and Europe, especially Germany. However, both economies viewed production differently than did U.S. firms in not only what was produced but also how it was produced. American corporations had dominated the world marketplace by producing standardized products under the NLRA framework. By contrast, the Japanese and the Europeans focused far more on producing a variety of differentiated products for niche markets under systems of labor relations vastly different than the NLRA framework. Their systems of labor relations are generally classified as employee involvement systems in which the workforces assume productive importance far beyond that found in routinized standard production.

The NLRA framework primarily rests on collective bargaining agreements that contain elaborate workplace rules and that define highly detailed and specific job classifications with mobility between them based largely on seniority. In the competing economies, the relatively short runs of differentiated products require a broadly skilled workforce with a flexible job assignment system that permits the shifting between a variety of tasks on short notice. In addition, the somewhat greater fragility of that production approach requires shop-floor workers to make quick decisions that under the NLRA system would be a prerogative of management.

Beyond technical descriptions of markets and work processes, perhaps the greatest contrast between the NLRA framework and EI models, especially those found in Japan and Europe, is the climate of labor relations. The NLRA framework is based largely on adversarialism; the relationship is one primarily of a contractual, economic exchange. However,

81

in the EI model labor relations must be harmonious because of the dependency of the firm on the commitment of the workforce to make sound decisions; the relationship must tend toward that of a social exchange based on trust. The relationship of trust is furthered by the commitment of the firm to providing enhanced employment security. Under the NLRA framework, the detailed contracts reflect the lack of trust among the parties; from a worker standpoint, management must be constrained by work rules from arbitrarily changing workplace procedures (Mahoney and Watson 1993, 156–64).

By the late 1970s, U.S. corporations, especially those experiencing the greatest erosion of markets to global competitors, were feeling pressure to modify their industrial relations systems to resemble those of their successful international competitors. EI models were introduced into both union and nonunion settings. Frequently, the threat of layoffs or plant closure owing to the alleged competitive pressures was used to secure the support of a workforce or an entrenched union to accept an EI system.

The EI models introduced ranged from quality circles and production teams to forms of joint management, but they have several features in common. The number of work rules and job classifications are greatly reduced to limit restrictions on managerial flexibility; usually enhanced employment security of some type is offered as a quid pro quo for that increased managerial flexibility. Mainstays of EI programs are the regular meetings attended by workers for review of work group and individual performances. Workers' suggestions concerning means to increase productivity, to enhance product quality, and to deal with production problems are solicited. In essence, workers assess the performance of coworkers and pressure each other to meet the goals of the firm. An insidious side effect of these team meetings is that the worker solidarity needed to broaden the scope of EI beyond the narrow agenda of management is disrupted.

While employers and workplace consultants freely draw upon democratic concepts and terminology to describe EI processes, key elements of genuine empowerment are missing: there is no independent right of speech or means to affect the workplace agenda. In most EI programs, worker input outside of parameters defined by management is considered to be inappropriate. Also, with few exceptions, the implementation of worker suggestions is at management discretion. The worker empowering or democratic aspects of the various EI models have generally been minimized by management to a level where workers will still acquiesce to the EI plans and increase efforts to raise productivity.

The auto industry has made perhaps the most extensive effort in implementing various forms of the EI model in its facilities. Those EI plans vary considerably in the extent that workers are empowered. The General Motors-Toyota joint venture in Fremont, California, called NUMMI is a distinct form of EI referred to as a Toyota system, a lean production system, or, as Mike Parker makes a strong case for, a "management-by-stress" (MBS) system (Parker 1993, 261–72). It is a team-based form of production, but the teams are not autonomous: they do not independently control their own production. By breaking the assembly line into team-sized sections, it becomes easy for management to find idle time in the teams. The teams and workloads are continually readjusted to ensure 97 percent productive effort. The teams meet regularly to find quicker methods of assembly; in essence, the workers conduct Tayloristic time-studies on themselves. Although most standard union contracts contain limits on the pace of work, since MBS is a continuous improvement system there are no such limits.

Ultimate flexibility in shifting workers between jobs has been achieved at NUMMI because the multiplicity of job classifications found in standard auto plants has been reduced to only one. All workers on a team are required to be able to perform all of the jobs assigned to the team and to adhere to the prescribed techniques for the job. The MBS system touts the worker multiskilling that is necessary for such flexibility, but the reality is that the jobs have very carefully been robbed of virtually all complexity.

Just as surplus time has been squeezed out of an MBS system, so too have relief workers and inventory levels. Each team is headed by a management-selected employee who acts as a team leader, coordinator, and relief man. In the event of team absences, the team leader must replace the absent member, thus stressing the team by not being able to coordinate or relieve the remaining team members. As a result, there is far less tolerance for absenteeism on the part of coworkers as well as management at NUMMI than found in traditional auto plants. Extreme pressure is put on suppliers to supply parts only as needed with no buildup permitted. The firm is saved investment and storage costs, while the supplier must continually scramble to provide parts just-in-time (JIT).

An MBS system is very fragile, but that fragility is used to compel performance from workers and suppliers. Unless workers maintain a feverish pace, the system can readily collapse, endangering the employment of all. The union at NUMMI has far less leverage to counter speedup when compared with traditional auto plants. The major source of grievances in traditional auto plants—that is, violations of work rules and job classifications—has been virtually eliminated at NUMMI. Also, committeemen are not as readily available, and employees must discuss their grievances with management before officially filing a grievance. The result is that few grievances are processed at NUMMI. It is claimed that an MBS system is effective primarily because of the enhanced commitment of employees who have been given a voice in production matters, regardless of the regu-

83

larity or extent of that input. An alternative explanation is that an MBS system operates from a base of both fear of job loss and peer pressure.

A far more substantial form of EI has been implemented at the new [late 1980s] GM venture called Saturn; it is a comanagement system (Rubinstein, Bennett, and Kochan 1993, 339–67). The Saturn model is similar to the NUMMI model in that it uses team-based production, but from that point there is considerable divergence. There are contractual limits to the pace of work. The number of work rules and job classifications have also been reduced at Saturn, but the work itself has not been relentlessly deskilled. Teams have independent responsibilities to schedule work and to attend to personnel matters. Team leaders are elected, not selected by management, and they are not expected to perform the role of relief worker to the exclusion of other team activities.

However, the truly innovative feature of the Saturn system is that union representatives comanage the firm at all levels. Union representatives literally work side by side with management personnel in the business units of body systems, power train, and vehicle assembly, and the union is fully represented on the strategic and manufacturing action councils. Virtually all of the areas that have been upheld by the NLRB and the Supreme Court as the exclusive domain of management under traditional NLRA relationships have been opened to joint management at Saturn. Such matters as product design, marketing and sales strategies, supplier and dealer selection, and subcontracting decisions are now jointly considered and decided. The workforce at Saturn has achieved significant empowerment in immediate, shop-floor operations as well as considerable say in matters that have long-term effects on workers.

At Saturn, grievance handling, as at NUMMI, rarely goes beyond the first stage. But the union at Saturn has not been marginalized as at NUMMI. The union in its position of comanagement has the authority to ensure that the EI program at Saturn does not acquire the manipulative characteristics of the EI program at NUMMI. In addition, there is no need to stress pseudodemocratic rhetoric; both workers and the union have real obligations that can only be discharged through substantial participation and decision making.

The Saturn EI system is hardly typical of EI in the United States. Its establishment was owing to the existence of a strong union, the United Auto Workers (UAW), with a somewhat progressive history and a company, General Motors, whose desperate market situation in the mid-1980s created a willingness to share power in a new approach to production. The proposed AFL-CIO EI model obviously draws from the Saturn model, but there is no acknowledgment in the 1994 report of the special circumstances on which the Saturn EI model is based.

On the other hand, the NUMMI labor relations system is far more typical of the many EI programs found not only in the auto industry but in other industries as well. For example, work organized along NUMMI lines, that is, highly fragmented, de-skilled, and performed at an intensive pace, has been introduced into any number of clerical situations. In nonunion firms, such systems are unilaterally imposed by employers who are concerned with firm competitiveness and productivity. Worker cooperation is stressed, not worker empowerment. In addition, employment security quid pro quos have no legalistic standing. These management-defined EI programs have proven to be largely ineffective. The protection and enhancement of employee voice that a union provides appears to be fundamental in securing the employee commitment that is necessary for the hard bargaining that productivity improvements require.

Charles Heckscher has identified a form of EI in nonunion firms that he refers to as "managerialism" (1988, 93). There has been a tremendous rise in the number of so-called knowledge workers in the last thirty years; they now constitute over one-third of the workforce. These workers include semiprofessionals in areas such as administration, engineering, health care, and others requiring advanced education. By the very nature of their work, they are decision makers; de-skilling is not an option in controlling these workers (69–70). More sophisticated human resource techniques are typically used. Much as under "welfare capitalism" of the 1920s, extensive benefits and worker-friendly environments are provided.

But even beyond tangible benefits, an entire corporate culture is often created and promoted. Corporate values and statements of purpose are promulgated that put the corporation on a moral plane higher than, say, competitors. There is a decided attempt to prevent outside influences, especially unions, from injecting alternative ideas into that carefully crafted corporate world. These corporate efforts are designed to achieve the unquestioned loyalty and commitment of the workforce (Heckscher 1988, 106–7); in many cases, virtual lifetime employment is promised in exchange.

As with any firm, labor relations policies must be able to deal with employee problems. A major tenet of human resource management is that employee problems can be managed; failure to do so is the fault of management. Furthermore, employee problems are seen generally to fall in the category of a minor psychological maladjustment or personality clash to be resolved by counseling. The open-door policy is a preferred method of resolving such minor disturbances where the counselor is a sympathetic, paternalistic manager (Heckscher 1988, 103–4). However, employee criticism of the corporation's structure, values, or fundamental policies is not countenanced.

Managerialism is basically a model of benevolent authoritarianism; it rests only on a foundation of employer goodwill. Workers are not empowered beyond narrow areas of technical expertise; there are no formal and independent means for workers collectively to inject alternatives to mana-

85

gerial policies or decisions. When IBM, the exemplar of managerialism, eliminated tens of thousands of jobs in the late 1980s and early 90s, employees found that their loyalty and dedication did not translate into enforceable rights, such as being able to insist that IBM honor implied promises for lifetime employment or to make counterproposals to IBM's downsizing plans.

It is widely claimed that there is a huge representation gap for employees in the United States. Typically, attention is focused on the fact that most workers are not represented by either an EI plan or a labor union. However, increased attention on various forms of employee representation requires that the concept of a "gap" be extended beyond rates of membership in unions or EI plans; actual employee empowerment is an important determinant in ascribing a representation gap. A gap could be said to exist when employee representation is of either questionable validity (that is, based on employer goodwill) or is highly constrictive (that is, under the traditional NLRA framework).

Genuine participation by workers at the level of the firm requires rights of assembly and expression, rights to information, rights to propose alternatives to policies and strategies, and workplace structures that facilitate the exercise of those rights. In addition, an independent structure for the adjudication of violations of those rights is essential.

Nonunion and managerialist firms do not erect independent systems of rights or procedures on which to ground worker participation. Employees are routinely subjected to subtle pressure or manipulation to increase their output or dedication in exchange for vague commitments from management that frequently disappear on a whim.

However, the traditional NLRA framework does, through support of organizing, collective bargaining, grievance procedures, and resort to the NLRB and the courts, constitute a legal structure that is somewhat worker-empowering. But under that framework workers are carefully constrained in private employer-union agreements circumscribed by status-quo or proemployer rulings by the state.

As the Saturn EI model clearly shows, an empowering form of representation within the NLRA framework also requires strong unions. But it is only when workers are allowed fully to exercise their organizing and collective bargaining rights under the NLRA that unions gain sufficient leverage to negotiate agreements with Saturn-like empowerment for workers. However, as the political environment has become more conservative over the decades since World War II, employers have become more willing to violate workers' rights to organize for collective bargaining. The remedies under the NLRA for workers who are victims of these employer UFLPs are virtually useless in deterring these violations. While technically in compliance with provisions that eliminate managerial employees from coverage under the NLRA, employers abuse those stipulations by preventing the unionization of employees who make management-like decisions but, in fact, are not managers. Clearly, amending the NLRA is needed to bolster and extend the organizing capabilities and domain of unions and, ultimately, to close the representation gap for American workers.

Especially in the face of dramatic union decline, it is contended that the NLRA framework is a failed model for employee representation. Further justification for that contention is acquired by focusing on the widespread employee participation that supposedly exists within nonunion and managerialist versions of EI. However, it is evident that substantive worker participation must be based on rights that are political-like in nature and enforceable through legalistic structures and procedures. The only candidate among existing forms of representation that can provide such support for workers is an expanded version of the NLRA model. At a minimum the following amendments to the NLRA need to be made: extend coverage to all employees below middle manager level, permit card-check recognition, return employer UFLP adjudication to the NLRB, make the presumption that court injunctions should be sought for employer UFLPs, permit punitive damages in employer UFLP cases, require at a minimum first contract arbitration, disallow striker replacement for at least ninety days, and significantly extend—if not eliminate the categorization altogether—mandatory bargaining subjects.

There are other proposals for diminishing the representation gap that now exists in the United States. One of the principal objectives of the Dunlop Commission formed by the Clinton administration in 1993 was to consider the repeal of Section 8(a)(2) of the NLRA, which prohibits management-initiated employee representation schemes. However, the evidence from the vast majority of currently implemented EI plans indicates that the repeal of Section 8(a)(2) would only encourage the establishment of some variation of pseudorepresentation (evocative of employer-dominated representation plans of the 1920s).

Heckscher proposes reliance on associational unionism (nonmajority unionism is an instance) in a multilateral negotiation process (177–200). However, historically, associations of workers have had to operate as unions to be effective; relying on employer willingness to accept associations has little precedence. There have also been numerous calls for German-like works councils to be legislatively mandated for workplaces (Weiler 1993, 97–99; Freeman and Rogers 1993, 61–64). But German works councils exist in a context of strong extra-firm, industrial unions. Moreover, state-mandated social benefits eliminate many issues that are highly contentious at the enterprise level in the United States. There is little validity in selecting only one aspect of a balanced representation system, not to mention the huge legislative effort in a generally hostile political environment that would be required to bypass the NLRA framework.

The realization of significant worker participation in shop-floor and strategic decision making is dependent on the attitudes and understandings of American workers concerning the power dynamics of the labor relations environment. Some consider the 1930s to be the foremost example of a period where workers sought to gain control of workplaces. Perhaps a more realistic explanation is that the NLRA framework came about primarily as a result of efforts by the state to protect the economic order against the narrow economic interests of corporations. In the present era, it is difficult to find highly coherent calls by workers for substantive empowerment.

Survey data obtained from workers reveals feelings of both difficulty and confusion over representation issues. Over 60 percent of workers regard unions as "basically good" for working people and the nation as a whole (Freeman and Rogers 1993, 30–31), yet the unionization rate in the United States stands at no more than 11 percent of the private workforce. However, it is estimated that 40 percent of workers, including current union members, would vote for union representation (Freeman and Rogers 1994, 12). The fierce opposition that employers invariably mount against union organizing drives is not lost on American workers. Nearly 80 percent of workers find employer opposition to be unfair and believe that laws protecting workers' rights to organize should be strengthened. Yet among nonunion employees such laws would persuade only an additional 15 percent to join a union (Freeman and Rogers 1993, 30–31).

As many as 90 percent of American workers desire some form of worker committee "to discuss and resolve concerns with their employer" (30). In addition, most workers desire independence for such committees by opposing management selection of committee members and by favoring outside arbitration for unresolvable conflicts. But curiously, over 70 percent of workers find management cooperation as the key to the success of a committee. Nearly that same percentage, if given a choice, favor a worker committee with no decision-making power over one that has such power if necessary to prevent management disapprobation. By a three-to-one margin, workers favor joint employee-management committees over unions (Freeman and Rogers 1994, 9–13).

There is a huge disconnection between the recognition by workers that employers are quite willing to take severe actions to prevent unionization and a preference for joint committees where a cooperative management gives workers "independent input into workplace decisions" (Freeman and Rogers 1994, 15). There seems to be little appreciation that unions, especially if backed by stronger labor laws, are the only worker organizations that have the standing to obtain significant worker decision-making power. Wishful views of cooperation disguise the fact that genuine cooperation usually requires relative equals; long-lasting accords cannot be based on the benevolence of a superior party.

Survey data shows that a large percentage of management favors some form of nonunion employee representation. But their opposition to outside arbitration, reluctance to supply company confidential information, and dismissal of the need for legal sanctioning of worker committees is ample demonstration of the traditional management position of not surrendering workplace power to workers (Freeman and Rogers 1994, 14–15). The survey data lends credence to the historical observation that management will only tolerate pseudorepresentation for workers.

The AFL-CIO recognizes that traditional craft unionism is of minimal usefulness to enterprise-based workers who desire, if not need, to have voice in controlling their work. Also, it is realized that reliance on standardized production will relegate the U.S. economy to second-rate status. But more is needed from the AFL-CIO than declaring or hoping that the time has come for the support of newly structured workplaces by enlightened management and the state.

The current labor relations landscape is terrain where worker democracy has proven extremely difficult to establish. The evidence is overwhelming that virtually all employers oppose any significant form of workplace democracy; instead, they favor the substantial manipulation and control of workforces. Also, state decisions have invariably carefully circumscribed worker rights, subordinating them to employer private property rights. The NLRA framework needs substantial modification to permit workers to negotiate systems of workplace rights that permit significant worker participation in decision making.

But such a transformation will not occur without tremendous effort by the AFL-CIO and the entire labor community. Appealing to the goodwill of employers has never worked for employees nor will it work for the AFL-CIO. The only possible means of achieving significant workplace democracy is by waging a highly organized campaign within the general political process to reform the NLRA. However, the electoral approach is hardly as straightforward as implied.

It can hardly be discounted that workers as citizens and voters are manipulated by elites much as in the workplace. The existence of huge, centralized communications empires virtually guarantees a blanket of procapitalist, proemployer propaganda. For example, any state support of union rights to diminish the power of employers to operate with impunity is equated with the possibility that worker personal property will be next to undergo some form of state intervention. The effectiveness of such manipulation is readily seen in the electoral support of procorporate political candidates by large segments of the working class.

Any development of workplace democracy beyond current levels will require the emergence of vigorous proworker voices to counter simplistic procapitalist propaganda and to motivate and educate workers as citizens to insist on changes in the labor laws that will permit the American ideal of democracy to be extended to the workplaces of America. The AFL-CIO report does not address the severe legal and political environment in which innovative labor-management cooperation programs would have to exist; nonetheless, the AFL-CIO has a huge responsibility to be a leader in a political campaign to reform the NLRA. The alternative to a concerted effort is the continuation of the largely manipulative, pseudodemocratic EI schemes that are imposed with one hand, while peer pressure and fears of job security are used to squeeze workers with the other.

Bibliography

AFL-CIO Committee on the Evolution of Work. 1994. *The New American Workplace: A Labor Perspective.* Washington, D.C.: American Federation of Labor-Congress of Industrial Organizations.

Freeman, Richard B., and Joel Rogers. 1993. "Who Speaks for Us? Employee Representation in a Nonunion Labor Market." In *Employee Representation: Alternatives and Future Directions,* ed. Bruce E. Kaufman and Morris M. Kleiner. Madison, Wisc.: IRRA.

————. 1994. "Worker Representation and Participation Survey: First Report of Findings." Dec 5. Unpublished.

Greenfield, Patricia A., and Robert J. Pleasure. 1993. "Representatives of Their Own Choosing: Finding Workers' Voice in the Legitimacy and Power of Their Unions." In *Employee Representation: Alternatives and Future Directions,* ed. Bruce E. Kaufman and Morris M. Kleiner. Madison, Wisc.: IRRA.

Heckscher, Charles C. 1988. *The New Unionism: Employee Involvement in the Changing Corporation.* New York: Basic Books.

Mahoney, Thomas A., and Mary R. Watson. 1993. "Evolving Modes of Work Force Governance." In *Employee Representation: Alternatives and Future Directions,* ed. Bruce E. Kaufman and Morris M. Kleiner. Madison, Wisc.: IRRA.

Parker, Mike. 1993. "Industrial Relations Myth and Shop Floor Reality: The Team Concept in the Auto Industry." In *Industrial Democracy in America: The Ambiguous Promise,* ed. Nelson Lichtenstein and Howell John Harris. Cambridge: Cambridge University Press.

Parker, Mike, and Jane Slaughter. 1994. *Working Smarter: A Union Guide to Participation Programs and Reengineering.* Detroit: Labor Notes.

Rubinstein, Saul, Michael Bennett, and Thomas Kochan. 1993. "The Saturn Partnership: Co-Management and the Reinvention of the Local Union." In *Employee Representation: Alternatives and Future Directions,* ed. Bruce E. Kaufman and Morris M. Kleiner. Madison, Wisc.: IRRA.

Verma, Anil, and Joel Cutcher-Gershenfeld. 1993. "Joint Governance in the Workplace: Beyond Union-Management Cooperation and Worker Participation." In *Employee Representation: Alternatives and Future Directions,* ed. Bruce E. Kaufman and Morris M. Kleiner. Madison, Wisc.: IRRA.

Weiler, Paul C. 1993. "Governing the Workplace: Employee Representation in the Eyes of the Law." In *Employee Representation: Alternatives and Future Directions,* ed. Bruce E. Kaufman and Morris M. Kleiner. Madison, Wisc.: IRRA.

IV

VIEWS
FROM
THE FIELD

5

IDENTITY CRISIS: UNIONS IN THE WORKPLACE OF THE FUTURE

PETER DOWNS

Anyone who has worked in a factory probably knows from experience that plans that look good on paper don't always work out in practice. The image of a "new American workplace" presented by the AFL-CIO Committee on the Evolution of Work is one such plan. The image is very pretty, but for millions of workers the reality is far different.

The workplace at General Motors is one such reality. For two decades, the corporation and its largest union, the United Auto Workers (UAW), have jointly promoted quality of worklife programs, the team concept, and cooperative contract language purportedly to create a new American workplace. They subscribed to the goal advanced by the AFL-CIO of combining "individual participation through restructured work processes and redesigned jobs, with collective representation, through restructured decision-making processes from the shop floor to corporate headquarters" (AFL-CIO Committee on the Evolution of Work 1994, 9). It hasn't worked. For many workers, "redesigned jobs" have meant more work, faster work, and more injuries. "Restructured decision-making processes" have meant a loss of union representation as grievance handlers refuse to file grievances against changes to which they, or their superiors, had given prior approval.

The GM reality more closely approaches the statement on work reorganization issued by the Canadian Auto Workers (CAW) in 1993 than it does that of the AFL-CIO. The CAW noted that the new workplace differs from the old not in such developments as

> teams, suggestion programs, multiskilling or the like. The biggest differences are found in practices such as the massive outsourcing (contracting out) of parts and final assembly . . . [and] in technical developments such as the ease of making products (simple designs, fewer parts, quick assemblies). Most important, in terms of the labor process, is work intensification—tight work cycles, long hours, regimented work practices and significant managerial flexibility to use labour as it sees fit. (CAW-Canada Research Group in CAMI 1993, 3)

THE BRIGHT PROMISE OF THE TEAM CONCEPT

The GM assembly plant in Wentzville, Missouri, was one of the first organized around the team concept and cooperative decision making. The Wentzville plant opened in 1984 and added a second shift in 1985. Workers were carefully selected for the plant, then trained intensively in communication skills, cooperation, and teamwork before ever setting foot through the factory entrance. The author of this chapter is one of those workers.

The factory's "operating philosophy," which was engraved in plexiglass and touted to the world as a new beginning in labor-management relations, reads like it could have been written by the Committee on the Evolution of Work:

> We believe that all people have dignity and respond in the manner in which they are treated.
>
> Informed people working together with mutual trust and respect will create an environment that encourages support, participation, pride, craftsmanship and personal development.
>
> We are committed to the importance of individual involvement in decision-making in order to achieve common goals and to meet the challenges of the marketplace.

The similarities did not end there. The AFL-CIO committee notes that "the dominant system of work organization . . . requires a hierarchical, regimented environment in which layers of management are created to assure that the decisions of the thinkers and planners are correctly executed . . . [and] workers are seen by management and owners as merely another 'input' into the production process—a disposable commodity like any other production input. The employer's aim is to get the maximum output from the worker at the lowest possible cost" (AFL-CIO Committee on the Evolution of Work 1994, 3–4). Likewise, Wentzville GM trainer Dave Brandt told newly hired employees that the system of automobile production "was based on supervisors being dictatorial. They used intimidation, harassment, and favoritism. They treated workers as interchangeable parts of a machine, as if workers were lazy and stupid" (Downs 1988, 185).

The problem with that, concluded Brandt, is that it led to "unions, strikes and grievances . . . so the industry couldn't compete with the Japanese, the Swedes and the Germans" (Downs 1988, 186). Management had to change, he said. In the new workplace, workers would work in teams. They would be treated with "dignity and respect." They would participate in decision making, and management would listen to their ideas.

So What Else Is New?

Personnel managers have known for forty years that cohesive work groups promote better attendance, higher productivity, and more favorable attitudes toward the job and the company (Likert 1956; Seashore 1954; Kahn and Katz 1953). At first, however, managers were more concerned with the ability of such groups to restrict production (Hollander 1964, 32). They sought ways to prevent informal work groups from forming, or to break them up when they did form. Eventually, the idea percolated through managerial minds that such efforts were neither effective nor efficient. The alternative was to turn the human tendency toward group identification to the company's advantage. Psychology offered the tools for doing so, tools including what one psychologist calls "the weapons of influence" (Cialdini 1984). GM trainers proudly said at Wentzville that GM had brought in eminent psychologists to devise the training program.

The Psychology of Consent

When workers finally entered the factory in Wentzville, many did so full of enthusiasm for GM's new workplace. Ken Wiggers recalls that he was so impressed by what he was told in training "that I actually shed tears. They told us up front that we would be using our brains and not just our brawn. . . . They told us that what we said would mean something. . . . I was convinced that the team concept was the answer to our national economic and industrial ills, because the ideas and efforts of each individual worker would be sought out and appreciated. This would strengthen our economy and preserve our jobs" (Downs 1988, 189). Management was similarly impressed with Wiggers's attitude. They made him a team coordinator, a position he held for fourteen months before resigning in disgust to take a job on the assembly line. Wiggers was an older worker with experience on both sides of the old labor-management divide. He had belonged to the Oil, Chemical and Atomic Workers Union and the

United Steel Workers of America, and spent fourteen years in management.

Among the "weapons of influence" that Cialdini says are effective at getting people to agree to things that, on reflection, they would not like, are contrast, reciprocity, and authority. Wentzville trainers contrasted a brutal past of industrial work to an enlightened future where workers think for and direct themselves. They contrasted a hell of unemployment in a weak and enslaved America to a heaven of secure employment in a strong, free America. The method of the contrast is much like that of a real estate agent who shows you an overpriced, decrepit house before taking you to the one he wants to sell. GM offered us a golden future, on only one condition, that we trust management.

Another weapon of influence hinges on reciprocity, the rule that when someone does something for you, you must do something for that person in return. That rule appears to be fundamental to all functioning human societies (Gouldner 1960). It is so powerful as to be almost automatic (Cialdini 1984, 30–46). Push the right button and *click,* the rule is engaged. GM management reminded the thousands of us it hired off the street in 1985 that GM was "giving" us higher wages and more benefits than we had ever seen before. It was "giving" us the opportunity to be treated as thinking human beings instead of drones or cogs in a machine. It was "giving" us a chance to be industrial heroes who save America from foreign domination. It was "giving" us the opportunity to escape financial worry with a job for life. All it wanted in return was that we do what we are told and trust management to work out any problems that arise. Years later, there were still workers who told me that they would do whatever management asked them to do because they never made anywhere near as much money at any other job in their lives.

The deal began to fall apart, however, when management didn't live up to its side of the exchange. Millie Donnelly was another person whose excitement about the new workplace had led to her becoming a team coordinator. She gave up that post after eight months. "They don't want to accept our ideas," she said of management. "They always say they wanted our input . . . [but] what we said went in one ear and out the other. They did whatever they wanted." Wiggers had gone into the factory on his own time while he was team coordinator to try to resolve problems that arose on the line, but management rejected his suggestions out of hand. That, he said, "was the culmination of my frustration" (Downs 1988, 190).

Part of the problem was that "quality" to GM meant something different than it means to the rest of us. It was not the same thing as performance, appearance, or comfort to a customer. "Quality," as defined on signs hung around the plant, meant "performing the operation according to specifications." In the less formal language used with work teams, "quality" meant "doing the job right the first time," or "doing it right in station." For the engineer, that meant a goal of designing jobs so that it was impossible for workers to make a mistake, designing tasks so a robot could do them. In other words, management wanted jobs designed for brainless zombies. The appeal to workers to use our brains meant to think of ways to make our jobs even more monotonous and mistake-proof, to think of ways to do our jobs without thinking. Many workers found it just a little hard to get excited about that.

A bigger rupture in the employees' reciprocal commitment to the company, because it affected so many more people, occurred the first time management laid off a shift without a call-back date. In angry, crowded union meetings, and in later discussions when people were back at work, workers opined that management lied about its commitment to give workers lifetime jobs, so workers no longer had a responsibility to management. Workers reinterpreted the company's use of reciprocity as an imperious demand to "do it my way or hit the highway."

Underneath all the psychological tricks lay a powerful motivator for cooperation: fear. When all else failed, management came back to one threat: if you don't do what we say, we'll close the plant, you'll lose your job. Appeal to the fear factor is so ingrained in auto company managers that in 1994 the Ford Motor Company told workers at its Lorain, Ohio, assembly plant that if they did not agree to the team concept they would not have a product to build. They did so despite the fact that Ford had been operating assembly plants at over 100 percent capacity for several years. Ford was desperately searching for ways to increase production and had publicly announced it was looking to add capacity. Workers in the Lorain plant, led by supporters of the New Directions Movement (a rank-and-file reform organization that opposes concessions and jointness) turned back management's demand, confident that Ford would not turn away sales in order to close a plant (Laney 1995).

Another psychological weapon is what salespeople call the foot-in-the-door technique. The idea is to get an initial commitment from an individual, no matter how small, that they can work on enlarging later. They try to sell a small, inexpensive item so that they can come back later to make more sales. They know that if one commits to buying from them, that person will probably buy from them in the future. Sometimes, they'll even sell an item at a loss to get that first business (grocery stores call such items "loss leaders"). Social psychologists discovered this phenomena in the mid-1960s (Freedman and Fraser 1966), when they discovered that people who agree to do something that appears harmless will later agree to do larger things consistent with it that they otherwise would have refused. In Freedman and Fraser's classic experiment, 76 percent of people who agreed to place a three-inch "Be a Safe Driver" sticker in their window later agreed to place a large "Drive Carefully" billboard across the front of their homes, while only 17 percent of a control group that had not been asked to use the sticker agreed to the billboard request. Psychologists call the phenomena "commitment" and "consistency." They have confirmed the principles many times. Commitment and consistency are central to the new workplace at GM. We can see how management tried to turn consistency to its advantage when dealing with union officers, team leaders, and the workforce in general.

The UAW-GM national agreement sets up a complex array of cooperative, or "joint," structures reaching from the factory or warehouse to the highest levels of the corporation and the union. These run the gamut from health and safety committees to attendance committees, from product promotion committees (which aim to increase sales of GM products) to sourcing committees (which decide whether work will be done in-house or by an outside vendor). Union officers also sit on local and national level quality councils, production councils, training councils, and corporate strategy committees.

A local union president or shop chairman (the top local bargaining official) sitting on such committees knows that the national union's position is that the company cannot pay or employ people if it does not make money, and it competes for customers with other companies for the sales that generate money. The national contract even provides for a paid educational leave program for union officers to learn more about how competition affects the economy and what it means for GM. On the surface, these hardly seem like concessions to management at all, but they lead union officers to agree to things that they would have abhorred if asked about them directly. The process goes something like this:

As a union officer, you have agreed that the company has to compete for sales to make the money to pay its workers.

Are the workers part of the company, management asks? Yes, of course, you answer.

Management: Then the workers also are competing against the other companies.

Union officer: Well, yes.

Management: These other companies can undercut us because they can get seats and headliners cheaper than us. Each percentage point of sales they take from us will cost us one thousand jobs.

Union officer: I didn't know that.

Management: We can match their price, however, if we switch vendors to this (nonunion) company from the (UAW-represented) vendor we have now.

Union officer: Okay. Let's do it.

There goes solidarity. Soon, you find yourself agreeing to outsource work done at your plant to an outside vendor, reasoning that it won't cost one hundred jobs, it will save nine hundred. Each such decision adds up, however, and you still face a loss of one thousand jobs. Then management comes to you and says: "The corporation doesn't really need all the factory space it has for these products anymore. It wants to consolidate. If we can show Detroit that we can do the work cheaper and better than Pontiac, they'll move it here, and we can save those one thousand jobs you're worried about. If we don't, they might move our work to Pontiac and you'll lose everybody." You agree. Of course, management in Pontiac is saying the same thing to union officers there.

Soon, you're bidding and rebidding against each other at cutting UAW-represented jobs. You can't even justify it anymore by appealing to the one thousand jobs you hoped to save, because the cuts you propose already are eating into that. Basically, you're doing it because once you accepted the premise of competition you wanted to be consistent.

The national GM contract commits the UAW to help the corporation "continuously improve" quality and operations to beat the competition. Plant-level union and management officers are required to report to national officers their plans for reducing waste and improving quality and "operational effectiveness." Once again management starts with the seemingly sensible proposition that "we can't afford to have people standing around doing nothing." Union officers agree. After all, it's meaningless, right? Later, management returns with data purporting to show that the plant is paying for thousands of hours of people standing around doing nothing. Union officials are shocked. "All we want from you," says management, "is an agreement to work with us to reduce this number by 10 percent a year that we can send up to the national production council." That doesn't sound like much, thinks the union officer. I can agree to that. Out comes the piece of paper. On go the signatures.

Months later, management reorganizes work on the assembly line. A line worker—let's call him Mike—finds himself virtually running to keep up with his additional work. He's twisting his wrists and shoulders to get his jobs done on one car before the next reaches his station. He's got the beginnings of a cold but doesn't have time to stop to blow his nose. He calls his committeeperson (the lowest-level grievance handler) and says he has too much work on his job. It's overloaded. The committeeperson talks to the supervisor, who shows her that the work adjustments are per a written agreement with the president and chairman to reduce wasted time. Mike had had seven seconds out of every minute in which he didn't have anything to do, says the supervisor, so all we added was this little piece to fill that time. Then she either tells Mike he hasn't got a grievance because the union already agreed to adding work to his job, or she writes a grievance but can't get management to settle it by removing work. In the latter case, she moves the grievance up to a higher level. When the chairman gets it, management reminds him of his agreement and assures him that Mike is just upset because he can't stand around doing nothing any more. Okay, says the chairman, and he withdraws the grievance. Paradoxically, involving union officials in the decision making actually closes the traditional avenue for individual and collective worker involvement: the grievance procedure.

The story above is basically what happened at the Wentzville assembly plant and other plants where committeepeople refused to file grievances because of prior agreements made by union officers. In such cases, many more than one person is affected, and plant injuries soar. At Local 1999 in Oklahoma City, union officers actually accepted the company argument that the workers themselves were responsible for their injuries because they were too soft, and agreed to a "work hardening" exercise program to toughen the employees (Downs 1994, 14).

WE'RE A TEAM: YOU DRAW THE WAGON, I'LL HOLD THE REINS

The Committee on the Evolution of Work prescribes four guidelines for the new labor-management partnership. One, management must accept and respect the union's right to represent workers. Two, changes in work organizations must be mutually agreed to, rather than imposed unilaterally. Three, unions and management must have an equal role in the development and implementation of new work systems, including equal representation and control over any bodies created as part of the work reorganization. And fourth, the partnerships must be dedicated to advancing certain agreed-upon goals reflecting the parties' mutual interests (11–12). None of these offer workers any protections if the union agrees that competitiveness is a mutual goal.

If any union and company have followed those guidelines, it is the UAW and GM. Yet, by expertly exploiting the psychological principle of consistency, management turns union representatives against the most basic goals of the union movement, which the same AFL-CIO committee notes are "to take wages and working conditions out of competition and negotiate labor standards that temper the market with human values." The logic of the new labor-management partnership spurs workers to compete with one another, instead of uniting to take themselves out of competition.

The CAW recognized this in 1991, when it stated: we have already lost if "competitiveness" is the agreed starting point. In subsequent discussions or negotiations based on competitiveness, the bottom line will always revert to "what's good for the corporation?" So it is critical we reject competitiveness as the dominant criterion guiding our actions.

Rejecting "competitiveness" is not the same as rejecting the importance of quality and productivity . . . competitiveness is something quite different: workers can produce high quality products, can be very productive, and can even show restraint in their wage demands—yet their competitiveness can be declining. The reason is that "competitiveness" is a relative concept. . . .

Accepting "competitiveness" puts us on a treadmill, a rat-race we can't win. It means trying to undermine fellow workers. . . . It forces us to compete with countries whose living standards remain below where we were decades ago and it leads to comparisons with regimes that keep standards low by denying basic human and trade union rights. It means concessions today and even more concessions tomorrow as other workers feel forced to join the downward spiral. Unlike quality and productivity, the logic of competitiveness adds a dimension that threatens all our achievements. (CAW-Canada Research Group in CAMI 1991)

THE HAZARDS OF FENCE-SITTING

Team leaders face some of the same pressures as union officers. Six months after Wentzville management organized the teams, they instituted elections for team leaders. Then they get new team leaders to read announcements or statements from management at the team meetings. From there, it is a small step to get them to report back at department meetings in general what people had said. Later, it is just another small step to get them to name coworkers who spoke in the meeting and tell specifically what they said. A later step gets the team leaders to make such reports in writing and sign them. Soon, team leaders have a reputation for being company snitches. That helps sustain the underlying atmosphere of fear on which management had played since team training. As trainer Brandt said: "Anyone defending traditional practices will not have a job" (Downs 1988, 187).

Team leader elections were supposed to generate commitment from the workers to the team process. After all, we were choosing our own representatives. A funny thing happened on the way to the new workplace organization, however. Teams took to voting out team leaders at every opportunity. Some even impeached their leaders and removed them. Workers did indeed view team leaders as their representatives, and not as management's. Every time management influenced a team leader to approach his duties from management's view, team members felt betrayed.

In 1991, supporters of the New Directions Movement explicitly called for workers to elect as team leaders the kind of people they would want as union representatives, and for committeepeople to treat such team leaders as union stewards. Many teams did just that. In some departments, enough workers elected enough union-oriented team leaders that they were able to elect one of their own as department coordinator. They turned department meetings into forums for demanding that management address workers' problems and meet with committeepeople to settle grievances. In the chassis department, team leaders and the department coordinator even organized a demonstration in front of the department

101

superintendent's office during team meeting time to demand the settlement of grievances.

That was not exactly what GM managers meant by worker participation. In June 1992, managers feared the trim department would go the same way as chassis. July marked the end of the department coordinator's term of office. When July arrived, a majority of team leaders demanded an election for department coordinator. Management refused, saying they had not followed proper procedures to request it. After weeks of arguing, team leaders and the department superintendent agreed on the petition process. During the first week of August team leaders again petitioned for an election. But, responded the superintendent, "elections are supposed to be in July. You're too late. We can't hold elections until next year." Management kept its chosen department coordinator but lost the facade of legitimacy.

In 1994, while the plant was closed for remodeling and retooling, plant management and the local union negotiated a new local agreement. The new agreement greatly extended a worker's right to bid for jobs within the plant and addressed some broad health and safety concerns. It also eliminated team leader elections and gave management sole authority to appoint and remove team leaders.

THE PROMISE IS EMPTY

The promise of the new workplace, in the words of the AFL-CIO, is "to provide new levels of individual worker participation in the workplace . . . [and] enhance collective worker representation," which serve "to increase worker opportunities, to enhance job satisfaction and to bring greater democracy to the workplace."

In actual practice, however, little effort was made to involve most workers in decision making at Wentzville in any way. Two workers were selected to go to Detroit during the design and engineering phase of each model change, but that did nothing to make the decisions which changed jobs any less foreign to the thousands of workers building the car. Another group of four to six workers was selected to backtrack quality problems, find the workers responsible, and tell them what they were doing wrong. A third team analyzed workers' job motions, then recommended ways they could perform their jobs in less time with less waste. The first group of workers called into the plant did help plan the lay out of the assembly line, but how many times in a generation does that happen? Once it's built, it's built.

In short, in the new workplace at GM, workers are performing functions traditionally part of management, but they are not the workers on the job. The actual workers on the job don't feel any more satisfied with the new system than they were with the old. Boredom and alienation remain endemic. Barely three years after thousands of new employees left team training and entered the Wentzville plant as true believers, attendance coordinator Jim May took to lecturing them at union meetings about their "excessive levels of absenteeism," which, though lower than absentee levels in the 1970s, remained high compared to the 1950s and 60s. Job rotation doesn't help. Getting to do six hard, monotonous jobs is no more fulfilling than doing one.

The main effect of "worker participation" seems to be to create more resentment of coworkers. In every GM-based local union with which I am familiar, workers revile and ridicule those "clipboard jockeys" who either "act like management and try to give us more work" or, at best, do nothing all day while their coworkers are sweating and straining on the assembly line.

Officials from the local union up to the highest levels of the national union like the new workplace because they appoint the clipboarders. The new system gives them broad patronage powers to reward their followers, who now have the time and freedom of movement to threaten and bully opponents. Such methods can bring quiet to the workplace but not worker involvement and satisfaction. The participation rate in automotive contract ratification elections, which for decades hit between 80 and 90 percent, has fallen in the last decade to 25 to 40 percent (Downs 1994, 12), while member appeals of grievance settlements and charges that union representatives are failing to represent members fairly are surging (Yettaw 1995).

Looking at the new workplace at GM from the perspective of the Committee on the Evolution of Work, a surprising result must be the number of people who look back on the old workplace with longing. Having looked more closely at the workings of the system, we can understand why that is so. For all its faults, in the old system individual workers had someone who would listen to them and an avenue for intervening in decisions to make their jobs better. That someone was their union representative. Collective bargaining and the grievance procedure provided them avenues for involvement in company decision making. The new system restricts those avenues without opening any new ones and turns the union hierarchy into just another layer of bosses. Meanwhile, jobs have become faster paced, more intense, and more repetitive.

The committee's perspective on the new American workplace recognizes that "involvement" and "empowerment" programs "which emanate from management and which stop at the task level cannot, by definition, provide workers with any real power over their working lives" (AFL-CIO Committee on the Evolution of Work 1994, 10). But the same is true if the programs emanate from management and high-level union officials. It is not enough that the union be recognized "as the representative of the workers in the process of implementing agreed-upon changes" (11).

103

Changes "mutually agreed to" by management and union officers will still seem to be changes imposed on the workers from outside if the workers themselves did not have the opportunity to discuss such changes and the power to ratify or reject them. This is especially true if union officials adopt "competitiveness" as the starting point of their partnership with management. When they adopt the ideology of "competitiveness," union officials automatically exclude worker participation on the basis of what is good for society, their community, or even themselves. When they accede to "competitiveness," union officials limit the basis of participation to what is good for the company. They implicitly agree that management will make all the important decisions (though perhaps with some input from a couple of high-level union officials) and workers will decide how best to live with them.

LOSING PRIVACY AND CIVIL RIGHTS

Not everyone resents the new workplace. Two programs that build on the psychological principles of commitment and consistency solidify a membership base for the new labor-management partnership. They are the "GM Ambassadors" program and supervisor training.

The GM Ambassadors grew out of a joint program called "Promote Our Products," which offered token rewards to employees whose referrals resulted in sales of new GM vehicles. Social scientists have shown that we embrace responsibility for a behavior when we think we have chosen to perform it in the absence of strong outside pressures, such as a large reward or a strong threat. A large reward might get us to do a specific thing, but it won't get us to accept the act as our own. We won't feel committed to it (Cialdini 1984, 96). That's why so many corporate worker-motivation programs rely on such inexpensive prizes as pins, mugs, or T-shirts.

Union officials appointed people to coordinate GM's promotional program. They extolled the program as a way to "secure our jobs" by increasing sales in 1988, and continue with the same theme today. A "Special Report" sent to all GM employees in March 1995 states, "The GM Ambassadors campaign offers each of us a way to secure the futures of all GM people. . . . Your involvement is critical to . . . the future of GM and the people whose livelihoods depend on it." Underneath the message were the signatures of Tom Weekley, assistant director of the UAW GM Department, and Jay Wilbur, executive director of the Quality Network.

A 1987 agreement establishing the UAW-GM Quality Network stated that the "leadership of General Motors and the U.A.W. is jointly committed to securing General Motor's position in the market and the job security of its employees. . . . The parties agree that the production of world-class quality products is the key to our survival and . . . [the] Voice of the customer is understood and drives the whole process." Tying job security directly to sales was not such a big step from the UAW's own "Buy American" emphasis, but it opened the door to a whole series of other issues. By throwing the weight of the union's authority behind the company's agenda, union leaders effectively limited debate about the company's agenda and set the stage for even the skeptics to conform with the true believers. (On the effects of authority, and disagreement among authorities, on conformity and compliance, see Cialdini 1984, 203–13; Kiesler and Kiesler 1969, 37, 90–92.)

The Ambassadors program expanded the sales=job security thesis of Promote Our Products. Arguing that sales depend on overall public perception of the corporation, the GM public relations department tried to convince employees that their future job security depended on how they comport themselves away from work. Employees are "ambassadors of the corporation." Accordingly, they should never speak ill of the company or its products. Whenever they see someone having trouble with a GM car, they should stop and help that person, at least by giving them a corporate number to call for assistance.

Over time, the number of things ostensibly affecting sales grew. Employees should never talk to the media. Never protest an action by management or talk about problems at work, because if people think there is labor tension they will think workers aren't doing their jobs right and they will not buy cars. Report to an anonymous tip line any employee you know who uses drugs, even if only on his or her own time, because if people think our workers use drugs they won't buy our cars. Don't go to federal agencies with your safety concerns, because if people think there is a safety problem they won't buy cars. Oppose clean air and fuel efficiency regulations, because they increase the cost of cars and so decrease sales. Vote for candidates who will reduce government regulation. In 1990, local union officials at Wentzville told members that passage of the new Clean Air Act would force the company to close the plant by August 1991. Union officials joined with plant management to bombard workers with video messages and handbills against the legislation. Then they sent nonunion employees and clipboarders to solicit employees on the assembly line for signatures for letters to Congress protesting efforts to strengthen the Clean Air Act. The UAW and GM exalted that effort as a model for every GM plant in the country. Equating sales with jobs opens the way for management to dictate to employees how they should behave at home and how they should act socially and politically.

Unionism is based on the thesis that owners and workers have interests that clash. The only power that workers have to force owners to compromise in such a clash of interests is the power to cost them money. Traditionally, that power was exercised by halting production, thereby depriving the owner of products to sell. In recent decades, in response to the growing concentration and geographic dispersion of corporate opera-

105

tions, unions put new emphasis on tactics that rely on publicity and public pressure to threaten losses of sales or investment dollars to pressure corporate managers to settle disputes with their employees. To the extent to which workers and their unions accept that they must not publicize their disputes or cost their employer sales, workers and their unions unilaterally disarm themselves in the event of a clash with their employer. Management shows no such inclination to disarm. Press releases still assert "assembly problems" and "the high cost of labor," and employers still oppose any restriction on their ability to hire replacement workers during a strike or lockout. As the CAW noted, if we accept competitiveness, "we have already lost."

The March 1995 "Special Report" to employees crowed that 27,000 workers had signed onto the GM Ambassadors program, or approximately 10 percent of the GM-UAW workforce. This is, in essence, a sizable "fifth column" within the union that has adopted management's agenda.

Another program building a promanagement base in the union is the supervisor training program. Management promoted this program widely at Wentzville, and hundreds of employees signed up for it, even though the chances of promotion to supervisor were slim. GM embarked on a quest to "downsize" operations, and one of the avowed purposes of the new labor-management partnership was to reduce the percentage of the workforce that was supervisory. Nevertheless, management knew that those workers who committed to go through supervisor training would tend to stick with that decision and identify with management in the future. They would tend to be more open to management's arguments than employees who never made that decision. Part of the training often included a few weeks back in the plant as a temporary supervisor, where the opinions of coworkers that trainees were "management" would tend to confirm trainee identification with the company line.

Management knows who enrolls in those programs and who is likely to be friendly to its claims. It can make that information available to friendly union officials. It did so on at least two occasions in Wentzville. In 1988, faced with a local union bylaws amendment to reduce the terms of grievance handlers from three years to one, management gave friendly union officers office space, telephones, and phone lists to call people to get them to the union meeting to vote against the bylaw. They argued that the amendment would increase uncertainty and bad publicity for the plant, which would cost people their jobs. In 1990, supervisors addressed selected workers about the importance of voting for candidates in the union election who favored labor-management cooperation.

Now we can see that the new workplace at General Motors is not designed to enhance worker participation. Rather, it is designed to enhance worker compliance. As part of that process it skews union politics, tending to discourage from union participation those who have problems

106

with the company, while encouraging participation by those who embrace management's agenda.

An Alternative Approach to Job Satisfaction

Few if any workers came to GM Wentzville because they always dreamed of building Buicks. Working for GM is not an end, it is a means for them to pursue other goals.

The Committee on the Evolution of Work states that in addition to seeking "to take wages and working conditions out of competition" (1994, 1), "the labor movement also has sought . . . to improve the quality of work life, to enhance the opportunities for worker to develop their skills and participate in the workplace, and to create industrial democracy." Indeed, the preamble to the constitution of the UAW states that "essential to the UAW's purpose is to afford the opportunity for workers to master their work environment; to achieve not only improvement in their economic status but, of equal importance, to gain from their labors a greater measure of dignity, of self-fulfillment and self-worth."

Such statements are too limited. They reflect a time when men defined themselves by their work and women by their families. Increasingly, workers of either gender seek fulfillment in both work and family. The above union statements also are incomplete. There have always been workers who seek fulfillment and self-worth outside of their workplace, through crafts, hobbies, education, community involvement, and independent business opportunities, to name a few. Many UAW members operate their own small businesses: a liquor store or a car wash, a cabinetry shop or a farm. They are construction contractors, athletes, musicians, and poets, besides working in an auto plant. Such are the things in which they find fulfillment. Such are the things in which they achieve their own measure of satisfaction and success. Very, very few of them want the factory to be their life.

It is past time for unions to recognize that there are many roads to self-fulfillment. A few workers may find fulfillment in greater involvement in the automotive production process, but it is presumptuous for the union to say that that is where all auto workers must find fulfillment.

A more inclusive statement of goals would claim for unions the purpose "to afford the opportunity for workers to master their environment, to gain a greater measure of dignity, of self-fulfillment and self-worth." This goal has three parts. One, to improve the economic status of workers, to give more options to their lives. Two, to increase the time away from work available to workers, to give more time to their personal lives or for pursuing their own options. And three, to increase opportunities for workers to participate in decisions affecting their jobs or their workplace.

107

Recognition of the pluralism of self-fulfillment requires that unions pursue all three objectives together.

It is also time for the AFL-CIO to recognize the dangers in a labor-management partnership based on enterprise goals or management's agenda. Even the Committee on the Evolution of Work admits that the objective of increasing the opportunities for worker participation in decisions at work requires "free and independent labor unions" that the workers control. It fails, however, to note what that means. It fails to note that a union that lacks democratic procedures is one that the workers do not control.

The AFL-CIO want workers to be satisfied with their lives, but they cannot be satisfied without union democracy. Research has shown that worker satisfaction is higher when workers participate in decisions in both the company and the union in an atmosphere in which they feel free to express themselves (Hollander 1964, 38–41).

The two poles of authority at the workplace are management and the union. When unions clearly define their objectives separate from management, it creates a broader range of acceptable opinion at the workplace. A broad range of opinion is an essential component of an atmosphere in which people feel freer to express themselves and to make their own decisions (Kiesler and Kiesler 1969, 91–92; Cialdini 1984, 209–10). A union that seems to have no goals of its own, but embraces management's agenda, collapses the range of acceptable opinion to one. This inhibits workers from expressing themselves and makes it more likely that they will simply do what they are told instead of making their own decisions. The opposite, however, a strong stance independent of management's and internal democracy, will actually tend to make unions stronger (Kiesler and Kiesler 1969, 31; Jacobson 1951). Thus, the same organizational qualities that make for a strong, independent union also promote employee participation and job satisfaction at work.

In summary, a union must do four things to promote opportunities for workers to master their environment:

1) It will clearly state its goals, which are independent of management's, such as the one offered above.

2) It will reject secrets. Union officials must insist on the right to share with their members any and all information given them by management. They must resist pressure to make decisions on the spot, insisting that their membership has the right to discuss the information before a decision is made. (This will also give union representatives the opportunity to examine management's appeals to see if management is trying to manipulate them psychologically.)

3) All worker representatives in the new labor-management partnership must be accountable to the members they represent. Members must have the right to reject agreements their representatives make and the

right to remove representatives from office and select new ones to take their place.

4) The process must be democratic. Workers must have the right to discuss options before decisions are made. They must feel free to question and disagree with their representatives. They must have the right to affirm or reject agreements and the right to expect their representatives to carry out their decisions faithfully.

These things will do more than enhance the quality of worklife. They will enhance the viability of unions.

BIBLIOGRAPHY

AFL-CIO Committee on the Evolution of Work. 1994. *The New American Workplace: A Labor Perspective.* Washington, D.C.: American Federation of Labor-Congress of Industrial Organizations.

CAW-Canada Research Group in CAMI. 1991. *Statement on the Reorganization of Work.* North York, Willowdale, Ont.: CAW Research Dept.

———. 1993. *Work Reorganization: Responding to Lean Production.* North York, Willowdale, Ont.: CAW Research Dept.

Cialdini, Robert B. 1984. *Influence: How and Why People Agree to Things.* New York: Quill.

Downs, Peter. 1988. "Wentzville: Strangest Job Training Ever," in *Choosing Sides: Unions and the Team Concept,* ed. Mike Parker and Jane Slaughter. Boston: South End Press.

———. 1994. "UAW: Death of a Union?" *Against the Current* 51 (July/Aug.): 12–17.

Freedman, Jonathan L., and Scott C. Fraser. 1966. "Compliance without Pressure: The Foot-in-the-Door Technique." *Journal of Personality and Social Psychology* 4, no. 2 (Aug.): 195–202.

Gouldner, Alvin W. 1960. "The Norm of Reciprocity: A Preliminary Statement." *American Sociological Review* 25 (Apr.): 161–78.

Hollander, Edwin P. 1964. *Leaders, Groups, and Influence.* New York: Oxford University Press.

Jacobson, E. H. 1951. *Foreman-Steward Participation Practices and Worker Attitudes in a Unionized Factory.* Ph.D. diss., University of Michigan.

Kahn, Robert L., and Daniel Katz. 1953. "Leadership Practices in Relation to Productivity and Morale." In *Group Dynamics: Research and Theory,* ed. Darin Cartwright and Alvin Zander. Evanston, Ill.: Row, Peterson.

Kiesler, Charles, and Sara Kiesler. 1969. *Conformity.* Reading, Mass.: Addison-Wesley.

Laney, Tom. 1995. "Take Heart." *Ford Worker,* Mar.

Likert, Rexsis. 1956. "Motivation and Productivity." *Management Record* 18: 128–31.

Seashore, Stanley E. 1954. *Group Cohesiveness in the Industrial Work Group.* Ann Arbor: University of Michigan Press.

Yettaw, Dave. 1995. "President's Report." *Headlight* (UAW Local 599, Flint, Mich.), Mar. 23.

6

PARTICIPATING IN LABOR-MANAGEMENT
INITIATIVES TO BUILD THE UNION

MAUREEN SHEAHAN

In June 1990, the United Auto Workers' Region 1A (covering the west side of metropolitan Detroit), under the leadership of Bob King, launched a Labor-Management Council Project using a grant program intended to sponsor interfirm networking as an economic development strategy for small and midsized businesses. The project was aimed at the region's more than 150 independent parts and suppliers (IPS) units (that is, non–Big 3 or Agricultural Implements manufacturing employers, usually sites with fewer than five hundred workers). I write this essay as a unionist who has served as director of the project since its inception, following four years in joint UAW-Ford education programs.

THE U.S. LABOR MOVEMENT AND THE NEW AMERICAN WORKPLACE

The AFL-CIO's Committee on the Evolution of Work published its document, *The New American Workplace,* in February 1994. Since unions have been participating in joint activities and work reorganization efforts since the late 1970s, what accounts for the delay?

One reason for the lack of a cohesive strategy was how quickly polarized the discussion became about labor's role in joint activities. Those

110

who opposed involvement couched their criticism in heated, scathing language and analysis (Parker 1985; Parker and Slaughter 1988). Many of those who advocated joint partnerships angrily dug in their heels in defense of cooperating with management's agenda and counterattacked with venom. Political caucuses became identified with one stance or the other, heightening the split. The middle ground seemed lost, and substantive dialogue that could have incorporated the merit in each side's position didn't happen.

Meanwhile, the initiatives grew and expanded. In workplace after workplace, management came to local leaders and/or their members talking about employee involvement, total quality management, team concept, self-directed work teams, lean production, continuous improvement, and a host of other ideas. Initiatives were being launched—with or without the union's active involvement. Most unions were sorely lacking in the capacity to provide information or direction to these local leaders and their servicing representatives, leaving them to cope as best they could and to learn by the seat of their pants.

The *New American Workplace: A Labor Perspective* is therefore significant for what it represents—a growing sense of urgency and concern that the union movement carve out a positive role for itself in workplace change—as well as for its defining some of the terms and conditions of a strong, independent labor role in joint work reorganization efforts.

The paper reaffirms the union goals of promoting democracy in the workplace and ensuring more dignity for workers through greater use of their skills and minds. It acknowledges the unendingly adversarial nature of labor-management relations at the same time it advocates more constructive relations under proper conditions. It offers a critique of Taylorism, and emphasizes that many of the problems that now beset U.S. business were created by U.S. businessmen. It also points out the failure of many workplace reform efforts in the 1970s and 80s, and lays out five principles for new work systems and four conditions for partnership that can guide local efforts. It then goes on to identify a number of the obstacles to workplace revitalization, including how threatening change is to members, supervisors, and union leaders.

The New American Workplace offers a good overview of the issues and is a useful tool for outlining to local labor and management leaders the parameters for workplace change efforts. Its appearance is all the more exciting in that it both reflects and legitimizes increased action. Since it came out, a variety of unions have added staff dedicated to the union's role in workplace change, including the Steelworkers, Communications Workers (CWA), the Service Employees International Union (SEIU), and the American Federation of State, County, and Municipal Employees (AFSCME). The Amalgamated Clothing and Textile Workers Union (ACTWU), one of the first unions to assign a staff person the responsibil-

111

ity of providing technical assistance to joint initiatives, has recently expanded its staff. (This function is being supported by UNITE as well). Others, such as the International Association of Machinists (IAM), have reversed previous positions against involvement in favor of a union-building agenda for high-performance workplace change.

In 1995, four unions are piloting a leadership training program at the George Meany Center (the AFL-CIO's national training institute, which is open to all affiliated unions) in cooperation with the U.S. Department of Labor, and the center is now offering weeklong programs for local leaders on their role in workplace change. The University College and Labor Education Association (UCLEA) is exploring—together with the AFL-CIO—how it can offer services and resources to its members who are trying to help local union leaders. This is the kind of capacity building that is essential to using the union's role in joint workplace change initiatives as a strategy for building the labor movement.

These public developments—and the paper itself—grew out of a myriad of experiences within individual unions, but also as the result of concerted effort by a cross-section of union staff who have worked hard to develop a united labor strategy. In 1991, a Technology Working Group (TWG), coordinated by the AFL-CIO Industrial Union Department and made up of representatives from more than a dozen unions, began meeting bimonthly to develop strategies, share and build resources, and organize more services for members. The result was a series of regional conferences that were held throughout 1994 and during the spring of 1995 to introduce local leaders to a union-building approach to participation in workplace change. The TWG also advocates capacity-building legislation and develops grant projects with federal agencies, including the U.S. Department of Labor and the National Institute for Science and Technology.

The Work and Technology Institute (WTI) was also established as an independent nonprofit organization with assistance from the AFL-CIO in 1993 and is conducting research and support projects to guide unions in workplace change. One promising initiative promoted by WTI has funded "labor specialists" at a number of manufacturing extension centers to encourage union awareness and use of these federally funded services.

After *The New American Workplace* was published, the AFL-CIO Human Resource Development Institute immediately began work on *Changing Work: A Union Guide for Workplace Change*. Published in 1994, it offers an overview of the new terms and ideas being used by management, a rationale for union action, references and tools for strategic planning, and bargaining ideas. The AFL-CIO Research Department has also been offering research directors from affiliated unions information and strategies on the issue.

Given the length of *The New American Workplace* and its nature as a consensus document among so many independent union organizations, it

112

is not a guidebook or a comprehensive analysis of the issues. It is an ambitious vision statement. Practitioners and individual union organizations must work out the nuts and bolts of change and handle some of the more difficult and complex aspects of joint workplace initiatives. Problems that have been encountered include local leaders' lack of the power and skills needed so that they can truly participate as equals; members' difficulty with expanded jobs and responsibilities; access to a role in strategic business decision making; and developing good ways to share rewards of efforts with workers.

One way to consider the issues is to review some of the criticisms and concerns that have been lodged about participation and to try to address them substantively. The valuable analyses that have been developed by those critical of past labor-management initiatives can be used to strengthen future work. (A local plant chairman who felt that his site had negotiated a good team concept once waved Mike Parker's book, *Choosing Sides*, at his audience and said, "We used this book as a checklist of what we wouldn't let happen at our site.")

For instance, critics of labor involvement in joint activities have stated that these programs encourage union participants to identify with management goals. More fundamentally, they argue, since labor-management initiatives require members to review working conditions from a competitive vantage point, they inevitably betray and undermine union values. While the AFL-CIO report touches on these issues and asserts another basis for participation, it does not confront them in depth, and the risks are real.

Yet, a critique that lays the blame for member and/or leader alignment with management values on joint programs is too narrow and simple. An analysis that suggests that unions not participate in such initiatives because of the risk of undermining union values is, in the long run, damaging to the labor movement.

The risks *are* great because the terrain of joint programs is so much about business. Even if the union is participating on the basis of a distinctly developed agenda, the day-to-day discussion is usually about improving quality, reducing downtime and setup time, increasing efficiencies, and eliminating waste. In smaller shops, where loss of business and/or moving operations are constantly threatening job loss, union members and leaders want their facilities to be competitive. Even though, with strong union leadership, participants in workplace change can learn to conduct job impact studies as well as quality and efficiency analyses, it is still the production performance indicators that generally drive the programs. So it is a major task to see how members can participate without becoming detached from union values.

The risks are greater still because management tends to dominate the workplace. The company pays our members to listen to its information, and it has the resources and time to gather and package that information. Management threatens, punishes, and rewards workers in ways that strengthen its hold on them. Most of the time, management controls the resources used to conduct joint activities—the information gathering, the training programs, written communications, and planning capacity. Its staff often has more opportunity to learn about change initiatives, more office time to strategize and plan, and more skills for organizational activities. Since the union (particularly in smaller sites) usually has to depend on donated time for education, meetings, and planning, and on leaders who may change every three years and don't have comparable preparation opportunities for their role in joint activities, it is at a severe disadvantage.

However, losing members' and leaders' hearts and minds to management purposes is not a phenomenon that occurs just because of joint program participation. It might even be argued that if it does happen within joint programs, it is largely because of preexisting conditions in the labor movement. There has been widespread discussion about the high defection rate among union members from labor's political candidates. Elected union officials and staff bemoan the attendance levels at union meetings and union-sponsored programs and activities. Divisions along lines marked by race, sex, age, sexual preference, job classifications, uneven treatment, and the perception that the union only protects lazy workers and substance abusers are rampant in our workplaces. Half a century of service-model of unionism has left us with a disaffected membership and, often, a disaffected leadership as well.

To argue that we must hold true to the principle of taking wages and working conditions out of competition at the expense of strategies that might protect members' interests through other means is only fair to them if we have some chance of success. While we ought to continue to struggle for that ideal, we don't appear to have a hope of achieving it this year or next. Some would argue that we still have that power in industries where we control wages such as auto. But that is an empty claim to supplier industry workers who make as little as five or six dollars an hour. Now that capital finds it so easy to move operations to wherever in the country or globe it cares to, the task for labor is even more difficult.

While it's a valid argument that joint programs take advantage of members' willingness to compete with other workers for available jobs, it would be hard to say that they create this disregard for worker solidarity. Working-class people have experienced a terrible decline in their prospects and incomes over the past twenty years. It's reasonable for them passionately to defend the jobs they do have—particularly well-paying ones. If that means fighting over which plant closes, they will mostly struggle to see that it is someone else's. Their inclination to do so doesn't arise out of joint programs, and their outlook won't be changed without education and mobilization on a scale we can hardly imagine.

114

According to critics, work organization that relies on the commitment of workers (usually through some version of team concept) to improve performance poses another danger, which is commonly referred to as "taking the whip from management and putting it in other workers' hands." Again, this concern is often asserted as if it exists in a vacuum, as if there weren't problems with the issue outside of joint programs or new workplace change initiatives, or as if the status quo were acceptable. Yet, in many work sites, for many years, lots of workers have been picking up the slack from coworkers who are not doing as much, and the union movement has paid a price in those members' disaffection. Aren't members who are working an extra load worth defending as well? Does upholding union values mean perpetuating this type of unequal treatment? This is just another tough and complex issue that requires more than platitudes and admonitions about solidarity.

A number of critical analyses of new work organization highlight how stressful and intense the pace of work can be when employers successfully implement lean production or eliminate "waste" in the system (Robertson et al. 1993; Parker and Slaughter 1988, 1994). While the analyses are helpful in highlighting one extreme, the issues in many shops couldn't be more different. Workers would appreciate a management competent enough to organize production with less waste, or so that they made less scrap, or so that they spent less time waiting for QC, maintenance, shipping, or engineering. In this issue, as in all others, the point is that a balance must be struck that reflects both management's and the union's interests. Sometimes that will mean interfering with efficiency in the name of humane treatment, and sometimes it will mean interfering with poor management that threatens the business's viability and members' job security.

Even though joint involvement is full of dangers and complex balancing acts, to argue against anything other than active, independent involvement in them *does and has* undermined the labor movement. During the 80s, many unionists passively allowed joint programs to be launched, keeping their distance because they didn't really like or trust them. Other good, militant union leaders decided that noninvolvement was a viable strategy. Both approaches crippled labor and lessened the amount of effort and resources that unions dedicated to figuring out what their role in joint activities ought to be and how they could defend their interests in them.

Furthermore, to argue against involvement in these initiatives because they don't often succeed or are riddled with problems doesn't address the problem posed by the fairly lousy reality that exists within many workplaces. Critics argue for noninvolvement by pointing out the horrors of joint programs as if there were a more pleasant alternative. It isn't so. It is easy to allow long-term conditions to become invisible because they are the status quo. But how are members expected to cope day to day with

115

disrespectful management, stupidly organized production, uneven and unfair distribution of work, bad raw materials and scheduling, and poorly maintained equipment? How can the union put itself in the position of denying members the chance to participate in resolving these conditions? To argue against joint programs requires an alternative.

The New American Workplace acknowledges that the AFL-CIO's response to the demands of joint workplace change initiatives has been "insufficiently attentive to the needs of trade union leaders who are on the firing lines." The paper represents a recognition that it must help those local leaders, and its departments and independent unions are increasingly building resources for offering needed support.

Union-Building Approach to Labor-Management Initiatives

In 1990, as I began the IPS Labor-Management Council Project, I was convinced that labor participation with management-driven programs founded on cooperation was a damaging trend, and yet convinced that labor had to play a significant role in workplace change. I found Andy Banks and Jack Metzger's book Participating in Management, which came out in 1990, inspirational. It offered one of the first analyses of how the union could be involved in joint activities on behalf of its own agenda. In 1991, the Grainmiller's document about the Union's role in joint programs appeared and eloquently outlined why the union had to take an active role in workplace change, and under what conditions it ought to participate.

That fall, while writing a paper on "Preparing Local Leaders for their Role in Joint Programs and Work Restructuring," I spoke with dozens of unionists and labor educators to ask for materials and ideas. People shared what they had, but published resources were sparse. Most were excited about the paper and eager to see it when it was done. All over the country, activists were trying to forge a union-centered approach to involvement, and feeling isolated and lacking in resources.

The last few years have created more and more opportunities for unionists to network about labor's role in workplace change, and to develop strategy. In addition to the activities noted above, the Ecology of Work Conference organizers have begun holding annual meetings for unionists about the issue. People are sharing materials, such as "Bargaining for New Work Systems," a guide produced by Roberta Till-Retz at the University of Iowa that cites language from a variety of contracts. There is growing acceptance that a person can be a militant trade unionist and a proponent of the union's involvement in joint activities. The ideas that follow are the outcome of that networking, that sharing of materials and experience. It reflects the work of dozens of committed activists.

Beyond being involved in labor-management initiatives because they

116

are pervasive and capable of addressing real problems members have in their workplaces, there ought to be strategic, long-term reasons for participating as well. Unions need to use involvement in joint programs to benefit their organizations and members by consciously using them to achieve a variety of goals.

The first goal is to use the union's participation on behalf of workers' distinct interests as a means by which to moderate management's pursuit of its own agenda. In this way, the union will help develop workplace changes, policies, and programs that are wiser and more durable than they'd be without the union. Although the "distinct agenda" approach is perceived by some management representatives as adversarial, it is actually the approach that offers the best chance of success for change initiatives. The union's involvement should safeguard that higher efficiencies and less waste don't lead to overstress, that reduction of variance in product doesn't cause mind-numbing regulation of jobs, that team concept doesn't turn members into each other's cops, and that new technologies are deployed in ways that enhance work instead of "dumbing it down." Doing this through joint programs is just as valid a way of defending members' rights, extending bargaining power, and building better working conditions as any other.

The second goal is to influence management to take the high road rather than the low road to competitiveness. This means ensuring that members become more and more capable of and responsible for adding value to products and services. It requires advocating for substantive, long-term training opportunities with real breadth and depth, and more and more autonomy on the shop floor. Widespread access to training and opportunities to apply new skills can increase equity among members, and enhance their employment security in an era when job security is so tenuous. High-performance workplaces also require more information sharing and hold management more accountable for their actions, both of which can be used by the union to advance its interests.

Third, in order to advocate for the high-road strategy, the union must have a compelling vision of a prosperous and just society in which workers have decent jobs, management can make reasonable profits, and social problems are lessened by more justice and equity. By pursuing that vision through joint workplace change, the union has a larger platform from which to communicate its distinct role. The labor movement can use its participation in joint programs to build that vision, communicate it more fully than it has been able to lately, and use it in building its public image. Articulating a distinct union role in workplace change could be a powerful tool in outreach to other organizations and the general public. The Region 1A council's accomplishments have been covered by local media, just as ACTWU's role at Xerox has had a positive impact on the union's public image.

Fourth, since joint programs are often the focus of a lot of interest and action among the union, its members, and management, they offer a point of intervention that could be effectively used by national unions to work with and train local leaders and members more fully. At Region 1A, we argue that a local union that does not have an internally organized membership is not likely to fare well in joint initiatives, and so we offer training in internal organizing, as well as in involvement in the various aspects of workplace change.

There are also times when management will give time for the union committee to organize itself, as well as to meet with its membership. If the national or regional union is prepared to help the local committee use these opportunities for strategic planning and/or union agenda building, then a good opportunity is well taken. One program that has been delivered to a council work site entirely on company time walked union leaders through the following questions:

1. What are the Union's mission and goals? [Answers to this question usually include, "Creating the Best Workplace Possible" and "Job Security."]

2. What are the characteristics of the best workplace possible, one that's capable of providing secure jobs?

3. How can team concept help the union advocate for a better workplace and achieve its other goals?

4. What problems can team concept create for the union? How can it undermine the union?

5. What conditions does the union need to build into a team concept to gain the benefits and avoid the problems?

6. What are the problems in our workplace that will get in the way of developing a good team concept?

7. What are the positives in our workplace that we have to use to help develop a good team concept?

8. What proposals do we need to develop to handle those problems and take advantage of those positive factors?

9. How well prepared are our members to sustain union values and goals as we participate in team concept?

10. What action plan can we develop to prepare our members and stay on top of our role in the change initiative?

11. What are an ideal union leader's roles and responsibilities?

12. What skills, qualities and information do union representatives need to carry out their role effectively? [Committee members conducted self-assessments based on these lists.]

13. How well prepared is our union committee to play an independent role in the development of team concept?

14. What steps do we have to take to prepare ourselves to be effective leadership?

Fifth, unions need to use joint programs to learn more about business issues and how they impact workers. Through participation in joint activities and training, members and leaders can learn more than they've previously had the opportunity to. Advance knowledge of company financial issues, investment plans, and business concerns can assist in developing strategic responses. More ease and familiarity with the terrain of business could assist the union in educating members about how union and management interests differ in the national and international scene.

Charley Richardson at the University of Massachusetts-Lowell argues passionately on behalf of a sixth goal—understanding new technologies in advance of their deployment so that we can advocate for adequate training for members and union involvement in the design, selection, and implementation of them. The escalating rate of technological change is one aspect of the new demands that require "continuous bargaining," according to Richardson. (Richardson 1993–95). Unions must use joint activities as another means by which they gather information that will help them strategize and negotiate on behalf of members' interests, particularly since changes are occurring so quickly and pervasively that triennial contract negotiations are inadequate to protect them.

Knowing about technologies in advance of their introduction into the workplace is linked with another key goal. Unions can use their involvement in joint activities to protect and expand members' jobs. This is the seventh goal. By expanding the amount of training available and selecting programs based on anticipated process changes, members will be in a better position to argue for retention of work that is dramatically altered by new technology. Joint activities can give members more information about company outsourcing decisions than the union has traditionally been offered, and armed with the information, our members can make successful bids to insource and retain work.

Unions must also consciously use their involvement in joint processes to gain organizational power. As they illustrate their capacity to add value to developing participative processes by guiding and directing members' involvement, they can use this leverage to win larger gains from management. The ACTWU Partnership Agreement with Levi Strauss and Company, which defines the union's role in workplace change, also outlines how the union will have access to the thousands of workers in unorganized facilities and commits management to neutrality during the organizing and to recognizing the union when a majority of authorization cards have been collected. At Region 1A, organizers have Labor-Management Council for Economic Renewal (LMCER) brochures on hand to refute management lies about how the union doesn't care about the future of the business. The National Treasury Employees Union actively uses its involvement in workplace partnerships as a recruitment and publicity strategy. This is the eighth goal.

Taking advantage of the skills of participative process and organization development that can be learned through joint activities could have immense value for the union and should be the next goal. Although the potential (much less the theory) is rarely realized, the purpose of most labor-management initiatives is to reorganize the workplace based on "Theory Y" principles, which argue that people are intelligent, responsible, creative, and happy and willing to work if properly motivated. To make the transition to an organization that's able to operate as if this theory is real, leadership that can motivate, structure participation, strategically plan, and organize follow-through on input has to replace management that gives the orders.

These strategies can be effective for managing workplaces, but they are also exactly the skills that are essential for revitalizing the labor movement:

—Learning how to run meetings members want to attend, where they feel heard, but progress is made toward common tasks and goals;

—Creating structures that use members' interests and input to build the union's capacity for community and political action;

—Using strategic planning to balance and prioritize plans of action that can have broad and meaningful impact;

—Developing motivational skills so that members are re- inspired with the union's vision and develop commitment to the union cause.

—Gaining interpersonal skills that expand how much truth can be said and increase the chances of resolving conflicts and differences that divide the membership.

Although many joint programs are run so shabbily that such positive lessons seem absurd, they can promote these skills and strategies, if they are well done. That's increasingly important considering the implications of Charley Richardson's idea about continuous bargaining. He asserts, "We used to bring our members out of the closet every three years to scare management into satisfying our demands. Now, we have to keep them out of the closet so that we can continually defend union interests as changes are undertaken" (Richardson 1993–95). This requires a much more active level of member organizing than most unions are used to, and the skills outlined above can make efforts much more effective.

The tenth and last goal incorporates the points above but puts them in a larger context. Through participation in joint programs, it is possible for the union to advance members' skills as participants in democracy. This is crucial. As a society, we are in danger of losing any meaningful democratic process. Information is supplied to the public in packaged bits that serve the interests of the privileged that generate them. The volume of information and the complexity of issues is increasingly overwhelming and confusing. There's a growing tendency to turn to populists who promise simple solutions and who villainize the poor, whose increasing poverty is causing them to act badly. Most people, including our members, feel less able to participate in the political process, less confident of what they think and feel, more ready to rest upon their anger and frustration, and to turn over the decisions to others. This is dangerous.

So how does this relate to joint programs? First, because joint programs are (or have the potential for being) about differing interest groups seeking a common good by attempting to balance their interests. They are about having meetings where groups of people are supposed to have their say, reach a decision, and make plans for the future. They are about teaching people to analyze complex information and use disciplined problem-solving processes to reach conclusions. They are about people interacting across lines of class, race, sex, age, job classification, and lifestyle, with each supposedly having an equal voice, and using constructive conflict skills.

Through these experiences, our members could gain more confidence in their opinions, as well as learn how to express themselves in ways more likely to be heard. They could learn to listen to what others have to say, even if they don't like them or don't agree with them. They could have the experience of analyzing more and more complex information and issues. They could possibly see how the group is capable of coming up with ideas and solutions that are more creative and more beneficial than what one person could think of. They could enhance their ability to give and take in order to reach decisions that balance their needs with those of others. That's the potential.

That potential probably seems far-fetched. Most meetings don't function like the description above, and very few joint processes come even close to their potential. It is true that, in general, our society is terrible at the skills and practices listed above. This is why it is so important consciously to pursue them.

Part of the challenge, given the often dreary reality of how far short of the ideal labor-management activities operate, is to remember the vision. This essay has not focused on the multitude of difficulties a practitioner faces when he or she attempts to assist in a local work site. But the hurdles are daunting, and the horror stories that many people tell are real. On a day-to-day basis, the redeeming thought is "Keep your eye on the prize."

The key issue is "What is the union's business?" It includes defending members' interests for decent wages, working conditions, and benefits; educating and involving them in the struggle so that they are enriched by participation in the union; and extending the value of the union movement into society as much as possible. Regardless of the obstacles, it is the vision of that "business" that's the compass that must be used as we gain expertise at participation in joint initiatives.

121

A Case Study: The UAW Region 1A IPS Labor-Management Council Project

The Labor-Management Council Project launched by Region 1A, UAW, in 1990 began with grant funding from the state of Michigan. Funding was cut owing to a turnover in state administration that fall, and the project had to become self-funding through grant procurement; fees for training, consulting, and publications; and annual membership fees collected from firms, locals, and individuals. The council has collected a great deal of experience and many lessons over the past five years, and it has been good just to survive.

The LMCER, the lead agency, is organized as a tax-exempt membership organization, with firms and locals paying annual dues. Additional funding is raised from training, consulting, meeting, and publication fees, as well as through grants. LMCER focuses on education, research, and outreach and is heavily concentrated on labor-management relations. It currently has thirty-six firms and fifteen union member organizations. The UAW Region 1A IPS Labor-Management Council (UAWLMC) is not tax-exempt and has been less active. Its role is to sponsor interfirm business arrangements. Until January 1995, there was one staff person for both councils; now there are two. The office remains at Region 1A, which donates space, supplies, equipment, mailing costs, and xeroxing.

The introduction to the Region's IPS Mission Statement outlines why it launched the project:

> UAW Region 1A is committed to revitalizing and rebuilding the union so that we can better defend members' interests in the independent parts and supplier sector. History compels us to take an aggressive role.
>
> In 1976, 62% of IPS plants were unionized. By 1988, the rate had declined to 22%. UAW supplier plants continue to go out of business as the non-unionized sector grows. Suppliers face brutal competition for quality, reliability, innovation and low costs. The Union's ability to fight for good wages and working conditions and decent benefits is eroding under these conditions. UAW Region 1A believes that the Union must forge multiple strategies to rebuild our membership and our capacity to win good contracts.
>
> Aggressive organizing of non-unionized workers is one aspect of our fight for a better future. . . . [A group of] 400 volunteer members . . . helps carry out home visit blitzes, does research and office work, and joins in campaigns and rallies in support of organizing drives. The Union must also educate and involve our members in the critical political issues we face. . . . Most importantly, the Union must educate and reorganize our own members and activate them for consistent, ongoing involvement in shop floor issues, organizing and solidarity efforts [Region 1A launched a Support Group for a Salvadoran trade union federation in the summer of 1990, which is now operating as the UAW Region 1A

122

International Labor Solidarity Network], community action and political mobilization. With a revitalized membership, we can militantly defend the rights of the workers we represent and expand those rights to all poor and working people in our society. Finally, the Union must take initiatives in economic development and workplace organization to ensure that well paying, secure jobs are available to our members and their children.

Employers can choose one of two roads to gain a competitive edge. The low road builds competitiveness on the backs of workers—reducing their wages, eroding their benefits, and increasing the pressure to work harder and faster. The high road to competitiveness demands that employers create high performance workplaces that can respond quickly and effectively to changing market demands. The high road is created in workplaces which give workers job security, input into vital shop floor decisions, and training to maximize their ability to use new technology and participate in decision-making. It is for these conditions that the union must advocate.

The union has to fight to make employers see the benefits of choosing this higher path. In doing so, we can also extend democracy in the workplace, improve working conditions, and increase the dignity and respect our members enjoy on the job. Widespread access to training will also promote equity among all workers. In fulfilling the union's goals as we intervene in management's control of the shop floor, we can contribute to their competitiveness as we retain high paying, secure jobs." (United Auto Workers 1994)

The Labor-Management Council Project wasn't created because the Region thought that success would be easy. Staff and advisors were very aware of the research about the high failure rate of joint initiatives—and heard from dozens of local leaders in IPS shops within the Region of wasteful, half-baked efforts. Many sites had watched two or three programs launch and sizzle, explode or fade in the 80s. But the rain of programs was continuing, if not becoming a downpour, and they were having a profound day-to-day impact on local union leaders and members. Moreover, regardless of the history, the reality was that many of the shops suffered from poor management and working conditions, and the Region wanted to use whatever strategies were available to impact those sites.

In part the approach was built on an honest assessment of the union's strengths and weaknesses. It was not the Region's experience that the union could always halt poor efforts in its smaller sites, which often lacked the institutional clout the union enjoyed at the Big 3. At times, local union leaders didn't have the information or skills needed to defend members from badly designed efforts. At the same time as the Region pursued strategies to build the union's power in its relationship to management, it also built the council. It was hoped that providing desperately needed support to those smaller units as they attempted to respond to and maneuver through management demands and proposals, share information, offer guidelines, provide networking opportunities, and stop the endless repeating of the same mistakes in location after location would be a worthwhile effort. While the council has proven its value, it hasn't been a simple project to build and sustain.

From the start, the Region consciously built the union's capacity for thinking and strategizing about its role in joint activities. Andy Banks presented a workshop at Black Lake (the International UAW's Education Center in northern Michigan, at which the Region hosts two weeklong training programs for leaders and activists each year) in the summer of 1990 on the "Union's Role in Joint Workplace Initiatives." Then, beginning that fall, classes were organized twice a year at the Region, covering topics including team concept, understanding business, health and safety, training and technology, flexible compensation, the organizing model of unionism, and union-centered approaches to joint activities. It was from the discussions and debates within those classes that the Region's paper, "Participation in Joint Programs: Mission Statement, Goals, Guidelines, Action Planning," was developed.

I was chosen to direct the project after working as an education advisor for UAW-Ford programs at Local 600 while Bob King was president. One reason for my appointment was my commitment as a trade unionist. This identification was challenged within the first year of the project, when debate occurred among advisors and board members about whether or not I was operating as a "neutral professional." What began as a gut reaction about not wanting to misrepresent myself became an analysis of how dangerous and false the concept of neutrality actually could be in our work sites. (See the council's publication on "The Role of Consultants in Small and Mid-Sized Unionized Firms.") Bob King backed this analysis, and it prevailed within the board. Management in our council has still found it valuable to use the council's services, despite the openly avowed leanings of its director.

Another tension that simmered and has been somewhat resolved over the past five years has been between the "common agenda" versus the "distinct agendas" approach to labor-management initiatives. In 1990 and 1991, it seemed radical to assert that unions and managements had to pursue separate and unmerging goals in joint programs, and the Region was accused of being adversarial in its approach. Nevertheless, that has been the council's premise for its activities, and it has found increasing acceptance over the years.

Some managements have come to see the wisdom of this approach. At least two have been grateful for it, since it has offered a way to incorporate hostile or passive local leadership more constructively into workplace change initiatives that were under way. At one facility, management paid for an eight-week program in which union representatives developed their position for participation in a team concept plan by answering the questions outlined in the previous section of this essay. They returned to the work site with their own agenda for involvement, a list of concerns about the site's ability to succeed, and some "demands" about what they felt they needed in order to go forward.

When the "distinct agenda" approach is presented to labor-management groups, what is remarkable is that resistance to the concept is often based not on well-informed political analysis but on the wish to make things easy. Operating from dual agendas means that both sides have to take on independent responsibility for their own goals, that they can't expect the other to take care of them, and that there is a permanent kind of tension. People want a quick fix or simple answer. An honest approach to labor-management initiatives doesn't offer either. Instead, it can provide the skills to conduct the ongoing process of bargaining over workplace issues in a manner that's more constructive, less conflictual, and more inclusive of the membership.

Where we've seen the failure of this hope for an easy out is with the concern representatives from both sides have about "trust." At a recent workshop, participants were asked if they could think of the "deal" that's often being unconsciously struck when two sides agree to trust each other, and someone said, "That each side will look out for the other's interests." Labor- management teams with any amount of experience inevitably wind up betrayed by the deal, since it's absurd to expect people to know, recognize, and act on the other side's interests as well as their own. That's why beginning from a recognition of the distinct agendas is so important.

Acceptance of the distinct agenda approach has reached the point that labor and management representatives at the council's semiannual membership meeting in May 1995 adopted without debate (though not necessarily without behind-the-scenes grumping) the following new proposed publication:

Finding the Common Ground in Management's and the Union's Interests

Elected labor officials and hired management staff are in their positions to represent distinct, independent organizations with different missions and agendas. When Unions and business engage in constructive relations and partnerships for workplace change, the differing purposes of their organizations don't change or become merged. Instead, representatives work to achieve the goals of their organizations in the wisest, fullest way possible. Then, through dialogue, debate, discussion and compromising, they attempt to find mutual gains, and the goals of both sides are achieved.

Joint activities and constructive relations must be built on each side's understanding and respect for the other's interests, and in acceptance that each decision must serve some of the other's needs. If both

125

sides accept responsibility for representing their distinct interests while showing concern for those of the other, trust can be built and meaningful change can be accomplished.

This doesn't mean ready agreement or the lack of conflict, but it does require that conflicts are handled constructively—with a focus on solving the problem and not blaming or villainizing the other side. A dynamic tension is present in all decisions as the attempt to balance interests and find solutions for mutual gains is made. The graph below indicates the common ground around which labor and management can serve their distinct interests.

Table 6.1

Management Interests	Common Ground	Union Interests
—Profit —Good return on investment —Dividends for shareholders —Competitive edge	—Quality —Productivity —Waste reduction —Reduced absenteeism —Customer relations —Increased markets —Problem resolution —Proactive health and safety	—Good wages —Good benefits —Good working conditions —A meaningful voice in decisions affecting workers' futures —Protection against unfair discipline, favoritism —Job security

The council has offered dozens of training programs in health and safety, team concept, constructive conflict, workplace violence, the Americans with Disabilities Act, continuous improvement, QS 9000, employee assistance programming, and other topics. Semiannual membership meetings are often hosted at sites where labor and management have a good story to tell about joint efforts to improve the workplace. Task forces visit members' facilities to discuss specific efforts undertaken by the union with management and to propose council activities. Panel discussions bring together labor, management, and other speakers to debate hot topics. Task forces, interns, and council staff develop publications offering guidelines and recommendations and discussing topics of interest. Staff provide on-site consulting to local processes. The council helps members plan for and get funding for workforce training.

In the fall of 1994, the councils were funded through a federal grant project called Cooperative Network for Dual Use Information Technologies (CoNDUIT), which is designed to assist small and midsized manufacturers in adopting computer information technologies by developing computer-based training programs that can support the technologies. A steering committee made up of union and management representatives is learning about networking, simulation, Computer Numerical Control (CNC), and interactive computer training technologies, and considering how they can best be introduced into our work sites. In the spring of 1995, the council began hosting labor-management overviews of the Big 3's new combined quality standard, QS 9000. LMCER argued that the standard was so rigorous and demanded so much shop-floor participation that labor and management must work together to ensure successful implementation. One union representative, upon hearing of the program, asked if the new standard was a secret. He had heard nothing about it, although his shop's future depends on compliance.

Although the council doesn't have, at this point, exemplary work sites that have successfully made the transition to high- performance organizations with internally organized union memberships, our members praise our work. The council has been a consistent source of information, inspiration, and encouragement to a variety of members. It has been able to help individual sites get through conflicts that were frustrating both the union and management. Some of the union leaders from smaller shops who have had little opportunity to attend training sessions or meetings now participate regularly. Labor and management leaders get to see the world beyond their own site, and many have been amazed at what can be done.

The council is one model by which the union movement can extend its capacity to assist local leaders in the workplace. By leveraging funds from employers, private foundations, and public agencies, while keeping substantial control over the nature of the work, the Region has supported a staffperson dedicated to the issue of the union's role in workplace change. It is hard to reach into the thousands of individual workplaces throughout the country and convey the AFL-CIO's new consensus, or national unions' policies and agendas. Small- and medium-scale local and regional efforts are a key strategy for providing this direct, intensive support and communication; even a project the size of the council finds it difficult to provide the level of service wished for.

Perhaps glowing examples of successfully transformed workplaces are not the point. Even when there is a site that has done a great job of improving relations and conditions, its story is only a snapshot, a moment. A year or two later, the same site might be full of problems and conflicts. This is irrelevant, because there is no end point, there is only day-to-day participation in workplaces where people are well-intentioned, wicked, talented, and incompetent, and the union movement has a mission that demands that it participate to expand dignity, democracy, and good jobs.

The union movement can't walk away from labor-management initiatives. They are too pervasive. They appeal to too many needs and concerns of our members. And they have too much potential if they are used to advance union goals and build the movement. We must build our capacity to participate as independent players, clearly pursuing our own agenda.

BIBLIOGRAPHY

AFL-CIO Committee on the Evolution of Work. 1994. *The New American Workplace: A Labor Perspective*. Washington, D.C.: American Federation of Labor-Congress of Industrial Organizations.

American Federation of Grainmillers. 1991. *The Grain Millers' Role in Creating Labor/Management Partnerships for New Work Systems. A Statement of Policy and Guidelines for Local Unions*. Minneapolis: American Federation of Grainmillers.

Baugh, Robert. 1994. *Changing Work: A Union Guide to Workplace Change*, Washington, D.C.: AFL-CIO Human Resources Development Institute.

Canadian Auto Workers. 1993. *Workplace Issues. Work Reorganization: Responding to Lean Production*. North York, Willowdale, Ont.: Canadian Auto Workers.

Communication Workers of America. 1993. *Union Involvement in the Workplace of the Future: A Guide for Staff and Local Unions Representing AT&T Employees*. Washington, D.C.: Communication Workers of America.

International Association of Machinists and Aerospace Workers. 1994. *GL-6 IAM Policy: High Performance Workplace Partnership*. Upper Marlboro, Md.: International Association of Machinists and Aerospace Workers.

Labor-Management Council for Economic Renewal. 1991. *The Four Key Ingredients of Labor-Management Relationships That Can Lead High Performance Workplaces*. Taylor, Mich.: Labor-Management Council for Economic Renewal.

Labor Research Review. 1989. *Participating in Management: Union Organizing on a New Terrain*. Chicago: Midwest Center for Labor Research.

———. 1991. *An Organizing Model of Unionism*. Chicago: Midwest Center for Labor Research.

National Treasury Employees Union. 1994. *NTEU and You: Getting Involved for a Better Worklife*. Washington, D.C.: National Treasury Employees Union.

Parker, Mike. 1985. *Inside the Circle: A Union Guide to QWL*. Detroit: Labor Notes.

Parker, Mike, and Jane Slaughter. 1988. *Choosing Sides: Unions and the Team Concept*. Detroit: Labor Notes.

———. 1994. *Working Smart: A Union Guide to Participation Programs and Reengineering*. Detroit: Labor Notes.

Richardson, Charley. 1993–95. Interviews with author. Washington, D.C. and Silver Springs, Md.

Robertson, Dave, et al. 1993. *The CAMI Report: Lean Production in a Unionized Auto Plant*. North York, Willowdale, Ont.: Canadian Auto Workers-Canada Research Department.

Service Employees International Union. 1993. *SEIU's Experience with Work and Union Participation in Quality Projects*. Washington, D.C.: Service Employees International Union.

Sheahan, Maureen. 1994. *Preparing Local Leaders for their Role in Work Restructuring—A Strategic Approach.* Taylor, Mich.: United Auto Workers Region 1A.

Till-Retz, Roberta. 1994. *Negotiating New Work Systems: Contract Language to Protect the Union.* Iowa City, Iowa: Labor Center, University of Iowa, 4th revision.

UNITE. 1994. *Partnership Agreement: Levi Strauss & Co., Amalgamated Clothing and Textile Workers Union.* Oct. New York City: UNITE.

United Auto Workers. 1994. *UAW Region 1A IPS Council: UAW Region 1A's Independent Parts and Suppliers Mission. Participation in Joint Programs: Mission Statement, Goals, Guidelines, Action Planning.* Taylor, Mich.: United Auto Workers Region 1A.

United Steelworkers of America. 1993. *Twelve Point New Directions Bargaining Initiative.* Pittsburgh, Pa.: United Steelworkers of America.

7

WORKPLACE EDUCATION AND LABOR-MANAGEMENT COOPERATION IN SMALL- AND MEDIUM-SIZED URBAN MANUFACTURING

MAE M. NGAI

Since the late 1970s, many American workplaces have experienced a major transformation. In response to the competitive demands of the global economy, a new trend in business and industry advocates smaller units of production, multiskilled teams, employee participation in decision making, and labor-management cooperation in the interest of productivity, quality, and job security. The so-called "high performance workplace" theoretically comprises high skills, high wages, and high quality, and promises increased economic competitiveness for business and more secure and meaningful work for workers.

At present, the high-performance workplace remains more an ideal than a reality. Its practical articulation is limited by a range of factors, not the least of which is a political and business climate that undermines the ability of workers to participate in meaningful ways. For the labor movement, the theory and practice of the changing workplace raise challenges for policy and strategy. Should unions even be concerned with issues traditionally believed to be solely in management's domain, such as quality, productivity, and market share? Should unions push businesses to commit more fully to the new workplace, or try to retard its implementation? Are the tenets and methods of twentieth-century industrial unionism really too conflictual and rigid for the workplace of the twenty-first? Or can the values and principles of American trade unionism be articulated in ways that speak to secular shifts in the global economy and the concerns of workers today?

This essay considers some of the problems raised by these questions by examining the role of union education programs that support labor-management cooperation projects in small- and medium-sized manufacturing firms in New York City. The experience of unions in these projects suggest the high-performance workplace is not a total or complete system. Rather, it is a process that involves an ongoing negotiation between management and labor over the organization of work, the use of technology, the decision-making process, the terms of compensation, and other issues concerning the boundaries of power in the workplace. Like its antecedents—the craft workshop and the mass production factory—the high-performance workplace is a contested ground upon which employers seek to enhance profits and workers strive individually and collectively for a decent standard of living and dignity in their work.

The high-performance workplace is sometimes called the workplace of "the future." The description is apt insofar as the high-performance workplace is characterized by new work practices aimed at meeting needs that traditional methods do not. But the future is not preordained. Traditional workplaces still far outnumber high-performance ones, and high-performance practices are often only partially implemented within many workplaces. Workplace change is also influenced by conditions outside the workplace, such as a conservative political environment, the continued export of jobs and capital out of the United States, and declining union membership as a percent of the workforce.

Thus while business needs for increased productivity and quality and the advent of new technologies compel the trend toward high-performance workplaces, the shape of those workplaces is far from settled. The process of workplace change is incomplete and therefore at this time somewhat messy and unstable. Union policies for the changing workplace are thus at once constrained by the weight of present conditions and constitutive of new strategies for the future.

Workplace education and training programs offer unions a particularly useful method of intervention during this period when the process of drawing (or redrawing) the boundaries of power within the new workplace is incomplete. Workplace education and training not only teach workers new skills but play an important role in helping unions mobilize their membership and clarify solutions for the new workplace. An effective workplace education program can provide both the organization and methodology for understanding and influencing workplace change.

THE NEW WORKPLACE

The evolution of the new workplace has been driven in large part by fundamental changes in the global economy in which capital, technology, production, and information have become highly transportable. Long-term declining productivity in the United States, government deregulation, and demographic changes in the workforce have further increased the competitive pressures on American businesses. The dominant trend in corporate policy has been to increase competitiveness by moving production to low-wage areas in the developing nations or lowering labor costs in the United States, or both. The diversion of capital to speculative financial investment has further depressed wages and living standards for American workers and eroded the nation's productive base (Harrison and Bluestone 1988; Davis 1986). Some economic scholars and policymakers, including those in the Clinton administration, have argued that the low-skill, low-wage path is a losing proposition for American business and industry in light of the impossibility of matching wages in the developing countries, new technologies, and the maturation of advanced markets. They advocate that companies reject the low-skill, low-wage road and choose instead a strategy based on high, knowledge-based skills, quality, and customized goods and services (Piore and Sabel 1984; Kochan, Katz, and McKersie 1986; Reich 1992).

In this vision, the mass production work system that has dominated American industry since the early twentieth century is considered a barrier to economic competitiveness and workforce development. Some companies have thus sought to replace the Taylorized work system and its perceived weaknesses of inefficiency, waste, neglect of customer needs, and low worker morale with a more flexible system of production that can quickly and continuously redeploy resources in support of rapidly changing market trends. New business theories have emerged with concepts like just-in-time, total quality, continuous improvement, and employee involvement, some of which are drawn from work systems employed in Japan (lean production), Italy (flexible specialization), and Sweden (sociotechnology) (Kochan, Katz, and McKersie 1986; Appelbaum and Batt 1994).

For the high-performance work system to function, workers need analytical and conceptual skills so they can make judgments and decisions on the production and delivery process, a role rarely demanded in the past. In its ideal conception, the new workplace rejects the traditional separation between thinking and doing. Workers are more productive because they work in teams that design and manage their own work; at the same time they understand how their work fits into the overall process. They contribute their intelligence and creativity to that process, not only on the shop floor but in strategic areas of management as well. The implications of these changes are profound, for they challenge many of the assumptions that lie at the heart of the culture of work and the system of industrial relations in the United States (Marshall 1992; Bluestone and Bluestone 1992).

Notwithstanding the promise of meaningful work and worker empowerment, important features of the high-performance work model were conceived during the 1970s as management alternatives to unions (Kochan, Katz and McKersie 1986). Moreover, the new workplace, while theoretically offering greater job security owing to its competitive advantage, in practice sometimes threatens workers' economic security through downsizing and displacements by technology. Many unions, however, have adopted policies that embrace the high-performance model and attempt to influence its design and practice. Unions often cite the need for a proactive approach to changes in the workplace they believe are inevitable. Some see those changes as potentially positive for workers insofar as increased business competitiveness leads to greater employment security and labor participation in decision making limits the domain of management rights (Chase and Klein 1994; Appelbaum and Batt 1994; Bluestone 1989).

The AFL-CIO considers the new workplace to be not only necessary to meet the demands of global competition but more democratic and humane than the traditional mass production system. The AFL-CIO states that the new system of work organization "combines *individual participation* through restructured work processes and redesigned jobs, with *collective representation*, through restructured decision-making processes from the shop floor to corporate headquarters. The aim of this approach is to achieve work organizations which are one and the same time more productive and more democratic. Therein lies the source of its legitimacy and power" (AFL-CIO Committee on the Evolution of Work 1994).

The AFL-CIO's policy statement accomplished a number of things. It placed the new work system in historical context, as a democratic advance over the Taylorized mass production system. It presented a compelling argument for both individual *and* collective worker participation, that is, for the need for workers to have their own independent organization in order to have meaningful participation and input at all levels of the new work system. Research also demonstrates that new work systems and labor-management cooperation efforts are most enduring and effective when implemented in unionized settings, where workers have both independent representation and contractual protections (Mishel and Voos 1992; Appelbaum and Batt 1994).

But if business leaders, economists, and organized labor all advocate the new workplace, it is only slowly taking root. A 1987 GAO survey of Fortune 1000 companies estimated that 60 to 70 percent of American companies used new practices, like self-managed teams and quality cir-

133

cles, but most were limited to a single practice or department and did not involve most employees. A survey conducted by Paul Osterman in 1992 concluded that 37 percent of firms had 50 percent or more of their core employees involved in at least two new work practices (Appelbaum and Batt 1994). Using a more comprehensive definition of high performance, the U.S. Commission on the Future of Worker-Management Relations (the Dunlop Commission) (1994) concluded that only 5 percent of the nation's workplaces can be classified as such. The commission defined "high performance" as a "total system that rests on a foundation of trust and combines employee participation, information sharing, and work organization flexibility with reinforcing human resource practices such as a commitment to training and development, gain sharing, employment security, and where a union is present, a full partnership between union leaders and management" (1994).

There are several reasons for such limited practice. In the real world, most companies are not choosing between two distinct and total systems, mass production or high performance, but operate at various points along a continuum. Many companies remain focused on short-term results, and thus utilize new methods on a selective basis. Competitive pressures make companies resist commitments to training, gainsharing, and job security for employees; traditional ways of thinking limit managers' willingness to concede power or control in the workplace. Workers are often less than enthusiastic about new methods. They sometimes also feel uneasy about assuming more responsibility or anxious that increased productivity will lead to layoffs. And companies seeking to use employee involvement programs as a means of undermining workers' right to union representation often find workers suspicious and reluctant to participate.

Moreover, labor unions are wary about taking risks in a general climate of economic uncertainty and political conservatism. Accustomed to upholding strict work rules in a Taylorized context, unions are nervous about throwing out contractual protections when it is unclear what will replace them. The undermining of workers' legal rights collectively to bargain and strike influence the dynamics of change within any given workplace by giving companies additional leverage over their employees, making worker participation and empowerment seem like hollow promises.

Organized labor has called for labor law reform to strengthen *existing* labor rights, but it has not advocated for any larger reconsideration of the system of industrial relations established during the 1930s. The AFL-CIO's report on new work systems boldly embraces the new workplace but does not critically examine the reigning system of industrial relations—including many entrenched union policies—that many advocates of new work systems find disconsonant with their operating principles. Thus the AFL-CIO responded tepidly to the Dunlop Commission's *Final*

Report (1995) despite that report's recommendations for reforms that would encourage the development of democratic work practices, strengthen workers' rights to organize, and give greater protections to contingent workers. Unions were most critical of what they perceived to be the commission's equivocation on Section 8(a)(2) of the National Labor Relations Act, the ban on company-dominated unions.

There is legitimate concern that tampering with Section 8(a)(2) is dangerous in a Republican-controlled U.S. Congress.[1] Nevertheless, the labor movement needs to move beyond a defensive position toward a policy on collective bargaining and labor law reform that addresses changes in the organization of work. Key features of traditional collective bargaining agreements include a hierarchy of job classifications, strict work rules, and clear distinctions between workers and supervisors—all important in mass-production industry but not well-suited to the new workplace. Survey data also show that many workers desire more flexibility, diversity, and decision-making authority in their work, as well as some form of union representation (U.S. Commission on the Future of Worker-Management Relations 1995). If, then, the current system of "workplace contractualism" developed out of the "logic" of the system of mass-production industry during the 1920s and 1930s (Brody 1993), the logic of new work systems should similarly compel unions to think about what ought to define the system of labor relations today. Only a bold, critical evaluation and self-evaluation on the part of the AFL-CIO and individual unions can make policy on new work systems fully relevant.

Moreover, union policy on workers' rights and just treatment in the new workplace needs to be linked to a proactive strategy to rebuild the labor movement. It is beyond the scope of this essay to elaborate such a program, but it might entail an aggressive commitment of resources to organize the unorganized, a political mobilization to elect prolabor candidates to public office, and a communications strategy that articulates the principles of unionism in ways that are relevant to workers' needs and concerns today.

Without a change in the political balance of power and a revitalization and growth of the labor movement, unions will find it difficult to make the new workplace truly democratic. Meanwhile, however, unions will continue to grapple with the demands of the high-performance workplace in all its limited and distorted practical expressions. Their efforts constitute an important ingredient in the development of union strategies for the future.

EDUCATION AND TRAINING IN THE NEW WORKPLACE

The Consortium for Worker Education (CWE), a not-for-profit organization comprising the education programs of thirty-four New York City

135

unions, has worked with unions, companies, and trainers in small- and medium-sized manufacturing to develop a model of education and training for workplaces that aspire to high-performance status.[2] Much of the experience—and the literature—on labor-management programs in high performance workplaces is in large corporations in basic industries like auto, electrical, and telecommunications (Appelbaum and Batt 1994; Rosow and Casner-Lotto 1995). Those programs are often negotiated at the highest levels of the company and the union and then brought into the workplace. In small- and medium-sized urban manufacturing, the process of workplace change is often more fluid. Changes in the organization of production and work practices are often introduced with limited strategic planning and without benefit of a labor-management process or agreement. However, because the urban manufacturing workforce often lacks sufficient English-language, literacy, and numeracy skills needed for new work systems, many employers are receptive to establishing a joint labor-management education program even when they have made no commitment to a strategic partnership with the union.

In this context, education and training provide unions with a particularly useful instrument to address issues of power and control in the changing workplace. Workplace education teaches people discrete skills, equipping them for new work requirements and enhancing their prospects for job security. An effective education and training program also helps workers understand the changes taking place around them, enhances their ability to participate in that process, and helps them make thoughtful decisions about their individual and collective futures. The classroom becomes a locus for critical discussion of the changing workplace from the perspective of workers on the shop floor. The changing workplace itself is the content of workplace curriculum. Certain features of the new workplace, such as continuous improvement and employee participation, are consonant with principles of workplace pedagogy, such as continuous learning and participatory education.

The CWE education model is based on several general principles. First, we understand that workplace learning is different from generic, school-based instruction. Workers are experts in the jobs they are doing. They find ways to adapt to the literacy and language requirements of the tasks they do and to the social environment at work. While learning or literacy problems may surface when new work tasks or organizational forms are introduced, workplace education should not be approached with the idea that workers suffer from educational deficits. Workplace instruction should build on the knowledge workers have and on the strategies they use for sharing and acquiring information from and with their coworkers. In addition, the organization itself should be assessed to see if it can utilize, develop, and apply the existing and proposed skills and knowledge of workers and management alike.

136

Another critical difference between workplace education and generic education is that the former typically involves a number of stakeholders, each of whom bring different goals and expectations to the workplace program. For example, management may see an education program as a way immediately to improve production, while workers may feel stigmatized by being placed in a literacy or English class. The union may see the classes as a way to help members become more active; teachers may associate the class with advancement and opportunity for the individuals participating. Often, the assumption in workplace programs is that literacy or English language instruction is the only kind of classes needed. In fact, workers may be interested in acquiring a high school equivalency degree or going to college, and some may need instruction to meet these goals. Supervisors may need a writing class; front-line workers may need computer skills. These varying assumptions and goals need to be discussed, and the stakeholders need to assess the class regularly to determine whether or not it is fulfilling its purpose for learners and for the reorganization process.

An educational assessment based on a participatory structure ensures ongoing input from representatives of all sections of the workplace. Managers, supervisors, workers, and union representatives participate through interviews or focus group discussions. To get all perspectives on each important issue, the same (or basically similar) questions are asked of all the sections of the workforce. This helps identify differences in perception that may come from existing gaps in communication (Folinsbee and Jurmo 1994).

The assessment findings may also point to other organizational and communication needs that should be addressed before any basic skills instruction can effectively take place. For example, in one workplace the language of the training manuals was considered by most workers to be unclear and unnecessarily complex. When the manuals were rewritten, many of the previous training problems vanished. In another workplace, what appeared to be a problem with an English as a Second Language (ESL) class turned out to be a misunderstanding relating to cultural differences. One ethnic group believed it was being discriminated against under a personnel practice relating to vacation time. As a result, the group did not want to participate in education programs. When the vacation issue surfaced during the assessment, it was addressed satisfactorily, and the group then participated in the program planning.

Second, we advocate a structured three-way partnership among labor, management, and educators to manage workplace education programs. Many large companies with dedicated training resources establish parallel training organizations to manage education programs. Joint training programs are now common in large unionized firms (Ferman et al. 1991; Roberts and Wozniak 1994). Smaller companies often do not have the resources or even the need for a discrete training organization. In these situations, workplace-based education committees comprising management, union representatives, and teachers provide organization for training assessment, design, and evaluation. A structured relationship is especially important for teachers, who may be from an outside training organization like CWE and not familiar with the workplace. Workplace education committees are particularly useful in workplaces where workplace change is partial or incomplete and broader labor-management cooperation structures are lacking. In some instances, education projects have served as a catalyst for greater cooperation by labor and management and the resolution of larger issues in the workplace.

Third, while training and education should be mixed, there are important distinctions between the two. Training instructs people *how* and *what* to do; education is the understanding of *why* we do something and how it fits into a larger purpose. Training may be narrowly appropriate to particular workplaces, tasks, or situations, while education that improves English-language skills, reading and writing, critical thinking and problem-solving abilities transfers to other domains of life. In the context of the changing workplace, education about the process and what it means for everyone involved provides the understanding of purpose that can motivate workers being trained to do specific jobs or tasks differently. Education situates the restructuring of the workplace within the larger economy and the forces driving the company to reorganize. It also provides a way for workers to understand what change at work means for their futures.

Finally, we advocate integrated and participatory education and training. Our experience has shown that basic education overlaps with all other needs related to workplace change. ESL and literacy instruction should not be taught in a vacuum but are effective when integrated with other aspects of the education and training project. For example, ESL can be developed in connection with the development of leadership and teamwork skills in a multilingual workplace. Basic reading or math instruction needs to go hand and hand with instruction on how to use new computerized equipment.

Some workplace educators advocate "functional context" instruction, which combines basic literacy instruction with job tasks and performance. Though nominally work-based, it is limited because it ignores the larger social and political context of the changing workplace. Moreover, functional context education tends to rely on outside experts and evaluators, undermining the involvement and respect for workers' knowledge associated with team-based work systems (Jurmo 1994).

Our model is both more participatory and more integrated. If workers need English-language skills to communicate in teams, the ESL curriculum has to focus on the role of team members in production on the shop floor *and* in decision-making meetings. Thus, rather than offering a ge-

138

neric ESL class focused on either a school-based model emphasizing grammar or a functional context model focused on work tasks, we recommend classes combining ESL with leadership or communications skills.

Curriculum is often open-ended, utilizing methods that enable workers to write their own lessons and critically evaluate the workplace. For example, a class in communications skills for group leaders at a cookware factory in the Bronx analyzed the culture of the workplace. Workers did their own ethnographic study of the factory, considering its demographics, values, rules, myths, and lines of power and communication. Ideally, workers and supervisors who attend classes related to their work should be able to integrate what they've learned immediately. CWE designed a cell training program for management and union at the a factory in Queens where little English was spoken. The program was designed so that speakers of different languages practiced communicating with each other in the classroom while they were learning cellular manufacturing concepts. Each session was then followed by an on-the-floor test of the concepts, skills, and language learned in the classroom.

Participatory education also utilizes techniques such as dialogues and role-plays. Dialogue themes emerge from classroom conversations and reflect participants' concerns relating to work, family, and other issues. Classes might also incorporate presentations by union and management spokespersons, health and safety experts, industrial engineers, and other relevant speakers. Workers thus utilize the classroom to discuss and evaluate issues important to them and often devise solutions to problems.

The above model is an ideal drawn from the collective experience of several companies and unions in manufacturing industries in New York City. The practice of implementing the model is much more uneven, and it is in the practical struggle to realize the high-performance workplace and high-performance education that unions wrestle with issues that embody questions of power, control, and purpose.

In New York City, which has lost more than 500,000 manufacturing jobs since 1966 (Fitch 1994), unions are acutely aware of the competitive pressures on industry that drive down wages and labor standards. Some unions have concluded that it is in their interest to support efforts to establish a high-skills and high-quality workplace. While some unions have long had industrial engineers on their staff, local union managers, business agents, and education staff have now gotten directly involved in modular manufacturing projects and the like. These trade unionists articulate traditional values of the labor movement—security, dignity, quality of worklife—in context of the problems posed by new conditions in the economy and the workplace. In the past, for example, employment security was generally assured by an expanding economy and growing markets; unions were concerned with regulating cyclical layoffs by seniority. Many unions now believe they have to take some responsibility for the

139

economic survival and viability of their companies. In the apparel industry, union leaders have educated themselves in the technologies of modular manufacturing and insist on playing a proactive role in the design and implementation of new systems. At one apparel shop in Brooklyn, the company first implemented modular manufacturing without input from the sewing operators; as a result, sewing methods were inefficient, and workers lost income from the new piece-rates. The workers protested with a work stoppage. The union helped resolve the crisis by negotiating a joint labor-management committee that involved workers in correcting the problems in the system and adjusting the piece-rates. The ESL class in the factory assisted the process by helping workers organize their ideas and articulate their concerns. For the union, the process involved a complex integration of education in ESL and teamwork skills, strengthening the union's shop organization and developing rank-and-file leaders, and ongoing negotiation and intervention with the company.

In exchange for assuming greater responsibility for enhancing productivity and quality, unions want commitments to just compensation and job security as much as possible. However, companies are not always willing to make such commitments. The issue is one of fairness and creating an environment where workers feel they have an investment in the new work system. At a factory in Queens, the union was confronted with layoffs from downsizing at the same time that the employer requested a training program for self-managed teams in the new work system. Workers were unenthusiastic about the new setup because they associated their increased productivity with layoffs. The union was willing to participate in the training program but demanded that the employer place the training program under a labor-management structure where its design and implementation would be considered as part of a the larger picture. Because the company would not agree, the training program did not take place.

The same issues emerge at the very basic and practical level of organizing a class in the factory. For example, unions are not always able to get the company to pay release time for instruction. The practice is common in large corporations, but in small manufacturing, where the workforce is small, deadlines are tight, and resources are marginal, the issue of release time can be problematic. Union educators point out that workers are less able to participate in education programs after work hours owing to family responsibilities, transportation difficulties, or other issues. They also argue that employers need to view education as an investment and not merely another cost. In some factories, unions have negotiated full release time for ESL or other instruction; in others, two-hour classes are scheduled between shifts, with workers receiving one hour of paid release time and contributing the other hour on their own time.

At all levels—strategy, policy, and daily practice—unions are struggling to articulate their basic values to meet the demands of the changing workplace. In all of the above examples, unions took positions based on a general commitment to productivity, quality, and cooperation with management, all nontraditional concerns for unions. At the same time, their positions were based on basic trade union principles of safeguarding jobs and demanding that the employer respect workers' knowledge, interests, and rights to have a voice in the workplace. Education programs often served as the impetus for defining workers' positions on those issues and as a vehicle for strengthening the union's shop-floor organization and developing rank-and-file leadership. Ironically, while management initiated new work systems based on "teams" and "employee involvement," in each case the union had to struggle for "cooperation" to have any practical meaning. In fact, productivity, quality, and cooperation took place only to the extent that workers and their unions effectively negotiated with management over issues of power and control, and made the principle of workplace justice that lies at the heart of trade unionism relevant to the changing workplace.

NOTES

1. Research also suggests that employer claims that Section 8(a)(2) hinders labor-management cooperation are largely groundless. The overwhelming number of employee involvement committees ordered disestablished by the National Labor Relations Board (NLRB) because of Section 8(a)(2) violations were in cases that also involved other unfair labor practices by management (Rundle 1994).

2. The model described here is drawn from "Education and Training for the Changing Workplace: A Practical Guide for Managers, Unionists, and Teachers" (1995), produced by the New York Area Labor Management Educators Committee, a project of CWE directed by the author and funded by the Federal Mediation and Conciliation Service. Members of the project included ACCO-USA, Beth Israel Medical Center, Farberware, Inc., Mademoiselle Knitwear, Inc., Magic Novelty Company, Inc., Marcus and Wiesen, Inc., and Sequins International, Inc. (management partners); Teamsters Locals 815 and 808, International Ladies Garment Workers Union Locals 155 and 62–32 and ILGWU Education and Organizing Departments, 1199/National Union of Health and Human Service Workers, and Retail, Wholesale, and Department Store Workers Union Local 377 (union partners); the Alliance for Employee Growth and Development, Consortium for Worker Education, Garment Industry Development Corporation, and New York City Industrial Technology Assistance Corporation (training and education partners).

BIBLIOGRAPHY

AFL-CIO Committee on the Evolution of Work. 1994. *The New American Workplace: A Labor Perspective.* Washington, D.C.: American Federation of Labor-Congress of Industrial Organizations.

Appelbaum, Eileen, and Rosemary Batt. 1994. *The New American Workplace: Transforming Worksystems in the United States.* Ithaca, N.Y.: ILR Press.

Bluestone, Barry. 1989. "Goodbye to the Management Rights Clause." Participating in Management, Union Organizing on a New Terrain. *Labor Research Review* 14 (fall): 66–72.

Bluestone, Barry, and Irving Bluestone. 1992. *Negotiating the Future: A Labor Perspective on American Business.* New York: Basic Books.

Brody, David. 1993. "Workplace Contractualism in Comparative Perspective." In *Industrial Democracy in America: The Ambiguous Promise,* ed. Nelson Lichtenstein and Howell Harris. New York: Cambridge University Press.

Chase, Thomas, and Janice Klein, eds. 1994. *The Role of Unions in New Worksystems.* Northwood, N.H.: Ecology of Work.

Davis, Mike. 1986. *Prisoners of the American Dream.* London: Verso.

Ferman, Louis, et al., eds. 1991. *Joint Training Programs: A Union-Management Approach to Preparing Workers for the Future.* Ithaca, N.Y.: ILR Press.

Fitch, Robert. 1994. "Explaining New York City's Aberrant Economy." *New Left Review* 207 (Sept./Oct.): 17–38.

Folinsbee, Sue, and Paul Jurmo. 1994. *Collaborative Evaluation: A Handbook for Workplace Development Planners.* Don Mills, Ont.: ABC Canada Literacy Foundation.

Harrison, Bennett, and Irving Bluestone. 1988. *The Great U-Turn: Corporate Restructuring and the Polarizing of America.* New York: Basic Books.

Jurmo, Paul. 1994. *Education in the New Workplace: Literacy at Work.* Don Mills, Ont.: ABC Canada Literacy Foundation.

Kochan, Thomas, Robert Katz, and Robert McKersie. 1986. *The Transformation of American Industrial Relations.* New York: Basic Books.

Marshall, Ray. 1992. "Work Organization, Unions, and Economic Performance." In *Unions and Economic Competitiveness,* ed. Lawrence Mishel and Paula Voos. Armonk, N.Y.: M.E. Sharpe.

Mishel, Lawrence, and Paula Voos, eds. 1992. *Unions and Economic Competitiveness.* Armonk, N.Y.: M.E. Sharpe.

Piore, Michael, and Charles Sabel. 1984. *The Second Industrial Divide: Possibilities for Prosperity.* New York: Basic Books.

Reich, Robert. 1992. *The Work of Nations.* New York: Vintage.

Roberts, Markley, and Robert Wozniak. 1994. *Labor's Key Role in Workplace Training.* Washington: AFL-CIO Economic Research Department.

Rosow, Jerome, and Jill Casner-Lotto. 1995. *Strategic Partners for High Performance, Part II: People, Partnership and Profits, the New Labor-Management Agenda.* Scarsdale, N.Y.: Work in America Institute.

Rundle, James. 1994. "The Debate Over the Ban on Employer-Dominated Labor Organizations: What Is the Evidence?" *Restoring the Promise of American Labor Law,* ed. Sheldon Friedman, et al. Ithaca, N.Y.: ILR Press.

U.S. Commission on the Future of Worker-Management Relations. 1994. *Fact Finding Report.* Washington: U.S. Departments of Commerce and Labor.

———. 1995. *Final Report.* Washington: U.S. Departments of Commerce and Labor.

V

IN
THE PUBLIC
SECTOR

8

REINVENTING THE FEDERAL GOVERNMENT: FORGING NEW LABOR-MANAGEMENT PARTNERSHIPS FOR THE 1990S

EDWARD L. SUNTRUP AND DAROLD T. BARNUM

INTRODUCTION: FEDERAL LABOR-MANAGEMENT PARTNERSHIP POLICY SINCE 1993

Since the advent of the Clinton administration, there has been a distinct change in federal policy concerning U.S. workplace relationships. From its commencement in early 1993, the administration has put great emphasis on encouraging cooperative relationships between employees (and their unions) and employers, with such arrangements sometimes called union-management partnerships. Much of the new policy originated in the U.S. Department of Labor, where respect for, and even the encouragement of, unionism by the secretary of labor has surpassed the expectations even of many unionists. In line with this attitude, the administration has argued that labor cooperation spawns more competitive employers, makes for more satisfied employees, and leads to higher profits and, potentially, richer stockholders.

The Dunlop Commission[1] was appointed early in the Clinton administration. It was viewed by some as a policy initiative on labor-management cooperation by the Department of Labor, although the Department of Commerce also nominally signed on as cosponsor of the commission's work. The commission was charged with exploring methods and practices that would enhance labor-management cooperation inside and outside the collective bargaining arena and with examining how such cooperation could be attained without the intervention of the government or the courts. The commission released its *Fact Finding Report* in May 1994, several months after the AFL-CIO's Committee on the Evolution of Work issued *The New American Workplace: A Labor Perspective*. After checking the work of scholars, as well as conducting many public fact-finding hearings on its own, the Dunlop Commission noted that U.S. workplaces already had many cooperative work arrangements of various kinds. The report concluded that "the best available estimates suggest that between one-fifth and one-third of the work force is (already) covered by some form of employee participation," with some thirty thousand cooperative workplace arrangements already existing in the United States (Dunlop Commission 1994). Further, the commission reported that a substantial number of American workers wanted even more input into decision making, suggesting that U.S. employees hunger for more partnerships, at least in those circumstances where both cooperative arrangements and employee decision-making input are present.

In sum, the basic message of both the Department of Labor and the Dunlop Commission is clear. As a matter of federal policy and workplace fact, partnerships are in. Autocratic management styles and monocratic work structures are out.

THE CHASM BETWEEN LABOR-MANAGEMENT COOPERATION AND U.S. LABOR LAW

If workplace cooperation and partnerships are an improved way of operating the American workplace, and if such arrangements already exist in abundance, it would seem that lawmakers might want to create legal supports for such a work system. Such support, however, has not been forthcoming.

It might not be so obvious at first view, but workplace partnerships can mean two quite different things. One type of partnership includes quality circles, self-managed work teams, and quality-of-life committees. The other type is synonymous with collective bargaining. Therein lies the difference. The former grouping represents cooperative arrangements that may or may not include independent decision-making input by employees. The latter grouping requires independent decision-making input by employees and may or may not include cooperation, but is most typically characterized by conflict.

All labor laws written to cover the private sector in the U.S. assume "partnerships" characterized by conflict. This is true of the Railway Labor Act of 1926, as well as the National Labor Relations Act of 1935, and all their amendments. This is true of all state laws passed for public sector employees since the early 1960s, as well as Title VII of the Civil Service Reform Act of 1978, which covers federal employees. Our labor laws were not written to regulate cooperative workplace arrangements, although they permit it in some cases. Nothing has happened to change this in terms of legal developments in the United States since early 1993, despite the new national policy encouraging partnerships and the widespread existence of workplace cooperation.

In fact, the two major efforts to amend the National Labor Relations Act since 1993 represent very traditional solutions to labor-management issues. Further, they do nothing to encourage productive partnerships between managements and employee unions.

In the first instance, Worker Fairness Legislation was defeated in the U.S. Senate early in the Clinton administration by means of a filibuster by its opponents. This legislation would have eliminated the practice of permitting employers permanently to replace workers who are striking over economic issues (as opposed to unfair labor practice strikes). Worker Fairness Legislation was meant to eliminate this situation but had nothing to do with union-management partnerships or cooperation.

The second attempt to amend the National Labor Relations Act was the Team Act. A bill dealing with this legislation first passed the House of Representatives in September of 1995 and was considered in the Senate in the spring of 1996. But this proposed legislation also has little to do with enhancing union-management cooperation in the workplace, or with encouraging labor-management partnerships. Among other things, the act would make it legal for managements to avoid dealing with independent employee unions when discussing traditional collective bargaining matters with groups of their employees. Thus it would eliminate the legal assurance of true decision-making input by employees, making partnerships between equals less likely to occur. More basically, concerning the topic of this essay, it does nothing to protect or promote efforts by employers and unions to move from conflict-based bargaining to interest-based cooperation and partnerships. Indeed, because it would make unions less secure in their dealings with managements, the legislation would likely make unions more belligerent and less likely to take a chance on cooperation.

There continues to be, therefore, a chasm between current policies in Washington that encourage cooperative union-management partnerships in the U.S. workplace, and any labor law remotely related to such policies. Nothing has happened, in terms of either amendments, or any fundamental changes in the orientation of the intent of any of our labor laws since 1993, to change that.

This is why President Clinton's Executive Order 12871 of 1993 is an important document. This order not only diverges from mainline labor law tradition but is an attempt to put into sync the Clinton administration's support for cooperative union-management partnerships and the legal coverage aimed at encouraging and supporting such partnerships.

147

Obviously, the order is not a statute. And its application is limited to the federal sector. But it does establish, for this one sector, unambiguous support for union-management cooperation. Importantly, Executive Order 12871's intent is not to regulate union-management conflict but to encourage partnerships between equals and cooperative behavior.

THE FEDERAL REINVENTION INITIATIVE AND LABOR-MANAGEMENT PARTNERSHIPS

It is difficult to understand the thrust of the order and its companion federal reinvention initiative without considering how the two are linked together.[2] Nor can the innovative roles of several federal unions be undervalued as participatory members of this cooperative reinvention effort that has been going on for the last several years, albeit, truth to be told, they did not have much choice but to participate.[3] We think here of the involvement particularly, but not only, of the National Treasury Workers' Union (NTEU), the National Federation of Federal Employees (NFFE), and the American Federation of Government Employees (AFGE).[4]

When it was determined, early in the Clinton administration, that the federal government was allegedly too big, too expensive, too bureaucratic, and not as efficient as it could be—accusations that have always been levied against it—Vice President Al Gore drew the assignment of recommending what should be done. The charge given to Vice President Gore in March of 1993 was outlined by President Clinton as follows:

> Our goal is to make the entire federal government both less expensive and more efficient, and to change the culture of our national bureaucracy away from complacency and entitlement toward initiative and empowerment. We intend to redesign, to reinvent, to reinvigorate the entire national government. (Gore 1993)

Gore's initiatives resulted in the September 1993 *Report of the National Performance Review* (NPR). At first glance, this report reads like a proposal for reengineering and dumbsizing that has become the employer's panacea, and the employee's plague, of so many large companies in the U.S. since the early 1980s. The NPR report dealt with putting customers first and improving services, eliminating waste and streamlining purchases, decentralizing and shaking loose from the frozen rules of bureaucracy, and improving productivity and holding employees accountable for their work, which is all pretty standard stuff for improving any large work organization.

However, close observers of the work of the NPR began to realize early on that the originality of its report centered on the meaning of newly minted terms such as "reinvent" and the novel way the report was using terms such as "partnership" and "culture." How did the intent of such terms, used to describe vast organizational change, differ from such terms used in corporate America such as "downsizing" or "reengineering," which more properly described how so many industrial organizations became leaner in the 1980s and into the 1990s in response to deregulation, threats from imports, and changing culture and technology? How were President Clinton's goals to be met without this whole process turning into yet another monocratically executed exercise of across-the-board mass layoffs, speeded-up attrition rates through imaginative or otherwise buyout and early retirement programs, the closure of one work site after another, and so on? Questions such as this did not center on goals. Rather, they centered on the means to achieve the goals outlined in President Clinton's charge to the NPR. And the key to understanding these means centered on what the NPR report called the formation of "a labor-management partnership." The NPR report on this issue states the following:

> federal employees want to participate in decisions that affect their work ... (and) ... no move to reorganize for quality can succeed without the full and equal participation of workers and their unions. ... the primary barrier that unions and employers must surmount is the adversarial relationship that binds them to noncooperation ... [and] ... title VII of the 1978 Civil Service Reform Act presents such a barrier. ... [Therefore,] we can only transform government if we transform the adversarial relationship that dominates federal union-management interaction into a partnership for reinvention and change. ... The President should issue a directive[5] that establishes labor-management partnership as an executive branch goal. ... The National Partnership Council will propose the statutory changes needed to make labor-management partnership a reality. (Gore 1993)

Thus the NPR report not only stressed the need for a change of management-labor culture in the federal government based on a cooperative model characterized by partnerships, which is what reinvention means in this context, but it also recognized that change would be difficult to bring about without the cooperation of federal unions for the obvious reason that three-fourths of federal employees eligible for union representation are covered by union contracts.[6] There is no assumption in the report that federal unions might not participate in the process. The stumbling block, or the "barrier" to partnerships as the report put it, was the law under which federal unionism functioned heretofore, which assumed an adversarial relationship and only presented procedures for regulating such conflict.[7] To date, no statutory changes have been enacted for federal management-labor relations. But what does exist is an ethos of partnership outlined in Executive Order No. 12871, which did follow closely on the heels of the NPR report.

149

EXECUTIVE ORDER NO. 12871: POINTING THE WAY

The title of Executive Order No. 12871 is "Labor-Management Partnerships." In its introductory statement, it sets the stage for cooperative partnerships as vehicle for change in the federal government. The executive order states the following:

> The involvement of federal government employees and their union representatives is essential to achieving . . . reform objectives. Only by changing the nature of federal labor-management relations so that managers, employees, and employees' elected union representatives serve as partners will it be possible to design and implement comprehensive changes necessary to reform government. Labor-management partnerships will champion change in federal government agencies to transform them into organizations capable of delivering the highest quality services to the American people. (President 1993)

The executive order then lays out the mechanics of achieving change by means of partnerships in the federal government.

First of all, a higher-echelon partnership will be created, to exist for two years or more (it continues to exist as of this writing), called the National Partnership Council. Its functions include, but are not limited to, providing support and guidance for lower-echelon working partnerships throughout the executive branch; collecting and disseminating information to assist these latter partnerships; and proposing statutory changes to the president consistent with federal partnership objectives. Eleven individuals serve on the National Partnership Council: the directors of the Office of Management and Budget (OMB) and Office of Personnel Management (OPM); the deputy secretary of labor; the chair of the Federal Labor Relations Authority (FLRA), which administers the 1978 law that regulates federal union-management relations; the director of the Federal Mediation and Conciliation Service (FMCS); the deputy director for management, Office of Management and Budget; and the presidents of the three largest federal labor unions cited earlier, the NTEU, the NFFE, and the AFGE. The council also includes the secretary-treasurer of the Public Employees Department of the AFL-CIO, and the deputy secretaries, or some other officer, of two other federal agencies. Both management and labor are represented, therefore, at the upper policy levels of the federal partnership.

On what might be called the operational level, the head of each federal agency or department is then mandated by the executive order to create labor-management partnerships by forming committees or councils, if they do not already exist, in order "to help reform government." The functions of these partnerships are to "involve employees and their union representatives as full partners with management representatives to identify problems and craft solutions to better serve the agency's customers and mission" (President 1993). Obviously, these partnerships can go to the National Partnership Council, if needs be, to obtain guidance, assistance, and so on.[8]

As a logistical matter, in order to bring about change to "better serve the agency's customers and mission," these partnerships can function in two quite different ways.

Parties to partnerships can engage in collective bargaining and negotiate over mandatory items of bargaining at the bargaining table.[9] With respect to negotiations, Executive Order 12871 opens the door on the scope of mandatory items. This expansion of the scope of bargaining, only alluded to in the executive order, is outlined in another federal document that was issued approximately two months after the order. This latter memorandum, directed to all federal agency and department heads as well as to federal unions, was issued under title of a "Guidance (document) for Implementing Executive Order 12871" (King 1993). This document renders moot, in one fell swoop, many aspects of a pattern of legal bickering in federal labor-management relations that has been going on since 1962[10] involving control of decision making over a whole plethora of issues regulating the labor-management relationships in the federal workplace. By widening the scope of bargaining, the guidance document, of course, greatly enhances employee input into the arena of managerial decision making through the collective bargaining (now viewed as a partnership) process.[11] The guidance document states the following:

> the numbers, types and grades of employees or positions assigned to any organizational subdivision, work project, or tour of duty, and the technology, methods and means of performing work . . . are directly related to specific agency reinvention initiatives and to achieving the National Performance Review (NPR) goal of making government work better and cost less. Bargaining over these subjects will also be a new experience for virtually all management and union representatives. Until [the SCRA of 1978] was passed, bargaining over these subjects was prohibited; since 1978 such bargaining has been permitted at agency discretion but only rarely has that discretion been exercised. Under Executive Order 12871 bargaining over these subjects . . . is now mandatory. (King 1993)

Do we not have here simply another version of the old adversarial approach, but with widened bargaining scope, which partnerships were precisely meant to replace? On the face of it, this might seem to be true. But we do not believe this to be the case because the bargaining method proposed by Executive Order 12871 is different than traditional adversarial bargaining. On this count, the executive order states the following:

> [on the operational level the head of each agency or department] shall provide systematic training of appropriate agency employees (including

151

line managers, first line supervisors, and union representatives who are federal employees) in consensual methods of dispute resolution, such as alternative dispute resolution techniques and interest-based bargaining approaches.

At the bargaining table, therefore, the partnerships are to use consensus and interest-based bargaining.[12]

On the other hand, partnerships must also perform the function of "craft[ing] solutions to better serve the agency's customers and mission" in some manner and by methods that are clearly different from collective bargaining. This has been interpreted to mean partnership exercises in organizational design that also use consensus and interest-based bargaining techniques. The authors of this chapter believe that the exercise of union-management partnership relations in this manner, which implies joint decision making in an informal manner, outside the formal collective bargaining format, is novel and unique. For such an approach to work the partnership participants, theoretically at least, ought to have a working knowledge of organizational theory and organizational behavior and some understanding of strategic management and organizational development principles. Obviously, federal partnership participants involved in an exercise in organizational design also have to be familiar with consensual and interest-based bargaining methods since these are the methods driving a cooperative partnership approach. We believe that this is a great deal to ask. From our experience, some agency employees simply misunderstand and/or confuse collective bargaining with interest-based procedures applicable to organizational design and tend to treat organizational design exercises as confrontational collective bargaining sessions.[13] Others, however, are able to make the transition and keep the two separate. In one of the organizational design exercises that we participated in as outside facilitators, federal employees at one agency were able to take their agency through a veritable metamorphosis of structural change in approximately one concentrated week of work. This included the changing of lines of authority, the redesign of supervisory positions and reassignment of supervisors, and the redistribution of functions. In another agency, a "partnership" between some supervisors and union leaders who did not want to change the organizational structure played a role in retarding the progress envisioned for reinvention efforts, as did the notions on the part of some participants who confused the interest-based processes of organizational design with the former confrontational processes of traditional collective bargaining.[14]

THE AFL-CIO CALL FOR PARTNERSHIPS AND FEDERAL REINVENTION

To what extent are the AFL-CIO's recent call for partnerships and the federal reinvention initiative in sync? A review, and comparison, of both warrant conclusions that there are many similarities, but also some differences.

For our purposes here, it is sufficient to note that the AFL-CIO 1994 Partnership Report underlines that labor-management partnerships worth that title must include employees who have decision-making rights. This is why the report is critical of forms of employer-employee cooperation that are employer-dominated. Those are not true partnerships, according to the report. The report views them as "mirages" that offer the appearance, "but not the substance, of genuine worker involvement." Further, true partnerships are achieved only by means of "free and independent labor unions which [employees] control."

In this respect, the AFL-CIO report cites the federal reinvention program approvingly. The report states:

> What President Clinton said about the federal sector in creating his National Partnership Council is equally true of all sectors: "the involvement by federal governmental employees and their union is essential . . . Only by changing the nature of Federal Labor-Management relations will it be possible to design and implement comprehensive change. (AFL-CIO Committee on the Evolution of Work 1994)

The AFL-CIO report goes on to cite a variety of characteristics that make up true labor-management partnerships. Some of these coincide with those found in the federal mandates for reinvention, including the obvious acceptance of collective bargaining as the forum in which partnership activity should formally expresses itself. Further, the AFL-CIO report even appears to be consonant with federal reinvention's extraformal procedures related to organizational design, although the report does not exactly use those terms. It calls, in fact, the "designing [of] new work systems . . . a venture into uncharted terrain" for many unionists. There can be no doubt about the accuracy of that observation.

The report says, in this respect:

> partnerships must be founded on the principle of equality. In concrete terms, this means that unions and management must have an equal role in the development and implementation of new work systems, including equal representation and control over any bodies created as part of the work reorganization. Similarly, unions and management must have equal access to any information relevant to the issues they are jointly addressing. (AFL-CIO Committee on the Evolution of Work 1994)

If there is a difference between the manner in which the AFL-CIO report envisages labor-management partnerships, as opposed to the approach of the reinvention mandates, this appears to center, first of all, on the procedures to be used to attain agreed-upon objectives. Executive Order 12871 clearly emphasizes the use of consensual and interest-based bargaining methods for achieving mutual goals in a cooperative partnership. The AFL-CIO report says nothing about that. In fact, it speaks somewhat derisively of labor-management "cooperation," which it states should not be substituted for "adversarialism" in labor-management relations. The AFL-CIO report views conflict as endemic to the process of labor-management relations and, indeed, endemic to partnerships. The obvious bargaining tactic to accompany such a view is old-line positional bargaining. Only as a disclaimer does the AFL-CIO report stress that conflict does not necessarily mean that the parties have to be "antagonistic." In a direct reference to both conflict and power theory, the report states that "in the partnerships we envision, such conflicts of interest can be worked out in an atmosphere of mutual respect, trust and good will . . . since . . . unions cannot give ground on worker interests for some abstract notion of 'cooperation' as an end in itself" (AFL-CIO Committee on the Evolution of Work 1994).

Anyone studying the federal program on reinvention and/or involved in it would be hard pressed to believe that its constant references to cooperation represent "some abstract notion." Clearly, the federal reinvention mandates do not view partnership cooperation only as an abstraction. They view it as a realizable possibility. The FLRA even has a director of "Labor-Management Cooperation" (Federal Labor Relations Authority 1994).[15]

In the final analysis, cooperative thinking along the lines of federal reinvention, as this applies to partnerships, may be a commodity that private sector unionists believe they cannot afford, not only because of strong pockets of hostile managers in the U.S. industrial workplace but also because U.S. labor law, as written, does not provide protections for unionists who do not constantly guard their vested interests vis-à-vis such managers. Indeed, many unionists believe that if given a chance, these same managers would just fabricate another nail in the coffin of unionists under title of legislation. Proposed labor law in 1995 such as the Team Act does not exactly engender high levels of trust among industrial unionists who might otherwise be willing to participate in partnership behavior with American managers.

CONCLUDING COMMENTS

The AFL-CIO's view on labor-management partnerships is ultimately based on conflict theory and a theory of power politics. The federal reinvention view on labor-management partnerships, on the other hand, is based on a somewhat elusive, even somewhat quasi-utopian, theory of cooperation, whereby the notion of trust in the workplace is taken seriously by both managers and labor.

Nothing approximating federal reinvention, as it is mandated in President Clinton's Executive Order 12871, has ever been attempted in the history of U.S. labor-management relations. That reinvention might be a possibility at all is the result, of course, of it being proposed not by labor but by the executive branch of the federal government, whose officials happen to hold a particular labor-management philosophy.

But even if federal reinvention does not work as proposed, it may henceforth serve as an example for private-sector labor-management partnerships as an experiment, based in theory at least, on an assumption of mutual labor-management trust. It will have shown that labor-management partnerships based on a theory of cooperation, in lieu of adversarialism, may indeed present some possibilities not heretofore perhaps given their day in court. Federal reinvention is certainly an experiment that tends to reorient thinking about labor-management partnerships as well as about the underlying assumptions of U.S. labor laws generally.

Even if, in a future political era, the philosophy embedded in Executive Order 12871 is scrapped, some tangible results of federal reinvention will remain. As a practical matter, the widened scope of bargainable items, mandated by Executive Order 12871, will undoubtedly become institutionalized, and inroads by federal unionists into certain areas of shared governance will have been accomplished and will endure. Beyond that, both labor and management in the federal government may have to go through another cycle in the future and wait for the next utopia.

NOTES

1. The official title of what has become known as the Dunlop Commission, because former secretary of labor John Dunlop was appointed chairman of the twelve-member commission, is Commission on the Future of Worker-Management Relations. The commission was set up shortly after President Clinton's inauguration in 1993.

2. There are theoretical assumptions underpinning a document such as Executive Order 12871 that are not found in the body of U.S. labor law generally. The latter assumes that humans are to be mistrusted in their relations with each other in the workplace, that power politics will dominate, and that those in dominant positions would take advantage of those in subordinate positions, in the absence of enforceable rules, and so on. Such is inextricably related to conflict theory. The assumptions underpinning a document such as Executive Order 12871, on the other hand, are that humans can be trusted to cooperate with each other in the workplace, that they will be able to determine shared interests and common goals, and so on. Such is inextricably related to a theory of cooperation.

3. Approximately 60 percent of the federal workforce is under union contract. These 1.3 million federal workers comprise 80 percent of the federal workforce that is eligible for unionization. These do not include the workers at the U.S. Postal Service. Since the 1970 Postal Reorganization Act, postal employees have been covered by the National Labor Relations Act of 1935 and its amendments. Postal employees are not involved in the federal reinvention program.

4. There are some 125 different unions representing federal employees. The

lion's share of the employees under union contract, however, are represented by these three unions. NTEU has 150,000 members. It was founded in 1938 in Milwaukee, Wisconsin. Current president is Robert M. Tobias. NTEU is an independent union not affiliated with the AFL-CIO. NFFE has 150,000 members. It was founded in 1917 in Washington, D.C., and is the oldest of the three largest federal unions. Current president is Sheila K. Valazo. The NFFE is an independent union not affiliated with the AFL-CIO. AFGE has 200,000 members. It was founded in 1932 in Washington, D.C. Current president is John N. Sturdivant. AFGE is an AFL-CIO affiliate.

5. This directive was Executive Order 12871 of October 1, 1993.

6. Union involvement in industrial change, of course, is not new, as the changes that the auto, airline, and steel industries, for example, went through in the 1980s are witness. The Machinists and Pilots' unions engineered the largest employee buyout in American history at United Airlines in 1994 in a move that arguably permitted that airline to continue to be one of the dominant airlines in the world. With but an exception or two, there have been no organizational changes in the U.S. industrial workplace of individual large corporations, at any time, that have ever included the magnitude of the involvement of unions that the federal reinvention program contemplates. A well-known exception to such a generalization may be General Motors' Saturn division in Tennessee, where the UAW has been involved from the conception of that new GM division to the production of the finished product for much of the last decade. What may be the most extraordinary thing about Saturn, however, is that such levels of cooperation were achieved between GM and the UAW under a legal protective umbrella that assumed conflict. Clearly the Saturn experiment has been swimming against the legal stream from the beginning. Given a strong opposition group at the Saturn UAW Local that has emerged in the last few years and which is dissatisfied with the relationship between the Local and Saturn management, the cooperative relationship at Saturn may just peter out in the future anyway.

7. Indeed, a 1991 survey of union leaders, government managers, federal employees, and neutral experts by the federal government concluded that "the federal labor-management relations program embodied in [the Civil Service Reform Act of 1978] is 'not working well.' " The program characterized existing bargain practices as "too adversarial, bogged down by litigation over minute details, plagued by slow and lengthy dispute resolution, and weakened by poor management." One interviewee stated the following about federal labor-management relations up to 1991: "We have never had so many people and agencies spend so much time, blood, sweat and tears on so little. . . . it is an awful waste of time and money on very little results" (Gore 1993).

8. The agency-level teams can be further subdivided into types of labor-management teams with specific functions. For example, in the Department of Labor a three-pronged approach was developed "to review and approve employee proposals to improve DOL." This approach implies the existence of three types of teams: agency and functional reinvention teams, and what is called a leadership team. Agency teams lead an agency within the Department of Labor (DOL)—Occupational Safety and Health Administration (OSHA), Bureau of Labor Statistics (BLS), etc.—to examine its program and practices. Functional teams concentrate on crossagency issues such as employment and training. Finally, the

leadership teams oversee the other two, review changes proposed by the others, and serve as liaison between the agency and the National Performance Review Council (U.S. Department of Labor 1993).

9. This aspect of the partnership thrust gets fairly complicated in view of the fact that a union such as the AFGE, for example, which is the largest federal union representing federal employees, negotiates contacts both for specific federal agencies and across various agencies.

10. Federal unionism in the United States received its first legitimization with the issuance of Executive Order 10988 by President John F. Kennedy in 1962. Without getting into the somewhat complex history of the ulterior "amendments" of that original order by subsequent ones issued by President Nixon and so on, which would not be appropriate for an essay such as this, it suffices for our purposes here to note that many of the ideas and procedures of these earlier executive orders were co-opted into Title VII of the 1978 Civil Service Reform Act (CSRA), which was the first statute, per se, in the United States regulating federal unionism. (For a good explanation of the CSRA see Federal Labor Relations Authority 1992.)

11. Federal employees do not bargain over economic items such as wages and benefits, which are set by Congress.

12. This essay is not the place for a detailed explanation of the differences between interest-based bargaining, as a technique, as opposed to what some refer to as adversarial or positional bargaining. While running the risk of oversimplification, some information on the differences of these two bargaining methods are, however, in order. There are some variants of interest-based bargaining, but when parties use this technique they generally search for underlying interests and goals as a preliminary matter when they meet and then attempt to come to mutual agreements that meet everyone's interests. Adversarial bargaining, on the other hand, which is the most commonly practiced in labor-management relations, is bargaining by specific proposal and counterproposal. The latter is sometimes called bargaining by position. We would argue, as the federal reinvention initiative also implies, that interest-based techniques are more in sync with a theory of cooperative partnerships, and bargaining by position, as a technique, is more in sync with a theory of adversarial partnerships.

13. Others may simply not want to participate in such activities because any "redesign" of their agency might be viewed by them as threatening to their current job status. This is particularly so for supervisory employees whose position might be either eliminated or downgraded by means of an organizational design exercise.

14. We are academics with a combined experience of more than thirty-five years teaching labor relations, organizational theory, strategic management, and human resource management at various universities. We are also practitioners who have worked as trainers in dispute resolution techniques and have practiced all variants of dispute resolution over the past twenty years: mediation, fact-finding, interest arbitration, grievance arbitration, as well as alternative dispute resolution techniques (ADR). We were solicited by a number of federal agencies to assist partnerships in exercises of organizational design as facilitators, which also included training the partnership participants in consensual and interest-based bargaining techniques. We continue to work in that capacity as "Federal Restructuring Associates."

15. A brochure entitled "Cooperative Crossroads" published by the FLRA states, among other things:

> Parties seeking to embark on labor-management cooperative efforts should first become clear about their goals and constraints in achieving them. Many labor-management cooperative efforts in the federal service begin when:
> —high costs of an adversarial relationship become apparent; . . .
> —top agency and union leadership desire the creation of joint partnerships;
> —"Reinvention" and declining resources necessitate collaborative problem-solving. (Federal Labor Relations Authority 1994)

BIBLIOGRAPHY

AFL-CIO Committee on the Evolution of Work. 1994. *The New American Workplace: A Labor Perspective.* Washington, D.C.: American Federation of Labor-Congress of Industrial Organizations.

Dunlop Commission. 1994. *Fact Finding Report.* Washington, D.C.: U.S. Departments of Labor and Commerce.

Federal Labor Relations Authority. 1992. *A Guide to the Federal Service Labor-Management Statute.* FLRA Doc. 1213. Washington, D.C.: U.S. Government Printing Office.

———. 1994. *Cooperation Crossroads: Developing Labor-Management Partnerships.* Washington, D.C.: U.S. Government Printing Office.

Gore, Al, Vice President. 1993. *Creating a Government That Works Better and Costs Less. Report of the National Performance Review.* Washington, D.C.

King, James B. 1993. "Memorandum for Heads of Departments and Agencies and Presidents of Federal Employees Unions." Subject: Guidance for Implementing Executive Order 12871, December 12. United States Office of Personnel Management, Washington, D.C.

President. 1993. "Executive Order 12871." *Weekly Compilation of Presidential Documents* (Oct. 1).

U.S. Department of Labor. 1993. *Agency Reinvention Activities.* Washington, D.C.

9

LABOR-MANAGEMENT PARTNERSHIPS IN STATE AND LOCAL GOVERNMENTS

LEE BALLIET

INTRODUCTION

The AFL-CIO's 1994 publication of *The New American Workplace: A Labor Perspective* (NAW) is a welcome, albeit belated, response to forces at work in the U.S. economy for more than two decades. Looking back, U.S. employers, especially in the private sector, have been responding to pressures of growing competition and technological change at least since the early 1970s. Responses range from union avoidance and union busting to management attempts to convince workers that employers and employees basically have more interests in common than not.

Paradoxically, workers and unions increasingly have found their employers offering a "kinder and gentler" workplace with one hand while turning the screws of wage and benefit concessions, downsizing, outsourcing, and plant closures with the other. Whether to take the "high road" to greater efficiency through worker/union involvement or the "low road" of cost-cutting through command and control has become an important aspect of the debate over workplace reorganization (Bluestone and Bluestone 1992; Mishel and Voos 1992). Interestingly, some employers appear to be trying to travel both at the same time.

The assertion that labor's and management's interests are basically the same should have been dismissed as untenable at the outset of what has become a continuing and often rancorous debate over how employees can best protect and promote their welfare in the workplace. As emphasized in the NAW, there are fundamental distributive issues that divide all workers and employers into adversarial camps, regardless of the labor relations system in place (AFL-CIO Committee on the Evolution of Work 1994, 12). Lacking an independent political voice such as exists in many industrialized countries, the U.S. labor movement relies on collective bargaining as the principal means of advancing its distributive interests.

A key question for the NAW is whether it is possible within an adversarial collective bargaining environment to lessen antagonism while still maintaining the integrity (and benefits) of the process for workers and the larger society. The NAW assumes, perhaps hopefully for most current labor-management relationships, that its guidelines for achieving new models of workplace organization (mutual recognition and respect, a legally enforceable bargaining relationship, equality of roles in the change process, and agreed-upon goals) are applicable for a majority of U.S. workers (AFL-CIO Committee on the Evolution of Work 1994, 11–12). The NAW guidelines are irrelevant to unorganized workplaces, and arguably difficult if not impossible in organized shops facing the management sleight of hand referred to above.

Given the overall decline in the percentage of U.S. workers under union contract and the current hostile legislative climate (for example, the 104th Congress's defeat of Workplace Fairness legislation and efforts to pass the Team Act), there is little on the horizon to encourage labor's hope for a friendlier labor relations climate—especially in the private sector. The public sector, however, presents a different set of parameters regarding the prospects for meaningful labor involvement in workplace change: differences that are not fully addressed in the NAW.

First, compared to steady decline in the private sector, union membership among public employees has increased dramatically in the last three decades. In the last ten years alone, private sector membership has declined by 1.8 million while public sector membership has risen by 1.2 million (Hirsch and Macpherson 1996). Second, there has been greater employer acceptance and recognition (by statute and/or executive order) of the legitimacy of the union's role in the labor relations process. Third, and flowing from the first two differences, the posture of public sector managers (many of whom themselves are bargaining unit employees) toward worker/union involvement in workplace operations has tended to be more neutral and inclusive than in the private sector.[1]

Fourth, and perhaps most important, the public sector generally has not been subject to the same "bottom-line" drive for cost cutting and revenue enhancement that has occurred in the private sector. The public sector is judged primarily on its delivery of services, while private sector "success" depends on profitability. While private sector workers are basically the "prisoners of profit," public employees (the "prisoners of politics") have other, noneconomic ways to influence the terms and conditions of their employment—for example, as voters and, where organized, by union lobbying of the political process.

These differences combine to lower the risk of "enterprise unionism" and other management-dominated employee involvement schemes in the public sector—which, by definition, preclude the possibility of meaningful labor involvement in workplace change. Therefore the prospects for realizing the NAW guidelines should be better for organized public employees than elsewhere. And, if this is indeed the case, there should be evidence to support it.

The remainder of this essay focuses on apparently successful workplace change at the state and local level. It is drawn primarily from the findings of the U.S. Secretary of Labor's Task Force on Excellence in State and Local Government Through Labor-Management Cooperation (U.S. Secretary of Labor's Task Force 1996), and my own experience as director of the Indiana State Employee Labor-Management Project from November 1994 through mid-1996.

Labor Relations at the State and Local Level

Since 1980, public sector employees have accounted for some 15 to 16 percent of total U.S. employment. Of roughly 19.6 million public sector employees in 1995, 59 percent or 11.6 million (mostly teachers) were in local government and 25 percent or 4.9 million were in state government. The remaining 16 percent or 3.1 million were federal employees (U.S. Secretary of Labor's Task Force 1996).

In 1995, union membership in the public sector was 6.9 million or 37.7 percent of total employment, compared to the private sector where there were 9.4 million union members (about 10.3 percent of total employment).[2] Since state and local government workers are not subject to national law or executive order covering federal and private sector employment, union organization and representation among these employees varies widely from state to state.

All but fourteen states, mostly in the South and Southwest,[3] have some form of legalized bargaining for state and local government employees. In twenty-three states and the District of Columbia, virtually all eligible public employees are covered. Thirteen others have laws or executive orders covering at least some occupational groups—typically in education and public safety. In those states that do provide for public sector bargaining, nearly 60 percent of eligible workers are covered by union contracts.

Imagine what the U.S. labor movement might be like today if it represented 60 percent of the country's total labor force. In the heyday of its strength in the mid-1950s, this figure was some 35 percent. Given the

161

nearly sixfold difference in the levels of state and local vs. private sector union organization, one can begin to grasp labor's greater voice in government employment, as well as the greater strength of employers in the private sector.

PUBLIC/PRIVATE COMPARISONS

Following release of reports by the U.S. Commission on the Future of Worker-Management Relations (Dunlop Commission 1994, 1995), the Secretary of Labor's Task Force commissioned a parallel study of worker attitudes in state and local government (U.S. Secretary of Labor's Task Force 1996, 50–52). The findings of the task force study reinforce the view that prospects for meaningful change are better in organized workplaces at the state and local level.

The task force study found that, compared with the private sector, state and local government workers have higher overall levels of education and job satisfaction and that they rate their managers as competent and concerned, although lacking in leadership and decision-making skills required of a highly effective service delivery system. The incidence of participative labor-management programs was found to be higher in state and local government than in the private sector. However, worker satisfaction with these programs was considerably lower, which the task force attributed to lesser experience and/or attention to working out program details. Or possibly, public sector workers have set higher standards for evaluating such efforts.

As in the private sector, state and local government employees were found to desire less confrontational relations with management; but the public sector was seen as a better environment within which to undertake collaborative workplace change. State and local government employees also expressed a strong desire to be more involved in organizational change and to have a greater voice in decisions that affect their workplaces. Finally, the task force study found these workers to be strongly in favor of retaining their union representation and, if needed, for their unions to be more independent of management (that is, less collaborative) than in the private sector. Although the task force did not attempt to explain this particular tendency toward confrontation on the part of state and local government workers, it may well be related to more extensive union organization and political influence, which results in a heightened sense of both institutional and individual security. This certainly fits with explanations of power and performance in organizational theory.

The task force concluded that "while existing private sector programs may often be more fully developed, there appears . . . to be a greater proportionate incidence and interest in participative programs in the public sector" (U.S. Secretary of Labor's Task Force 1996, 52).

HIGHLIGHTS FROM THE TASK FORCE REPORT

The U.S. Secretary of Labor's Task Force on Excellence in State and Local Government Through Labor-Management Cooperation was established in 1994. It was a logical extension of efforts by the Clinton administration to address collaborative labor relations issues, first in the private sector via the Dunlop Commission, and shortly thereafter through President Clinton's Executive Order 12871, which was issued as part of the administration's "reinventing government" strategy at the federal level.[4]

The fourteen-member task force was composed of labor, management, neutral, and academic representatives with experience in state and local government affairs. Its cochairs were former governor James Florio of New Jersey and Mayor Jerry Abramson of Louisville, Kentucky.[5]

Secretary Robert Reich directed the task force to address the following issues: 1) new methods or institutions to enhance the quality, productivity, and cost effectiveness of public sector services; 2) changes in civil service and collective bargaining legislation to improve the delivery of public services; 3) direct resolution of workplace problems, as opposed to seeking recourse through administrative bodies and the courts; 4) executive and legislative steps that could be taken to promote a labor relations climate that would encourage innovation and risk taking; 5) the conditions necessary for elected officials, managers, employees, and labor organizations to work toward the goal of excellence in state and local government; and 6) identifying successful models of cooperative effort, and explaining others' failure.

The work of the task force, which spanned a period of nearly two years, is outlined in its report to the secretary in May 1996. Below are highlights of the task force's findings pertaining to the six elements of its mission statement.[6]

Key findings of the task force on new ways to enhance quality, productivity, and cost effectiveness focused on the need for state and local government units to reconsider the way in which services are planned and delivered. In particular, traditional delivery systems, supervisory patterns, personnel and administrative structures, and collective bargaining practices were often found to be improvable through the application of new technologies, skill enhancement, and more effective internal communications.

The task force proposed changes in civil service and collective bargaining laws to encourage service-oriented bargaining relationships with an emphasis on organizational improvement. The guidelines challenge labor, management, and elected officials to commit themselves formally to goals of excellence and innovation, improving the quality of worklife, constructive problem solving and dispute resolution, and enhanced training—all in pursuit of improving service delivery systems. In particular, there is a special emphasis on expanding the scope of bargaining to include the broadest possible consideration of organizational flexibility.

The task force also produced guidelines to develop alternative dispute resolution (ADR) mechanisms to supplement rights and practices under existing collective bargaining agreements. Emphasis was placed on the expanded use of mediation and arbitration as alternatives to resorting to the courts and other lengthy expensive administrative procedures. Ideal, according to the task force, would be the negotiated establishment of an ADR system based on local conditions and subject to periodic review and evaluation. Finally, the task force strongly asserts that any ADR process should be held to the highest possible standards of independence, neutrality, and accessibility.

The task force report tries to encourage innovation, which, by definition, involves elements of risk taking. The call for a facilitative legislative environment has already been mentioned. The task force also saw the need for executive-level and other leadership commitment to address openly the prospects for change within an environment of respect for the existing roles and interests of all concerned. Key elements identified as required by this process, besides leadership commitment, include appropriate training and technical assistance, a sensitive approach to issues of trust and legitimacy, and a firm commitment to job security.

The conditions required for such processes to work are summarized in a task force listing of typical barriers to establishing labor-management partnerships (U.S. Secretary of Labor's Task Force 1996, 6). Some have already been mentioned, above; but together, they clearly parallel the NAW guidelines referred to at the beginning of this essay. They also are a near match of the NAW's own list of obstacles (fear of change, authoritarian control by management, shorter- vs. longer-term horizons, the requirement of new union leader/member roles, and operating by command instead of respect) that it claims must be overcome in order to effect meaningful workplace change (AFL-CIO Committee on the Evolution of Work 1994, 12–13).

The first barrier is *mistrust,* which, in the view of the task force, typically exists as a result of previous conflictual labor-management relationships. The second is a *lack of skills* needed for new forms of communication and problem solving. Here, the view of the task force is that, lacking such training, the parties seeking change will continue hierarchical and confrontational practices that, at least in part, may well have contributed to the problems they are trying to resolve.

Third is the *failure fully and equally to involve all affected parties* in the development of programs for workplace change. Simply put, workers should be involved in the *process* of policy development and strategic planning, not just in the implementation of decisions made by others. Fourth is *continuing reliance on formal bargaining and administrative procedures*

164

where less formal and more innovative solutions could be used while still protecting the integrity of the formal relationship.

Fifth, *fear of job loss*, and in some cases even of significant changes in operational procedures, can foster resistance to both worker and manager involvement in participative problem solving. Sixth is the *unwillingness of union leadership to support reorganization* if their institutional roles are ignored, or if changes under consideration can be viewed as union avoidance. Seventh is a *perceived threat to the status of both union officers and midlevel managers* who may see their traditional roles being lessened through reorganization.

Examples of State and Local Government Reorganization

Through field visits and testimony the task force examined some fifty cases of innovative labor-management relationships that, in its view, involved the creation of service-oriented work environments. Programs studied were from all regions of the country and included both organized and unorganized workplaces, with many employment settings in state, county, and local government. The task force findings were categorized by "improvements," including service, quality of worklife, cost control, labor-management relations, safety and health care, and administrative procedures. In addition, issues of privatization and contracting out were treated separately throughout the task force report.

Foshay Middle School in south-central Los Angeles is cited as an example of service improvement through the establishment of an expanded, collaborative relationship between school administrators and the United Teachers of Los Angeles. The school, which in 1989 was among California's lowest in scholastic achievement and highest in student turnover, established a school-based management program that involved teachers for the first time in curriculum development and overall decision making. From these efforts, a school leadership council of parents, teachers, community leaders, staff, students, and union representatives was established to govern the school. As a result, the school's test scores are now approaching the state average. Its dropout rate has fallen from 21 to 3.5 percent; and suspensions have dropped from some four hundred to forty per year.

As part of a larger labor-management effort, the city of Madison, Wisconsin, and American Federation of State, County, and Municipal Employees (AFSCME) Local 60 jointly developed a training program to be delivered on-site to working electricians. The goal was to make the building inspection process more customer-friendly by changing the focus of operations from regulation to education and safety. As a result, the number of inspections to complete a project has fallen. Code enforcement has become more consistent and less costly. There is a growing knowledge base among contractors and the crafts. By changing the focus from regulatory oversight to consultative involvement, inspectors are now more likely to receive compliments than complaints for their efforts.

After nearly a century of contentious bargaining, King County Metro, provider of public transit and sewer service in the Seattle, Washington, area, and its three unions (Amalgamated Transit Union [ATU], International Brotherhood of Electric Workers [IBEW], and Service Employees International Union [SEIU]) used interest-based bargaining and participative problem solving in the early 1990s.[7] As a result, the parties attest to improvements, not only in their bargaining relationship but also in the cost-effective delivery of services and in the overall culture of the workplace. For example, tunnel maintenance formerly contracted out is now done in-house and at considerable savings, through a combination of jointly developed new work methods and the redeployment of metro employees previously subject to seasonable downtime. Transit teams have found ways to limit power outages to electric buses by nearly 75 percent and otherwise greatly improve customer service and relations. Sewage treatment operations have been overhauled, with major savings being shared by employees and ratepayers per a gainsharing agreement between Metro and SEIU.

As a consequence of new leadership, the Phoenix, Arizona, Fire Department and International Association of Fire Fighters (IAFF) Local 493 decided in 1978 to close the book on what had been a forty-year history of acrimonious contract negotiations and administration. They held yearly planning retreats for the express purpose of redirecting their attention to organizational stability and customer service. The retreats develop an annual "action plan," which is then reviewed on a quarterly basis by a department-wide labor-management committee. Those responsible for carrying out the action plan are trained as needed; and other, more general training such as "Relationships By Objectives" has been widely offered apart from the bargaining process. As a result, department and union officials believe that they have institutionalized a more responsible bargaining relationship that will continue its stability and customer orientation beyond those presently involved.

The Connecticut Department of Mental Retardation and District 1199/New England Health Care Employees (SEIU) have a collectively-bargained quality of worklife program with funding for pilot projects in areas such as child care, training, absenteeism, and safety. In the safety project that focused on improvements at custodial facilities, labor-management committees were established to analyze time-loss injuries and develop accident prevention programs. The committees determined that most injuries occurred in the process of lifting and transferring patients and, accordingly, proposed solutions such as skid-proofing floors and using back supports. As a result of this training program designed and run by the workers themselves, the department's first-year results were a 40 percent reduction in injuries, a 25 percent drop in lost time (with commensurate savings in overtime), and a 20 percent ($5 million) decline in workers' compensation expenditures.

Despite an initially embattled relationship between Governor George Voinovich and Ohio's public employees, the state eventually agreed with its public sector unions to tackle bureaucratic roadblocks to a more efficient and citizen-oriented service delivery system. Now, according to Governor Voinovich and Ohio Civil Service Employees Association (AFSCME) union leaders, Ohio's Quality Services through Partnership (QStP) program has accomplished a great deal in just three or four years. QStP is a training-intensive process for developing joint problem-solving skills and integrating quality standards throughout state government. About a third of Ohio's nearly sixty thousand state employees have received QStP training, with a ten-year goal of reaching the entire workforce. With a guarantee of no layoffs as a result of greater efficiency, QStP committees in the department of transportation alone have reduced purchase order processing time from twenty-eight to five days; cut the time from bid request to purchase award from twelve to five and a half weeks; and found ways to add an average four years to the life of a dump truck.

On the particularly volatile topic of privatization and contracting out (Labor Research Review 1990), the task force took special notice of the partnerships developed by the city of Indianapolis and AFSCME Indiana Council 62. Over the past five years the city and its local unions have dealt with these issues probably more often and certainly with more success than in any other metropolitan area of the country. A carefully crafted labor-management process forced the city to acknowledge the value and commitment of its employees, and the unions to respond to the realities of increasingly cost-conscious government. A jointly administered Competition and Costing Program, using strategic initiatives for financial training and front-line involvement of employees, a level playing field for competition (such as for contracting out, and in), and a no-job-loss employee safety net has allowed the city to continue expanded service and infrastructure improvements without increasing taxes. For their accomplishments, the city and AFSCME Council 62 received a 1995 Ford Foundation/Harvard University public service award in the amount of $100,000. The money is being used for additional training, a worker education fund, and for hosting delegations interested in learning from the "Indianapolis Model."

Regarding the report as a whole, a note of constructive criticism appears to be in order. For political reasons, one can understand the task force's inclusion of "labor-management" programs in unorganized workplaces. Yet, by doing so, its efforts to defuse one powder keg may well have lit another. Given its repeated emphasis on the importance to mean-

167

ingful and lasting workplace change of establishing truly joint and equal labor-management partnerships, the attention given to reorganization efforts among unorganized workers seems inappropriate. This is not to suggest that nonunion employers, especially in public settings where organization and bargaining are prohibited, are necessarily uninterested in greater employee involvement in reorganization efforts. But despite any surface accomplishments, the underlying relationship between employers and unorganized workers is one of inherent inequality and subordination. Represented workers, both public and private, in many ways set the standards by which their nonunion counterparts work. Accordingly, the task force should have been more diligent in pointing out these important differences between union and nonunion settings for workplace change.

THE INDIANA STATE EMPLOYEE LABOR-MANAGEMENT PROJECT

The Indiana State Employee Labor-Management Project was established in September 1994 through an eighteen-month grant from the Federal Mediation and Conciliation Service (FMCS). The project sponsors are the state of Indiana (Office of the Governor) and the two unions representing state employees (AFSCME Indiana Council 62 and the Unity Team—Local 9212—UAW/AFT).[8]

The project operates at six Indiana sites: the Lake (Gary area) and Marion (Indianapolis area) County Offices of Family and Children (the "welfare department"), the Indiana State Farm and Westville Correctional Facilities (maximum security prisons), the Muscatatuck State Development Center (for the developmentally disabled), and the Logansport State (mental) Hospital. These six facilities have more than 4,800 employees, with all but supervisory personnel covered by statewide settlement agreements.[9] However, with no negotiated union security agreements, union membership is less than universal and varies from site to site.

The project is managed by a nine-member Statewide Leadership Team (SLT) of three representatives from each sponsor. The full SLT meets on a quarterly basis, and its executive committee, representing the leadership of the three sponsors, meets monthly. It is staffed by a full-time director and a part-time secretary.

Project labor-management committees exist at each site. Each local committee has fifteen members, with equal representation including the executive officer and four others chosen by each sponsor (subject to approval by the SLT) from management and the two unions. A three-member executive council, chosen in the same way, is responsible for overseeing the committee's work (agendas, minutes, and so forth). The committees meet monthly, and meetings are chaired by individual members on an agreed-upon, rotating basis.

At the outset of the project, the full SLT met with all local committees, to show its support and to provide guidelines for their work. Per the SLT guidelines, each committee then developed a set of bylaws for its operation. The mission statement clearly states that the committee is neither an extension of nor a replacement for the bargaining process that currently exits between the state and the unions. Rather, it is a consensual process for addressing issues that affect the overall working environment.

Both labor and management (in fact, any employee) can bring workplace issues or problems that are not covered by the settlement agreements to the local project labor-management committee. The only condition is that all three parties (AFSCME, management, and the Unity Team) must agree to the items being discussed (typically, to assure that they pertain to the larger workplace community); and any actions that are decided upon must be reached by consensus; no votes are taken. Committee business can be conducted under a quorum consisting of at least three members from each group. Proxies are prohibited, and any member who is absent agrees to abide by the consensus of those who were present. Perhaps most important, each local committee has the authority (and responsibility) to resolve any issue or problem brought to it, in whatever way it feels will be best for the facility as a whole, so long as there are no violations of law, agency policy, or the settlement agreements.

Training was an important aspect of the committee process from the project's inception. In the first three months, a two-day conference was held for all local and SLT members (attendance was mandatory), with initial training in communications, problem solving, and workplace diversity provided by union/management staff and outside consultants. Participants also held separate meetings with their agency heads, to reinforce the importance of the undertaking.

Midway through the project the local executive councils and the SLT held a two-day retreat to discuss the results of a six-month review and evaluation of committee operations, particular examples of success and failure, and plans for the remainder of the project. Near the end of the project, a three-day conference was held for all state and local committee members. Here, more advanced training was provided by university instructors, following a "lesson plan" developed from priorities set by the local committees. The training was then delivered using case studies that drew on operational experiences throughout the project.

For the first three or four months, a portion of each local committee meeting was set aside for "process" instruction using FMCS, U.S. Department of Labor (USDOL), and other committee effectiveness training (CET) materials. Later, at the request of local committees, daylong, "generic" grievance process seminars were held for stewards and supervisors at each site, with instruction provided by international union staff. This and other joint training, such as "managing in a union environment," are cited among the committees' self-declared accomplishments.

169

PRELIMINARY PROJECT FINDINGS

At the outset of the project, a detailed "Needs Assessment Question-naire" was sent to fifty represented and supervisory employees at each of the six committee sites. The results were used as a benchmark for project evaluation, and as something concrete for local committees to use in es-tablishing their own priorities.[10]

The needs assessment confirmed what the project sponsors knew when they chose the six local committee sites: labor-management rela-tions were less than ideal. In fact, the SLT reasoned that "if something positive happens with these six, then replication at other, less-troubled facilities should be a piece of cake."

Sixty-six percent of respondents rated the overall labor-management relationship at their workplace as either "fair" (30 percent) or "poor" (36 percent). Thirty-four percent viewed the labor-management relationship as worsening over the last three years. And 63 percent rated the combined skill and efficiency of labor and management in solving workplace prob-lems as "fair" (35 percent) or "poor" (28 percent) while only 10 percent rated it "very good" or "excellent."

An "Exit Survey" mailed eighteen months later to the same group who received the original needs assessment questionnaire produced a signifi-cant change in responses to the same basic questions. The percent of those ranking the labor-management relationship as either fair or poor dropped from 66 to 50. The percent who felt the relationship had worsened over the period in question fell from 34 to 24. And, most notably, the percent rating the combined skill and efficiency of labor-management problem resolution as fair or poor fell from 63 to 18 while ratings of improved performance rose from 10 to 42 percent.

While these survey results indicate modest to substantial improve-ment at the six committee sites, it also is obvious that the "problem has not entirely been fixed." Nor was that the intention or hope of the spon-sors at the outset. Other measures of "success," while varying from site to site, show the committee process to have had an overall favorable impact on both the quality and content of workplace relationships.

A complete listing of committee accomplishments would require more space than can be given them here. But it can surely be said that all six committees found ways to resolve workplace issues that had pre-viously been given up on, or were thought to be beyond resolution at their level of operation and decision making. Among the tangibles were numerous improvements in the design and application of personnel pro-cedures; the establishment of a health fair, wellness, scholarship, and other employee recognition programs; physical improvements to the workplace; and a nearly 50 percent drop in formal grievance filings and appeals.[11] Equally significant have been improvements in communication and problem solving at all six facilities.

170

As a whole, the project's sponsors and participants agree that a modest-or-better start has been made to involve more employees in decision making and improve the overall labor-management and workplace environments. Two of the six committees have been highly successful by any standard. The other four have made from some to considerable progress while working to overcome a variety of institutional and other more personal/organizational barriers to change. In sum, both the sponsors and participants are basically in agreement that the committees have begun a process of building new skills and tools for changing the workplace to the benefit of all employees. And they are committed to continuing and expanding this process beyond the six original project sites and the expiration of FMCS support.

LESSONS LEARNED IN INDIANA

From my experience dealing directly with state and local committees of the Indiana project, it is clear that committee progress and setbacks have been related to the NAW "guidelines and obstacles" and the "barriers" outlined in the task force report.

The level of mutual recognition and respect has definitely risen, especially among local committee members who have worked together on particular issues or problems. Since both union and management leadership are among the committees' members, local relationships have improved, most notably through the resolution of problems before they become formal grievances. Also, with numerous guarantees of equality and independence built into the committee process, the participants have had relatively few problems agreeing upon both goals and procedures. They have found that consensus (no winners or losers) can be a useful way to resolve certain workplace issues.

Setbacks for local project committees also have typically fallen into one or more of the obstacle/barrier categories outlined above. The most frequent and disruptive of these stem from the inability or unwillingness to keep adversarial postures and outcomes from "souring" the labor-management process. Perhaps most encouraging has been the willingness of at least some local committees to deal with such conflicts, using a process with entirely different ground rules from those on the shop floor.

Furthermore, mistrust and resistance to change, the reluctance to assume new roles (with accompanying skill and duty requirements), and perceived threats to the roles of midlevel management, line supervisors, and union stewards have all been experienced on various occasions during the project. Also, an unanticipated impediment to steady progress, not mentioned by the NAW or task force, was excessive turnover in the membership of some committees owing to position vacancies, promotions, and quits.

171

To deal with these impediments, the project sponsors' plans for the future will likely involve a number of refinements. First, to deal with mistrust and resistance to change, even more attention will be given to explaining both union and management goals for the committee process—to the entire workforce, but especially to line supervisors, midmanagement, and union stewards/activists.

Second, additional time will be spent on the selection and initial training of committee members, to allow them to begin the labor-management process with the greatest possible levels of understanding, support, and interpersonal/group skills. Third, more attention will be given to the work of the committees (both accomplishments and setbacks) by raising the level of communication, especially at the very top (such as agency heads) and among rank-and-file workers. Finally, to deal with conflicts within committees or between them and the bargaining process, the sponsors intend to establish a separate dispute resolution process, so as to preclude "shutting things down until this, that, or the other is resolved."

So, What Might All This Mean in Real Life?

The NAW accurately describes the current U.S. work system as retaining most of its "Taylorist" origins, that is, using workers for assigned tasks like any other factor of production, with planning and decision making also assigned to a separate managerial and technical hierarchy.[12] And, as anyone who has gone through the process of registering a vehicle, applying for some form of public assistance, or appealing a property tax assessment knows, government agencies are rightfully notorious for carrying the hierarchical specialization and division of labor to illogical (and often frustrating) extremes. Which is to say that the private sector is not alone in making workers the first and frontline victims of poor management and organizational dysfunction.

For the debate over union involvement in workplace change through labor-management partnerships, the overriding issue appears to be whether worker/union subscription to such efforts will necessarily serve to strengthen or weaken individual bargaining units and, ultimately, the larger labor movement (Parker 1985; Kochan, Katz, and Mower 1984; Banks and Metzgar 1989). For workers in state and local government, the answer is a definite "It depends!"

The NAW asserts that unions have a right to sit at the table of workplace change; and it sets forth principles for doing so. It suggests that these principles (rejecting the dichotomy between thinking and doing, redesigning jobs for greater individual responsibility, a flatter and more accountable management structure, worker involvement in decision making at all levels of operation, and the equitable distribution of gains) can direct the way to more productive and democratic workplaces.

172

Evidence from the task force report in general and the Indiana labor-management project in particular suggests that, while "easier said than done," union involvement in joint reorganization programs should be neither accepted nor rejected lightly, as a matter of policy or principle—at least in state and local government. Despite inherent demands and obstacles (any of which could be critical to the process), unionized workers in these sectors can in fact expand their organizational influence through negotiated partnerships to deal with matters previously considered to be the exclusive domain of management. Doing so can give organized state and local government employees another potentially powerful tool for directly affecting the design and control of work systems and other employment practices over which they normally, and legally, would have little say. And as shown by programs such as those of the Phoenix Fire Department and in Indianapolis, the labor-management process also can help unions refine their collective bargaining agendas and strengthen their case with management.

Nonetheless, labor-management partnerships are neither a panacea for contentious bargaining relationships nor a "magic bullet" that can produce a quick fix for particularly difficult or long-standing problems. They are a simply a strategic tool that, when used under the right conditions, can allow unions to approach their representational goals and objectives from yet another perspective.

Two pitfalls or barriers to meaningful union involvement in the public sector appear to be especially critical in deciding whether or not to engage in a collaborative labor-management process. First, management must clearly demonstrate that it is willing to concede a substantial portion of its present control and authority over decision making in the workplace. Second, labor must be willing to acknowledge that, in return, it will invest time and effort of its own in seeking innovative ways to change the overall workplace culture. If these fundamental requirements are met, there is at least the potential for resolving agreed-upon workplace issues and problems that previously have been excluded from the collective bargaining process.

A vitally important distinction should be made between negotiated participation in establishing a more facilitative environment for work and simply "cooperating" with management-controlled agendas for change. Negotiated participation can foster union-building, but cooperation for the sake of peace or to show "good faith" in pursuit of other goals will almost certainly lead to union decline. Negotiated participation is premised on the strength of the union; unilateral cooperation is likely to signal weakness and concession, to the eyes of both management and rank-and-file workers.

It is widely acknowledged that the U.S. labor relations system is basically inadequate to support fully the current organizing and representa-

173

tional needs of labor (Kochan, Katz, and McKersie 1994; Dunlop Commission 1994, 1995). Among these inadequacies are limitations on the rights of workers to have a greater voice in decision making at their workplaces, that is, legally to require employers to negotiate over issues such as the organization of work. Accordingly, the focus of this essay has been on the prospects for workers and unions in the public sector to overcome this barrier, at least in part, through negotiated labor-management partnerships that can lead to more effective bargaining.

In his 1994 book *Success While Others Fail,* Paul Johnston asserts that there are two U.S. labor movements: one in the private sector, the other covering public employees. And the way he distinguishes between the two relates directly to the issue of labor-management programs involving workers and unions at the state and local level. In Johnston's view, public sector unions

> are shaped by—and in turn shape—the distinctive context within and against which they operate: public organization. They depend for power less on their market position and on coalitions in their labor market than on their political position and involvement in the coalitions that govern public agencies. . . . [They] are involved not only in collective bargaining and lobbying over wages, benefits, and working conditions but also in broader political conflicts over the public agendas that guide and fund public sector work." (Johnston 1994, 4)

The detailed experience of the Indiana labor-management project suggests that there is indeed a "community of interest" among organized workers and management in public workplaces that is distinct from private sector employment. The same can be inferred from the task force reports of other labor-management programs at the state and local level. Likely, the most important determinant that sets the public workplace community apart from the private sector is the absence of private ownership of the "means of production." Accordingly, distributive issues, be they financial or otherwise, are viewed differently by public sector workers. For example, contesting the distribution of revenues in the private sector takes place in an environment surrounded by volatile issues of ownership and property rights. In the public sector, workers and managers alike rightfully tend to view themselves as owners (citizens/taxpayers), producers, and, often, consumers of the services they provide, in addition to being answerable to a larger constituency of other voters, taxpayers, and political interests. Nor do the extremes of compensation affect the public sector in the same way as they do the private sector ("CEO" salaries in the U.S. private sector are approaching 150 times those of hourly workers, while in the public sector the ratio is closer to 20 to one; and in local workplaces more like 10 to one).

This is not to suggest that issues of authoritarian control over decision making and the organization of work are any less problematic in government than in private employment. Rather, it is the context of political outlook, position, and coalitions in the public sector that, for organized public employees, creates a greater potential for change.

Perhaps most important to the prospects for organized state and local workers advancing their interests through negotiated labor-management partnerships is whether such a community of interest exists. The NAW suggests that unions, in general, give serious consideration to such opportunities for advancing their cause. The data gathered for this paper suggest that this is especially the case in state and local government.

NOTES

The author gratefully acknowledges many helpful comments and suggestions during the writing of this essay, from Michael Eisenscher, doctoral candidate in the public policy program at the University of Massachusetts-Boston; Steve Fantauzzo, executive director, AFSCME Indiana Council 62; Paul Rainsberger, associate professor, Indiana University Division of Labor Studies; and D. Sue Roberson, deputy director, Indiana State Personnel Department.

1. The National Labor Relations Act, which covers the private sector, basically excludes all supervisory employees from union representation. Accordingly, where supervisors are not excluded in the public sector, employees as a whole have greater representation and bargaining rights.

2. From Hirsch and Macpherson (1996), U.S. union density (membership as a percent of total employment) in 1995 was: overall, 14.9 percent; private, 10.3 percent; public overall, 37.7 percent; federal (excluding postal workers at 74.4 percent), 17.9 percent; state, 34.5 percent; and local, 43.9 percent.

3. State-level bargaining laws do not exist in Alabama, Arizona, Arkansas, Colorado, Georgia, Louisiana, Mississippi, North Carolina, South Carolina, Texas, Utah, and West Virginia. Arizona, Colorado, and Utah, however, allow bargaining at the local level.

4. President Clinton's Executive Order 12871, entitled "Labor-Management Partnerships," is certainly the most ambitious participative program initiated at any level in the U.S. public sector. Its intent is to expand greatly the scope of bargaining through the use of consensus and alternative dispute resolution techniques. It established the National Partnership Council, comprising agency heads and the presidents of the largest federal sector unions, to oversee the process.

5. Other members of the task force were Arvid Anderson, arbitrator; Martha Bibbs, state of Michigan, Personnel; Al Bilik, AFL-CIO, Public Employee Department; Hezekiah Brown, Cornell University, Industrial and Labor Relations; Lucille Christenson, state of Washington, Labor and Industries; Mary Hatwood Futrell, George Washington University; Arthur Hamilton, Arizona House of Representatives; Michael Lipsky, Ford Foundation; James Mastriani, state of New Jersey, Public Employment Relations Commission; Beverly Stein, Portland, Oregon, Multnomah County Chair; Kenneth Young, AFL-CIO, retired; and Kent Wong, UCLA, Labor Research and Education.

6. It should be noted at the outset that the task force chose to highlight only

successes and positive indicators. Its methodology makes it unsuitable for reliable generalizations to all cases. Despite this, its findings are useful if handled with care.

7. "Interest-based bargaining" and "participative problem solving" are consensual as opposed to adversarial techniques. They are the basis for "win-win" bargaining and a variety of alternative dispute resolution methods that have been developed and used in recent years, with varying success.

8. The Unity Team (UAW/AFT) is a coalition body of the United Auto Workers and the American Federation of Teachers. These two national unions joined forces during the organizing drives among Indiana state employees in 1990–91. Local 9212 operates statewide and represents a variety of employees in corrections, health, social services, transportation, and other executive branch units. Typically, AFSCME locals, under Indiana Council 62, represent workers in other job classifications at the same facilities.

9. Under the executive order signed by Indiana governor Evan Bayh in 1990, unions representing state employees are permitted to, " 'meet and negotiate' with the State Personnel Director on wages, hours and working conditions and reach a settlement on the issues, subject to approval of the Governor." The words "collective bargaining" do not appear in the executive order; thus the term "settlement agreements."

10. The response rate for the initial Needs Assessment Questionnaire was 50 percent (150 of 300). The response rate for the Exit Survey was 52.3 percent (134 of 256 valid responses). Survey participants were selected by the project sponsors (20 each from the two unions and ten from management, for each project site).

11. This significant drop in the "grievance load" has been especially heartening to the project sponsors, since the number of grievances being filed and appealed was one of the main criteria used for the selection of local committee sites. At the local level, the reason given for the reduction in the grievance load is that "people now know each other better. They have a clearer understanding of the roles that both sides play in resolving disputes. And, as a result of the committee process, they are better able to articulate their positions."

12. Frederick Winslow Taylor (1856–1915) is the acknowledged "father" of modern (traditional, hierarchical) workplace organization. His *Principles of Scientific Management,* published in 1911, is largely responsible for what is commonly referred to today as the "dumbing of work."

Bibliography

AFL-CIO Committee on the Evolution of Work. 1994. *The New American Workplace: A Labor Perspective.* Washington, D.C.: American Federation of Labor-Congress of Industrial Organizations.

Appelbaum, Eileen, and Rosemary Batt. 1994. *The New American Workplace: Transforming Work Systems in the United States.* Ithaca, N.Y.: ILR Press.

Banks, Andy, and Jack Metzgar. 1989. "Participating in Management: Union Organizing on a New Terrain." *Labor Research Review* 14 (Fall): 5–55.

Bluestone, Barry, and Irving Bluestone. 1992. *Negotiating the Future: A Labor Perspective on American Business.* New York: Basic Books.

176

Cohen-Rosenthal, Edward, and Cynthia Burton. 1993. *Mutual Gains: A Guide to Union-Management Cooperation.* Ithaca, N.Y.: ILR Press.

Dunlop Commission. 1994. *Fact Finding Report.* Washington, D.C.: U.S. Departments of Commerce and Labor.

———. 1995. *Final Report.* Washington, D.C.: U.S. Departments of Commerce and Labor.

Excellence in Public Service: Experiences From Ohio and Wisconsin. 1996. Washington, D.C.: State and Local Labor-Management Committee.

Hirsch, Barry T., and David A. Macpherson. 1996. *Union Membership and Earnings Data Book: Compilations from the Current Population Survey (1996 Edition).* Washington, D.C.: Bureau of National Affairs.

Johnston, Paul. 1994. *Success While Others Fail: Social Movement Unionism and the Public Workplace.* Ithaca, N.Y.: ILR Press.

Kochan, Thomas A., Harry Katz, and Robert McKersie. 1994. *The Transformation of American Industrial Relations.* Ithaca, N.Y.: ILR Press.

Kochan, Thomas A., Harry Katz, and Nancy Mower. 1984. *Worker Participation in American Unions: Threat or Opportunity?* Kalamazoo, Mich.: W. E. Upjohn Institute for Employment Research.

1990. "Privatization and Contracting Out," a special edition of *Labor Research Review* 15, no. 1 (Spring).

Mishel, Lawrence, and Paula Voos, eds. 1992. *Unions and Economic Competitiveness.* Armonk, N.Y.: M. E. Sharp.

Parker, Mike. 1985. *Inside the Circle: A Union Guide to QWL.* Boston: South End Press.

Schneider, Krista. 1994. *A Compendium of State Public Sector Labor Relations Laws.* Washington, D.C.: AFL-CIO, Public Employee Department.

Taylor, Frederick W. 1942. *Principles of Scientific Management.* 1911; rpt., New York: Harper.

U.S. Secretary of Labor's Task Force on Excellence in State and Local Government Through Labor-Management Cooperation. 1996. *Working Together for Public Service.* Washington, D.C.: U.S. Department of Labor.

VI

Opposing
Viewpoints

10

NEW UNIONISM AND THE WORKPLACE OF THE FUTURE

PETER LAZES AND JANE SAVAGE

Unions face significant challenges to their basic existence and to their ability to remain an important player in workplace matters. In its report, *The New American Workplace: A Labor Perspective,* the AFL-CIO outlines a new road map for unions. The report is an important statement in modern labor history. It offers a convincing case for unions' involvement in reorganizing their workplaces and clearly advocates that unions participate in managing the enterprises of which they are a part. Perhaps most significantly, the AFL-CIO has taken a clear stand about the principles on which *authentic* partnerships should be based. Its model offers sound guidelines for unions, yet acknowledges the difficulty of achieving the ideal.

The report, however, does not go far enough in presenting the new work systems and effective partnerships as a *strategy*—a radically different strategy for unions, and one that may be critical for their survival and relevance into the next century. Nor does the report define in enough detail what unions must do from within—either at the national or local levels—to position themselves as initiators and as competent partners in changing their workplaces.

In this chapter, we address these points directly. To establish the need

181

for a new union strategy, we begin the chapter by describing the current economic and institutional context unions face, which we view as a primary driver (as opposed to philosophical or management advances) for changes to American workplaces. We then share our own adaptation of the AFL-CIO model, developed from cases in the field, theoretical and empirical research, and our experience as practitioners working with labor and management in industrial settings. We present our version as a *strategy* for unions, one that is appropriate to the current context, that is based on the concepts of workplace and industrial democracy, and that is *unionbuilding;* it both serves workers' interests and builds union leverage.

The strategy has five components: 1) creating an independent union agenda, 2) bargaining for strategic alliances with management with clear areas of codetermination, 3) bargaining for compensation increases tied to the contributions that unions and workers make, 4) changing workplace structures, decision making, and the use of technology, and 5) restructuring union institutions. In the following five sections, we describe each part of the strategy, suggesting specific action steps for both union locals and internationals. We acknowledge that this strategy requires further testing and refinement. Thus, in the last two sections of the essay, we describe the limitations of the strategy and the difficulties unions are likely to encounter in implementing it, and we share our suggestions for what the AFL-CIO should do to strengthen its capacity to support the new strategy. Finally, we close with a brief statement placing our arguments, once again, in the context of the changing world of work.

We admit that the shift to greater decision making and new work systems may not be relevant for all work sites and that these strategies are complicated to implement. Nevertheless, we believe a discussion of the circumstances requiring these strategies, as well as an explanation of the strategies themselves, is important. We believe this exploration can help unions confront their own choices and clarify new ways of operating that are better suited to the current environment. Without this, it is our view that unions will continue to decline in their influence and ability to protect workers' rights in the twenty-first century.

A Dramatically Different Environment for American Workers

The environment in which unions operate has changed dramatically since the mid-1970s. From the post–World War II era until the 1970s, the United States was the dominant world trading partner, work was organized for mass production, and productivity grew as labor efficiencies steadily increased. A system of economic policies, labor law, and collective bargaining ensured that workers shared in the resulting prosperity (Marshall 1992).

The economics of that era, however, are being shattered. The "new economy," dating from the mid-1970s, is characterized by global competition and freer trade. The technology of mass production is available to newly industrialized and less developed countries, where wages are a mere fraction of those in the United States (Appelbaum and Batt 1994, 18). Meanwhile, rapid advances in technology have fueled recent domestic productivity growth more than the labor efficiencies that were typical of the postwar era.

In the U.S., these economic transformations are creating grave social inequalities: a steady drop in average weekly real wages, growing inequities in the distribution of income and wealth, a "shrinking" middle class, and numerous layoffs. For nearly two decades, the existing system of collective bargaining and labor law has not served well the economic interests of American workers. With very little input, they are bearing a significant portion of the risks and costs associated with the transition to a "new economy" and for regaining American productivity. They have borne these costs through losses in real wages, of jobs, and of union voice in ameliorating the social inequities created in the new economy.

In addition, these economic transformations have not been matched by the necessary *organizational and institutional transformations*—either of workplaces, industries, or unions. (It is beyond the scope of this essay to comment on the changes that may be needed in existing labor law and economic policy.) Although views about the "new economy" have varied widely (Prowse 1992), there is an emerging consensus that U.S. competitive advantage, and that of other advanced industrialized nations, relies on changing the mass production work organization (Appelbaum 1994, 18). While many new methods for managing and organizing work have emerged, they have not been widely adopted in a way that would indicate a clear new model for work organization (Osterman 1994) or that would strengthen domestic industries. U.S. companies have enhanced their competitiveness largely through greater use of information technology and downsizing rather than wholesale "transformation" of the mass production organization. Furthermore, while the institutional role for unions in these changes has been hotly debated, the traditional industrial relations model of labor practices has been weakened by management cost-cutting practices that combine low wages, little training, and fewer permanent employees and also by the emergence of nonunion "team" organizations (Appelbaum and Batt 1994).

Through much of the twentieth century, the domain of unions has been narrowly defined as wages (including benefits) and working conditions. The basic strategy for obtaining union rights has been through strong and hard-fought union recognition, collective bargaining agreements, and methods for administering the contract. Unions sought job classifications as a means to secure existing jobs and to create new ones. They bargained for extensive work rules to contain the supervisory abuses of management. They developed seniority systems protecting the jobs and rights of the most senior workers; and, they developed elaborate grievance processes. To a large extent, unions became experts at fighting the system. In exchange for progress in these areas and supported by labor law, management protected its rights to make decisions about the investment of capital and financial risk.

Through most of the postwar and Cold War era, the strategy unions followed was successful. It worked while workers' wages increased in accordance with their productivity gains and kept up with the real cost of living. In the new economy, however, many companies can no longer be counted on for employment security. And, while unions expend significant organizational energy servicing their members in the grievance process and protecting the rights of a minority of workers, plants continue to close their doors. Jobs and whole industries are lost. In the present context, the traditional strategies that unions have been armed with are not necessarily sufficient. Unions must develop contemporary approaches relevant to their new economic and institutional environment.

THE NEW UNION STRATEGY

In the present context, unions' interests extend a level deeper than wages and working conditions. They now include the critical decisions that *affect* workers' employment security and wages, such as the strategy of the company, its allocation of resources, workplace organization, the use of technology, and other decisions about quality and productivity. In the new economy, unions need to adopt strategies that can address these interests. They need strategies that enable them to influence critical business decisions, or to challenge those decisions before jobs are lost or wages cut. Thus, we recommend that unions develop *strategic alliances* with management to influence critical decisions and to develop more democratic workplaces. When they contribute to the viability and cost-effectiveness of the business, however, unions must do this in ways that not only serve their members' needs for job security, higher wages, and better working conditions but that also *rebuild the union*. Thus, we pose several requirements intended to strengthen unions in the process.

Our strategy requires that unions bargain for a voice in the *decisions* for changes to which workers contribute knowledge and ideas. It requires that unions bargain for their share of the *value* of these contributions as compensation. And, it requires that unions develop their own agendas, linking joint activities with management to the broader goal of building the union. By encouraging unions to develop a separate *union* agenda for these changes, this strategy helps to ensure that workers are not merely contributing to improving the production or service systems of the business but that they are creating a stronger union voice (Kaminski 1996). This new union strategy is as follows:

1. Unions must create an independent agenda for changing workplaces and for making their own union institutions more relevant.

2. Unions must bargain for the right to become partners with management in critical decisions that affect workers. They must create strategic alliances with clear areas of co-determination.

3. Unions must bargain for compensation increases tied to contributions that unions and workers make. These contributions may be in the form of improved business results, reduced total costs, reduced time to market, or the successful application of technology.

4. Through strategic alliances, unions must fundamentally change the work systems of their workplaces, including work structures, decision-making and the use of technology.

5. Unions must structure themselves differently and build new competencies to support these efforts.

Table 10.1 illustrates this new strategy juxtaposed against union goals and strategies of the past. The strategy we propose encourages unions to begin building alliances in areas over which management is *willing* to share power and to draw on this experience to expand to more significant areas of the enterprise. We acknowledge that while many companies are eager to have access to employees' knowledge and ideas to improve the business, they also are likely to resist unions' involvement in management of the enterprise beyond the traditional sphere of labor relations. More important, they are unlikely to share gains from workers' contributions equitably. This strategy does not necessarily mean that traditional union tactics such as work stoppages and strikes are not useful. In the new economy, such tactics can be used in the service of new aims.

Finally, our strategy is based on the notion that a democratic system in the world of business and work, just as in government, is the appropriate system to deal with the rapidly changing demands of the current environment. Research suggests that better quality solutions to problems arise when they are developed in a participative and democratic fashion and when they take into account the needs of those affected by changes. Research also suggests that participatory methods of decision making are effective vehicles for dealing with complex problems and that they lead to greater commitment to implementation. (See Vroom and Jago 1988, 5–14 for an historical perspective on this research.) In practical terms, this means enabling workers to contribute to decisions about jobs, the pace of work, and the work process. It also means providing workers with access to the information they need to participate knowledgeably and effectively in such decisions. In addition, creating greater decision-making opportunities and changing governance structures at work has not only helped organizations become more effective; it has also provided citizens with

185

Table 10.1
Union Goals and Strategies

	THE PAST	THE FUTURE
GOALS	1. Job security 2. Equity/Due process 3. Higher wages, better benefits 4. Better working conditions 5. Union building/ Stronger union	1. Employment security/Better jobs 2. Job creation 3. Higher wages and sustained benefits 4. Equity/Due process 5. Union building
STRATEGIES	1. Establishing job classifications, work rules, and seniority 2. Utilizing grievance procedure 3. Collective bargaining 4. Administrating the contract administration 5. Providing services	1. Create new union agenda for change 2. Bargain for greater say in business and economic decisions 3. Bargain for compensation on new bases 4. Develop new work systems 5. Rebuild and restructure unions

skills and experience to play an active role in government, civic, and community activities (Emery and Thorsrud 1976).

As we have indicated, rebuilding unions by strategically allying with management is new territory for many unions. Where do union leaders begin? How do they translate the lofty ideas of joint decision making and new work systems down to the politics and operations of their specific plants or workplaces? How do they communicate a new agenda and engage members in such activities? Moreover, how do such activities actually strengthen the institution of the union? Let us look at what unions can do at the local, and at the international, levels to implement this strategy.

1. Unions must create an independent agenda for changing workplaces and for making their own union institutions more relevant. In the current environment, unions cannot afford to leave critical business decisions entirely in the hands of management, only to fight to save jobs when a plant's doors are closing. Unions must prepare themselves to challenge management's business decisions and the potential impact of those decisions on workers. Furthermore, unions must position themselves with both the knowledge and leverage to do so.

At a domestic men's apparel manufacturer, it has been the union that has pressed for developing a flexible work system. Frustrated with frequent management changes and recent layoffs, the union believes the viability of the remaining five hundred jobs relies upon dramatic redesign of the manufacturing operation. More important, based on apparel industry research (Abernathy et al. 1995), the union is pressing for a new product and marketing strategy to which manufacturing changes are linked. With the help of the international business agent, a union engineer, and an external consultant, a representative group from the local developed its own set of goals, requirements, and activities. The group used information about other work systems, about the industry, and from a redesigned plant several had visited to develop a proposal. Their recommendations included a quick response manufacturing capability, greater disclosure of information, a new pay system, maintenance of annual earnings, joint problem-solving on specific quality problems, and restructuring of specific manufacturing areas. This group then shared and refined its ideas with the membership before presenting them to management. Joint efforts in several of these areas are now under way.

At Saskatoon Chemicals, the CEPU Local has developed a detailed union strategic plan to sustain employment security and obtain resources (CEPU Local 609 1994). The plan outlines clear action steps to address such strategic issues as greater worker involvement in decision making, skill upgrading and apprenticeships for members, and paid time and facilities for general union business and for union development. The union has made it clear that its strategic alliance *relies on management accepting and responding* to its needs and agenda for change. This requirement has been built into the joint process. The local tracks all goals and action steps on the union computer and assesses its progress at an annual strategic planning meeting.

The OCAW Local 4–367, which represents workers at multiple petrochemical plants in Texas with multiple employers, undertook a somewhat different process. The joint board, frustrated with the low level of member activity in union business and the union's poor relationship with the community, undertook an extensive process to make the local more relevant to its members. In addition to surveying and conducting small group meetings with members about their needs for change, the local held a three-day series of large group meetings, which more than 600 members attended. The conference led to extensive changes in the types of projects that the local undertook both in plants and in the community. Several major initiatives emerged: improving health and safety at each plant; increasing organizing activity at other sites without waiting for the international; increasing two-way communication with members; providing new member orientation; and reinventing the union's name in the community. Member subcommittees formed to address each area, and they function with little involvement from officers. In addition, a much greater proportion of members is involved in union business as well as a significant effort with the company to improve health and safety.

In all three of these cases, unions took a proactive role. In the first two cases, the unions responded to management initiatives and identified an independent agenda. They identified workplace changes that were important to them and to members. In the case of OCAW Local 4–367, the union built its own agenda, independent of management and work site priorities. Although this effort did not encompass extensive work system changes, we view it as an important case because it illustrates how a union can take the leadership in defining changes important to its members. In all three cases, the unions built their own union-oriented cases for change. In addition, they saw the importance of building authorization among members for a new agenda. Union leaders created a mandate for change, and, as a result, revitalized the role of members in union business.

LOCAL ACTION STEPS

We suggest the following action steps for local unions attempting to establish a union agenda.

Become knowledgeable about the enterprise. Unions need specific and up-to-date information about the company, its competitors, and its customers. They need to know management's strategic and operational plans, and to be able to assess the potential impacts on workers and the union. Local unions should not accept management's strategies at face value but research or question underlying assumptions and feasibility based on their own experience.

In many cases, unions can obtain copies of management's plans merely by request. In other cases, locals may need the assistance of independent financial or industry analysts to help them understand the present economic and market context. To the degree that the union-management relationship or proprietary information allows, this information should be shared broadly with the membership.

Identify your own union goals. Unions must define what *they* want out of a strategic alliance with management. Ideally, unions should start with a strategic plan (Weil 1994), as in the case of Local 609 at Saskatoon

Chemicals. A strategic plan should assess the economics and market dynamics of their industry, identify what is needed for a particular service or product to be competitive, and place the company in comparison to its competitors. It should identify changes needed in the systems of work, quality, or customer interface. The plan should also address broad issues for the union, not just work site issues. These might include community, social, and political initiatives that they wish to pursue either independently or with management.

In their plans, unions must use their knowledge about the current business and economic issues of the firm to identify the most critical workplace decisions in which they need to be involved. These may be as straightforward as getting better supplies or parts to operators or as complex as significantly reducing waste. For example, unions may desire less management control, more reliable work schedules, a role in specific operational decisions, funds for training (for example, in reading a control chart or analyzing a problem), paid time to meet with members, and paid time to learn about new work systems as well as to formulate their role in changing the workplace. In cases where assistance is needed, labor educators, responsive business school faculty, and/or consultants should be included in this process. The resulting product should be an independent agenda for internal and workplace reform.

Build support among the membership for a new conception of the union's role. Union leaders should engage their members in revitalizing the union and establishing a new role (Cohen-Rosenthal 1995). In many locals, building a new mandate requires an extensive information and education campaign. Members need to understand the industrial context in which their workplace functions and why change is needed. They need to understand that allying with management in targeted areas is a strategic option for the union; and they need examples illustrating how the union benefits, how this will increase the union's credibility with the public and unorganized workers, and how solidarity in these ventures *does* provide leverage to save jobs or create better jobs.

In many cases, union leaders will need to take a clear and visible stand that defines what they would like to achieve. They must be prepared for confusion and resistance from members. Acting as a strategic ally with management, after all, is a radical departure from the role most union members are accustomed to expecting from their leaders. Members will need to understand how their union leaders' time may be devoted to new tasks. To ensure their integrity with the workforce, union leaders must repeatedly define the union's interests and tie their actions, both with management and within the union, to those interests.

INTERNATIONAL ACTION STEPS

Local union leaders will often need the assistance of the international to develop effectively a union-building agenda and a clear case for appro-

189

priate labor-management restructuring. Moreover, international unions have a responsibility to provide local leaders with the same kind of training and support for new union strategies that they provide for functions such as grievance handling and safety.

While local unions struggle on the front lines with changing industry dynamics and changing worker expectations, what should international unions do? Or, as is more often the case, how can business agents and international representatives help poorly equipped union officials confront misguided management initiatives? Let us look at action steps that international unions can take.

Assist the local in translating from the current economic context to a union agenda. One of the critical ways the international can assist is by obtaining important financial, economic, and technical information about a particular work site and interpreting this for the local. The international can often leverage resources, within the union or company or with external consultants, to help the local evaluate the strategic issues facing a company, identify potential impacts on workers, and assess prospects for strategically allying with management. Internationals can also help the local formulate ideas into a written plan and position the plan appropriately with members and then with management.

Provide business and technical consultants. In addition to engineers and economic research departments, many international unions now have work system specialists or other assigned staff available to assist local unions and business agents. These specialists can identify workplace changes needed from the perspective of strengthening the industry or linking multisite union-building efforts.

Creatively use the media to reposition the message about "unionism" in the twenty-first century. Internationals provide credibility for a new union agenda with members, the public, unorganized workers, and even with the company. Unions should make greater use of the media to advertise how they are adding value in the new economy. Union publications should provide information about industry dynamics, partnerships, new work systems, and innovative models. In addition, internationals can tap local or regional media to show unions taking initiative to change workplaces and to improve business viability. This reinforces an image of unions saving jobs and creating a new basis for jobs that pay well.

2. *Unions must bargain for the right to become partners with management in critical decisions that affect workers. They must create strategic alliances with clear areas of codetermination.* In the ideal scenario, unions would have a role in the strategic decisions of the firm that affect the future of their members; unions and management would have an "enterprise compact" encompassing product quality, price-setting, and productivity goals (Bluestone and Bluestone 1992a; Bennett 1988; Lazes 1991).

190

Most companies, however, and probably many unions are not ready to move to this level of codetermination, especially if they have had a particularly adversarial relationship. Yet, we maintain that there can be advantages for unions to pursue strategic alliances with management—*provided the areas and terms of codetermination are clear.* Clarity about what activities will be jointly undertaken, what level of decision making will be used, and how rewards will be shared is essential. We have developed two tools that help clarify, on a practical level, both the scope of a partnership with management and the level of decision making that both parties can agree to.

DETERMINING AREAS OF PARTNERSHIP

We have defined five areas or "domains" for strategic alliance with management, moving in stages from traditional arenas of labor-management bargaining to developing business strategy with management. The five domains are shown in table 10.2.

At the left side of the table, labor and management operate in the traditional sphere of labor relations. Once the parties begin to define both mutual and divergent interests, they might experiment with simple joint problem solving in an area of mutual interest. The implication is that unions and management start in a domain most appropriate for them, and move to greater depths as they gain experience, skills, and the ability to negotiate interests in more complex domains. This spectrum, however, is intended as a vehicle for determining readiness and should be used with judgment. For example, economic distress may drive some unions and companies from stage one immediately to stage five.

This spectrum helps to illustrate the importance of experience to build the union's skills, members' support, and management's confidence to engage the union in important decisions. For instance, companies and unions who have not ventured into the arena of basic problem solving

Table 10.2
Domains of a Strategic Alliance

1 Traditional Labor-Management Domain	2 Joint Problem Solving to Improve Working Conditions	3 Projects Focused on Operations Improvements	4 Systems Changes	5 Business Strategy
Wages, work rules	*Health and safety committees, greater worker access to supplies*	*Equipment layout, statistical process control, worker skill training*	*Work and process design, information systems for shop floor, compensaion*	*Five-year planning, product development*

probably do not have the skills or sufficient understanding of each other's interests to venture immediately into strategic business issues. More important, each stage essentially involves greater numbers of members (and managers) in the bargaining process. As they engage in more complex decision making and workplace changes, unions must create new structures for bargaining and new educational vehicles that ensure that their interests and previously won gains are not eroded.

DETERMINING DECISION-MAKING LEVELS

The second tool we have developed is a decision matrix that defines the decision-making or "codetermination" level that management is willing to share with labor on any particular joint activity or traditional management issue. It reduces the confusion that often arises because parties have differing expectations of what a "strategic alliance" or "joint activity" means and of the responsibilities that go with it. It also helps unions to ensure that workers are not merely contributing ideas over which only management has the power to act. The five levels of decision making and decision matrix are shown in table 10.3 (Lazes 1995; Vroom and Jago

Table 10.3
Sample Decision Matrix

Key: Levels of Decision Making					
Level 1	Informed	Management shares information.			
Level 2	Consulted	The union has the opportunity to influence a management decision by giving feedback on what is already designed.			
Level 3	Developers	The union participates in developing solutions, changes, and proposals.			
Level 4	Input in Decision Making	The union has input in developing solutions and in final decisions; it participates in monitoring and taking corrective action.			
Level 5	Full Partners in Decisions	The union is a full partner in reaching final decisions, formulating plans, monitoring, and taking corrective action.			
Issue / Project Area	**Level 1**	**Level 2**	**Level 3**	**Level 4**	**Level 5**
Training employees on production jobs					X
Safety performance				X	
Reducing scrap levels				X	
Developing annual operating plan		X			

1988; Vroom and Yetton 1973). As table 10.3 illustrates, a strategic alliance may define joint activity at level five for new employee hiring and orientation, but at level two for business strategy.

The union-building strategic alliances we are suggesting are not the same as cooperation. They do not require that unions "sell out," "give in to," or "trust" management. Management and unions will continue to have interests that diverge. Strategic alliances necessitate responsible partners, each with something of value to bring to the table. They imply partnerships in predetermined areas, not across the board. They require partners who recognize individual as well as mutual interests. And they require clear agreements to which the partners can be held accountable if commitments are not met. In the new strategy, workers should not improve operations for management in exchange for the mere promise of a better place to work. Unions must use workers' collective ability to improve what management cannot, as leverage to influence far-reaching business decisions and to be rewarded for their contributions. Unions might, for example, bargain to improve a work system in exchange for level-five decision making over the new work system, combined with a productivity bonus and level-three input to the quality positioning of the product.

LOCAL ACTION STEPS

We suggest the following action steps for local unions attempting to establish strategic alliances with management.

Bargain for new contract language or side-bar agreements that frame a strategic alliance with management. Hold managers accountable to their commitments. Unions should present their own agenda for workplace change to management and seek a strategic alliance where appropriate. In most cases, it is wise to bind the strategic alliance in contract language or a written agreement capturing the expectations of both parties. Unions should bargain for language that commits the organization to a long-term change process with *specific goals* and that commits management to provide the *necessary resources*. Resource commitments might include working capital, training and education, work system, business or engineering consultants, and paid time for workers to participate on various task groups or committees. The agreement should also reflect in the parties' own words the kinds of principles outlined in the AFL-CIO model of work organization (AFL-CIO Committee on the Evolution of Work 1994). If consultants will be involved—both external and internal—the agreement should state that the union is to be a full and equal partner in selecting those consultants.

The easiest method for obtaining such an agreement is to negotiate appropriate language when the contract is renewed. Admittedly, this is not always possible or timely. In such cases, unions may initiate recommendations for their involvement and obtain an agreement to pilot a joint project. In cases where management is unwilling to share power, unions may need to force management to pay attention to these issues through more traditional means. In fact, some labor educators and unionists maintain that unions should make improving quality and avoiding mismanagement strikeable issues (Cohen-Rosenthal 1995; Bluestone and Bluestone 1992a; Bennett 1988).

Establish clear areas of codetermination. Use our partnership areas and decision matrix or similar tools to clarify areas of joint work and to decide upon specific levels of decision making. Not all activities or projects need to begin at level five. It is important, however, that management indicates at least a willingness to move to this level, in areas, over time.

Create new governance structures for codetermination. The collective bargaining language should clarify new decision-making and oversight responsibilities; in particular it should establish a joint working group to develop the strategic alliance. This is often referred to as a labor-management business council, steering committee, or the like. This group should include the key decision makers among both union and management. This group is an important vehicle for redefining the labor-management relationship. It must grapple with the terms, the scope, and the ground rules of the alliance, as well as the first areas of collaboration and any steps needed to prepare the organization.

Unions should also ensure that *joint* guidance and oversight of projects is established at appropriate levels of the organization. This can take the form of a union-management pair or a representative group. When the strategic alliance includes developing a new work system, unions should make sure that they are involved fully and should not leave parts of it to management alone. They should take a lead in monitoring all joint activities, regardless of scope, and should ensure that activities respond to specific needs or requirements of the organization (Lazes 1991) as well as the union.

When agreements are in place, unions should hold managers accountable to provide sufficient information, resources, and support to ensure that changes pay off. They should also establish ongoing access to financial and technical information regarding the plant or company. Such access is critical for tracking the outcomes of changes and identifying new strategic challenges.

Hold managers accountable to provide education and training. The new work organizations and strategic alliances with management require that workers and union leaders develop new skills. Although many companies do not invest in extensive training for workers, unions must press management for appropriate upgrading of worker skills. Supervisors and shop stewards should be provided with education, training, and support for a new role, as should union and management leaders.

INTERNATIONAL ACTION STEPS

The following are ways that the international union can assist locals in creating a strategic alliance.

Provide models and examples. Internationals should develop models and guidelines for strategic alliances with practices relevant to industries or regions. They might provide case write-ups or videotapes describing specific projects, with an analysis of the pros and cons for unions and specific recommendations for action steps.

Provide educational forums for locals. Internationals should provide regular educational and networking forums for local leaders to share their experiences, lessons, and concerns. They should regularly disseminate information about cases and engage locals and members in debates about the strategic merits and risks associated with these new strategies.

Assist in creating strategic decision-making boundaries. The international union can help to bargain for contract language or agreements that frame a strategic alliance with management. It can also help to define the membership and scope of authority for joint decision-making groups. Often it is useful to include the experience and influence of an international representative in the deliberations of a Labor-Management Business Council, particularly at the early stages, as this group informally negotiates important decisions. The international union can help to make sure that the union is kept informed about corporate decisions that will affect plant or site activities.

Keep the process on track. Sometimes pressure applied by the staff of an international is needed to get management back on track when plant-level activities are not well-focused or begin to drift away from their intended goals. Many efforts are considerably under-resourced and the international representative can be helpful in focusing or leveraging attention on these areas. Pressure or coaching may also be needed for union officials unaccustomed to the new demands of joint projects.

3. Unions must bargain for compensation increases tied to strategic alliances and contributions that unions and workers make. These contributions may be in the form of improved business results, reduced total costs, reduced time to market, or the successful application of technology. In the past, workers were rewarded on the basis of time. Unions bargained for wage increases and management afforded them through productivity increases driven by labor efficiencies in mass production. Workers can no longer count, however, on an "expanding pie" of labor efficiencies as a source of wage increases. Moreover, recent productivity gains have been driven in greater proportion by technological innovation. Although labor has had a share in successfully applying technologies and in providing data for sophisticated information systems, it is capturing little if any share of the resulting payoff.

By participating in improving the business, unions broaden the domain over which they can bargain for compensation. In the new work organization, the focus for workers' value shifts from solely "time work" to include knowledge work and the successful application of technology. These, rather than labor efficiencies, become the new sources of labor's part in productivity improvements; and labor should expect to share in the gains resulting from them.

More specifically, labor's added value may include helping to create and sustain a more flexible work organization; contributing ideas, knowledge, and skills to improve quality and work methods or to reduce material costs; broadening job and problem-solving responsibilities; effectively using information technology to reduce maintenance costs; and quickly bringing new products to the marketplace. In many cases, workers take on what traditionally were supervisory tasks. They may identify and solve their own problems or directly coordinate with the customer. Furthermore, workers enter data, make use of computers to schedule work, and use numerically controlled machines to perform operations once performed by hand.

The strategy we are proposing requires that unions bargain to expand the basis for labor's compensation before (or as a result of) engaging in significant improvements to the business. Given the multiple levels at which workers may be contributing to important solutions, unions may seek additional or alternative forms of compensation. These may include day-rate pay in a piece-rate shop, productivity-linked bonuses, gainsharing, stock investments, and employee ownership. In no case, however, should productivity-linked compensation replace regular wages and benefits.

Another important feature of the strategy we propose is that it increases workers' marketable skill base, which historically has been a competitive advantage unions offered over nonunion shops (for example, the building trades). The case can be made that many of the benefits of a broader skill base flow straight to the bottom line; thus, greater value per unit cost is achieved, which justifies higher wages paid to skilled union workers relative to their counterparts in lower-skilled jobs.

Obviously, unions must have useful financial information about the business in order to present a case for a greater share of productivity gains. In the role of strategic ally, unions do gain access to valuable financial information. They must, however, learn how to track the payback on changes involving workers in terms that managers cannot easily dispute. In addition, unions must negotiate upfront agreements that ensure that workers will be compensated for sharing their knowledge and information and for contributing to improvements in the business. They must hold managers accountable to these agreements and find creative ways to project future gains on which the union can deliver its members.

4. *Through strategic alliances, unions must fundamentally change the work systems of their workplaces, including work structures, decision making, and the use of technology.* From hard-pressed to emerging industries, it is quite apparent that the new economy requires more varied, reliable, and high-quality goods and services, as well as quick response delivery and the ability to adapt quickly in the marketplace. The bureaucratic tendencies of job classifications and rigid work rule structures will not secure employment in organizations that need greater organizational flexibility and better use of workers' skills, their knowledge, and technology.

To "transform" a work organization from a mass-production model to a flexible or high-performance model, the "whole system" must be part of the analysis, not just jobs and labor costs. By tapping workers' knowledge—which unions historically have protected—a broader set of costs and productivity factors can be addressed. For example, workers may develop ways to decrease material costs and waste, improve equipment efficiencies and processes, or respond to the customer more quickly; they may even participate in developing new products or in creating innovations in products, processes, or equipment. The outcome should be a work system that produces more effectively, with less management oversight and control. Moreover, the newly designed workplace should be able to respond much more quickly to changes in the marketplace, enabling it to compete against less flexible, low-cost mass producers.

It is not enough, however, for new organizational structures to be put in place. Unions and the workers they represent must be involved in designing, implementing, and improving them in order for these changes to impact the organization's economic performance (Bailey 1992). Furthermore, the union agenda must be built into initiatives. In many cases, managers will seek interim, suboptimal solutions, or they will attempt to apply the latest management fad. Unions must press for whole-systems change and for a focus on clear results and new measures of performance. Unions may also need to press for changes that strengthen their entire industry (that is, with customer-supplier links), as in the case of the apparel manufacturer we described.

LOCAL ACTION STEPS

The following are specific suggestions for locals unions attempting to develop new work systems.

Become knowledgeable about how to develop new work systems. Unions can only be effective in developing new work systems if they understand what new work systems can achieve and how they are different from the mass production model (Appelbaum and Batt 1993; Lazes 1991). Unions must learn from other unions who have experimented in these areas. They should see work systems in action and evaluate the outcomes. They should learn how other unions take part in designing and implementing them. Often this kind of sharing and learning takes place only among the top officers of unions. Unions must create ways for the leadership and rank-and-file members to learn together and to evaluate methods and ideas for their own workplaces.

Make sure that there are union developers to support organizational change. Unions should designate (either by selection or by election) members to act as skilled developers, guiding both union and management in developing agreements, redesigning work, and carrying out other improvement projects. These developers will need intensive and ongoing training and coaching from experienced specialists, including union international staff, other union leaders, labor educators, union-supportive consultants, and even engineers and accountants. Their skills should include problem solving, redesigning sociotechnical work, holding effective meetings, and presenting ideas as recommendations.

Provide ongoing two-way communication about changes to the work system. Locals should establish clear mechanisms to keep members informed and involved in changing their systems of work (as well as in refining their broader union agenda). They must provide the workforce ongoing access to production information, customer requirements, and competitors, as well as the status of restructuring activities. The best way to do this is through a face-to-face communication system that includes the union leadership and disseminates information at a regular weekly or monthly interval. Finally, union leaders must actively communicate the union's successes and take credit for changes that improve workers' standing in the new economy.

INTERNATIONAL ACTION STEPS

The following are ways that the international can assist locals in creating new work systems.

Provide new work system models. The international can play an important role in identifying work-system models appropriate for specific industries, including examples of work-unit structures, decision-making methods, communication and information-sharing methods, and training requirements. The international can also educate local leaders about how to design and implement new work systems.

Educate members about the impact new work systems can have on jobs, wages, and union strength. The symbolism and leverage of international staff may be needed to make the case with local boards and members that changing existing work systems can be a vehicle for rebuilding the union. The international can educate members about potential gains of better jobs, greater job satisfaction, and higher wages.

Identify resources. The international may be needed to identify labor educators, consultants, and even industry specialists to assist in the redesign at specific work sites. The international might also help to obtain state economic development and other public and private funding to offset the costs of redesign and training.

5. Unions must restructure themselves and build new competencies to support these efforts. For unions to be successful at changing workplaces in a meaningful way and rebuilding their own institutions in the process, they first need dramatically to restructure their organizations. They must start from within, breaking down their own bureaucratic tendencies and positioning themselves to be more flexible, responsive, and participatory. They must set new priorities, redirect the support they provide locals, cultivate leaders with a new skill set, and reposition their message.

At this point in time, most international unions' resources are deployed to support traditional goals, such as "organizing the unorganized," bargaining and administering contracts, and fighting unfair labor practices. The new focus should be on building internal capabilities to assess industry and business environments, to develop strategic plans at the regional and local level, to identify promising projects and leaders, to support those projects with skilled staff and extensive learning networks, and to train staff and local leaders in new skills. In addition, organizing strategies should be linked to these new capabilities and to successful outcomes of model projects.

Success with the new strategy will demand significant changes in how the departments and staff of internationals work together. In many cases, new staff members with different skill sets will be needed, and the criteria for hiring them will need to change. In addition to organizing skills, staff members may need technical and problem-solving competencies, a reasonable understanding of finances, the ability creatively to generate solutions, and the ability to negotiate in alliance with management while drawing on traditional adversarial methods when needed. Unions must also provide incentives for staff to reorient their priorities and energies. They must reward those who take risks and contribute to the unions' expertise in the new strategies.

A number of international unions have begun making these kinds of changes. Several have established specific departments to support partnership and restructuring activities. These unions include Union of Needletrades, Industrial and Textile Employees (UNITE; formerly ACTWU and ILGWU); United Steelworkers of America; Bakery, Confectionery and Tobacco Workers; Service Employees International Union (SEIU); and the American Federation of Grainmillers. Other unions have decided to restructure themselves in order to respond more effectively to these and other union issues. The American Federation of Teachers, the Communication Workers of America, Steelworkers, Union of Needletrades, Industrial, and Textile Employees (UNITE), Service Employees International Union (SEIU), the National Education Association (NEA), and the Carpenters all have established their own internal strategic planning as well as restructuring processes (Weil 1994).

THE LIMITATIONS OF THE NEW STRATEGY

It can be argued that some unions, attempting to work with management to improve operations, have actually engaged in activities that weaken their unions (Parker and Slaughter 1994). The strategy we are proposing does not come without risks to unions, and we do not wish to downplay these. In practical terms, there are significant barriers that originate both on the management side and on the union side.

MANAGEMENT ISSUES

In most organizations, there is a well-entrenched system of management decision making that extends beyond local plants into the corporate levels. Creating an authentic strategic alliance requires that management is aligned and supportive from multiple levels. This alignment is not easy to create, and often a visionary manager who is willing to take risks and to take stands is required. Our experience suggests that there is often more appreciation among local managers, as opposed to corporate managers, for the value of having the union as a strategic ally in endeavors; yet corporate managers may lend important leverage to get things done.

Another barrier is that managers and unions operate from two very different institutional perspectives. Managers generally operate from a "rational" model of management and organization, while unions operate from a "political" model. More often than not, misguided managers present workers with piecemeal initiatives and have no vision of an integral role for the union. Although they may recognize the value of worker input and the needs of workers, they often do not intuitively understand or account for the political cultures of unions. Furthermore, managers generally have a vested interest in minimizing the power of the union. It would not be well-regarded in most management cultures to advocate or allow an activist role for unions. The notion of sharing power is threatening, and most local plant managers would not assume the authority to take major steps in this area. Even sharing financial information can be a significant hurdle to overcome.

Management is often wary of its own risks in such a process. Because there are few models, embarking on these kinds of changes jointly is complicated and time consuming. It is difficult to predict outcomes without an extensive assessment process. Moreover, costs savings and overall improvements are not always well quantified and documented. Many companies, driven by the imperatives of short-term financial and accounting measures, will not allocate sufficient resources to support such systemic change. And, even where there are successful alliances, economic and market forces can overtake the gains achieved.

UNION ISSUES

Within their own ranks, unions face significant obstacles. In many cases, there is no clear mandate among members for a new agenda or for more influence over their jobs (Mills 1995). Dissatisfaction, however, with the lack of worker influence and with management's decisions is often ripe. Unions can build a mandate from such dissatisfaction. More important, changing work systems often results in "losses" to some members as new gains for the larger group are created. In some cases, members can lose overtime as a source of extra pay. In other cases, work schedules, high piece-rate earners, and even seniority as a basis for job selection have been affected. Unions will need to work with members to ensure that these kinds of losses are redressed in the new systems.

Union leaders embarking on these efforts must also plan how they will work with management. For example, in many cases, only an individual plant or human resources manager or a small group of managers understand why new work systems are needed and view the union as a valuable contributor to such changes. These managers may face considerable obstacles within their own ranks, and their tenure may be vulnerable to shifting views and political forces within management. Unions must identify these managers and may need to find ways to support these managers in order to sustain changes over the long term.

Table 10.4 illustrates the benefits and risks to unions engaging in strategic alliances with management.

A New Role for the AFL-CIO

We feel it is important to refer back to the AFL-CIO report and to make a few additional comments about the need for leadership from the AFL-CIO. The report does not clarify the AFL-CIO's role in developing partnerships and new work systems.

We feel the primary role for the AFL-CIO should be one of mobilizing international and regional labor leaders and setting a national agenda for union involvement in restructuring the workplace. Its secondary role should be advocating changes in management practices and public policy that hold corporations responsible for their actions and that are supportive of authentic joint processes for restructuring the workplace. The AFL-CIO should be developing policies that foster, if not mandate, the role of unions in strategic decision making and workplace restructuring.

We propose the following specific suggestions for the role of the AFL-CIO:

Table 10.4
The Benefits and Risks of Union Involvement
in Strategic Alliances with Management

BENEFITS	RISKS
• Most workers like the characteristics of new work systems better: —Less supervision —More decision-making opportunities —Connects them to the whole production process —Get immediate feedback and recognition of improvements • Workers gain dignity and self-esteem through more responsibility • Broadens workers' marketable skills • Unions with track record of success can offer new value to unorganized workers • Can reduce overall operating costs by 30% +; improves the quality of products and customer satisfaction. Broader union skills and contributions to business objectives become basis for secure jobs (without loss of wages and benefits) or for greater compensation • Can be used to help build a stronger union	• Unions have to restructure themselves to support the new strategy • Management may not be willing to share power or gains • Change is difficult for everyone • The membership may not understand the need for change or the union's new strategy and tactics • Management is unlikely to recognize the needs of the union as an institution, as distinguished from those of workers

POLITICAL ACTION

We recommend that the AFL-CIO advocate and provide evidence for the need for changes in national labor relations laws that increase the legitimate role of unions in strategic and shop-floor decision-making activities.

MEDIA OUTREACH AND PUBLIC PRESENCE

We recommend that, through a highly visible, organized media and information campaign, the AFL-CIO establish an updated popular picture of unionism for union members and unorganized workers. This "new unionism" should reflect an activist role on the part of unions to improve workers' control over their own jobs, their ability to influence business decisions that affect their employment security, their marketable skill base, and their opportunities to reap a share of gains to which they contribute.

LABOR EDUCATION AND OUTREACH

Our labor education and outreach recommendations are to:

Continue supporting Meany Center workshops on new work systems (for example, Union Leadership Series).

Provide additional funds or programs, especially for smaller unions, for educating labor leaders across the country in the new economic realities and for training and coaching them in new work systems and joint decision making. This training and coaching should be used to equip leaders to respond to management initiatives as well as to initiate their own. It should be available both regionally and in specific industrial sectors.

Work with labor studies programs across the country to establish regional educational programs and consulting outreach when the Meany Center is not able to provide such programs.

Provide funds for apprenticeships so that union leaders can learn from other sectors both in union-driven workplace restructuring and union restructuring activities.

Compile a referral network of skilled "consultants/advisors" recommended to unions for assistance on specific restructuring projects.

Develop programs to help individual unions examine the need for restructuring their own organizations. These programs should include the perspectives and experiences of internationals who have successfully undergone these changes.

RESEARCH

We recommend that the AFL-CIO encourage research in four areas. First, we recommend greater documentation of the contribution that labor is making to business results through knowledge work, use of technology, and new work systems. This can help to build a public case for labor's share in gains from improved productivity as a result of strategic alliances with management. It can also help labor rebuild its image and relevance within communities.

Second, we recommend more extensive documentation of existing experiments and evaluation of methods that work, those that don't, and quantifiable results. This research should also evaluate methods for rebuilding unions and engaging members in union business and community issues. It should include descriptive case write-ups that help to define the models. It could help to frame and guide the future development of labor-management strategic alliances.

Third, we recommend research that compares the European model of works' councils to the American model of governance and work-system design. Which gives greater voice to workers' concerns? Which yields greater benefits to unions? To society? Finally, we recommend research that defines the educational agenda for union leaders and members, with variations among industries or other subgroups.

CONCLUSION

The current challenges unions face are arduous, and there are no quick and easy solutions. Each day, corporate downsizing and the impacts of a global economy are having a significant impact on Americans. A poll conducted by the *New York Times* found that nearly three-quarters of all households have been or know of someone who has been directly affected by layoffs since 1980. One in ten adults indicate that their loss of a job has "precipitated" a major crisis in their life. In the last sixteen years, more than forty-three million jobs have been lost; and, although more new jobs are created, they do not return with the same wages (Uchitelle and Kleinfield 1996, 1, 26). The current job losses cause psychological, medical, and physical problems. In addition, job dislocation is a significant factor in the reduction of civic and social activism, which is the foundation for a functioning democracy (Uchitelle and Kleinfield 1996; Putnam 1996).

Unions have the choice, however, to remain bystanders or to engage and struggle with their own responses to the present economic and institutional changes. It is our view that the key to unions' survival and growth in the twenty-first century is to redefine what they are after and strategically to shift their resources, energy, and activities in new directions. Although organizing new members is a vital component of a new unionism and has been enthusiastically supported by AFL-CIO president John Sweeney, we believe it is equally important that unions obtain a role for workers in the fundamental decisions that affect their employment security, their workplace, and how they perform their jobs. We believe that only through participating in the management of the enterprises of which they are a part will unions be able to ensure that their interests and those of their members are met. The strategy we have outlined is intended not only to save jobs in a rapidly changing economy but also to create more meaningful and democratic jobs for workers, opportunities that are long overdue. Furthermore, the strategy is centered upon a clear identification of the union's interests. We believe that *union-driven* workplace changes are vital to the future of unions and should be a central part of a new union agenda.

BIBLIOGRAPHY

Abernathy, Frederick H., et al. 1995. "The Information-Integrated Channel: A Study of the U.S. Apparel Industry in Transition." In *Brookings Papers on Economic Activity: Microeconomics 1995,* ed. Martin Neil Baily, Peter C. Reiss, and Clifford Winston. Washington, D.C.: Brookings Institute.

AFL-CIO Committee on the Evolution of Work. 1994. *The New American Workplace: A Labor Perspective.* Washington, D.C.: American Federation of Labor-Congress of Industrial Organizations.

Appelbaum, Eileen, and Rosemary Batt. 1993. *High Performance Work Systems: American Models of Workplace Transformation.* Washington, D.C.: Economic Policy Institute.

———. 1994. *The New American Workplace: Transforming Work Systems in the United States.* New York: ILR Press.

Bailey, Thomas. 1992. "Why Change? The Breakdown of Mass Production." In *The New American Workplace: Transforming Work Systems in the United States,* by Eileen Appelbaum and Rosemary Batt, 14–25. Ithaca, N.Y.: ILR Press.

Baugh, Bob. 1994. *Changing Work: A Union Guide to Workplace Change.* New York: AFL-CIO Human Resources Development Institute.

Bennett, Mike. 1988. "The Changing Role of Union Leadership." UAW Local 1853, Mar. Unpublished.

Bluestone, Barry, and Irving Bluestone. 1992a. *Negotiating the Future: A Labor Perspective on American Business.* New York: Basic Books.

———. 1992b. "Workers (and Managers) of the World, Unite." *Technology Review* 95, no. 8 (Nov./Dec.): 31–40.

CEPU Local 609 (Communications, Energy, and Paperworkers Union of Canada, Saskatoon Chemical). 1994. Strategic planning proposal, working document.

Cohen-Rosenthal, Edward. 1995. *Unions, Management, and Quality: Opportunities for Innovation and Excellence.* Chicago: Irwin Professional Publishing.

Commission on the Skills of the American Workforce. 1990. *America's Choice: High Skills or Low Wages.* Washington, D.C.: National Center on Education and the Economy.

Dunlop, John. 1993. "Labor Productivity and Competitiveness: The Lessons from Apparel." Draft, Mar. 19.

Emery, Fred, and Einar Thorsrud. 1976. *Democracy at Work.* Leiden, The Netherlands: Matinus Nijhoff Social Sciences Division.

Freedman, Audrey. 1989. *Productivity Needs of the United States.* New York: Conference Board.

Freeman, Richard. 1992. "Is Declining Unionization of the U.S. Good, Bad, or

Irrelevant?" In *Unions and Economic Competitiveness,* ed. Lawrence Mishel and Paula B. Voos. Armonk, N.Y.: M.E. Sharpe.

Freeman, Richard, and Joel Rogers. 1994. "Worker Representation and Participation Survey: First Report and Findings." Dec. 5. Unpublished.

Howard, Philip K. 1994. *The Death of Common Sense.* New York: Random House.

Howell, David R. 1994. "The Skills Myth," *American Prospect* (Summer): 81–90.

Kaminski, Michelle, et al. 1996. *Making Change Happen: Six Cases of Unions and Companies Transforming Their Workplaces.* Washington, D.C.: Work and Technology Institute.

Kearns, David T., and David A. Nadler. 1992. *Prophets in the Dark: How Xerox Reinvented Itself and Beat Back the Japanese.* New York: Harper Business.

Lawler, Edward E. III, Susan Albers Mohrman, and Gerald E. Ledford Jr. 1995. *Creating High Performance Organizations: Practices and Results of Employee Involvement and Total Quality Management in Fortune 1000 Companies.* San Francisco: Jossey-Bass.

Lazes, Peter. 1991. "Unions and the Choice of Employee Involvement Activities." *Work Place Topics* 2, no. 2 (Dec.): 1–12.

———. 1995. "Building Effective Labor-Management Partnerships." *Journal for Quality and Participation* 18, no. 3 (June): 12–14.

Lazes, Peter, and Anthony Costanza. 1984. "Xerox Cuts Costs without Layoffs through Union-Management Collaboration." *Labor-Management Cooperation Brief.* U.S. Department of Labor, Bureau of Labor-Management Relations and Cooperative Programs. July.

Lazes, Peter, et al. 1991. "Xerox and the ACTWU: Using Labor-Management Teams to Remain Competitive." *National Productivity Review* 10, no. 3 (Summer): 339–49.

Marshall, Ray. 1992. "Work Organizations, Unions, and Economic Performance." In *Unions and Economic Competitiveness,* ed. Lawrence Mishel and Paula B. Voos. Armonk, N.Y.: M.E. Sharpe.

McKenzie, Richard B. 1992. *The "Fortunate Fifth" Fallacy.* St. Louis: Center for the Study of American Business, Washington University.

Midwest Center for Labor Research. 1987. *Mismanagement and What Unions Can Do About It.* Monograph from *Labor Research Review* 6, no. 1 (Spring).

Mills, Nancy. 1995. *Participating for Strength: A Guide to Worker Participation that Works to Build the Union.* Washington, D.C.: Service Employees Union.

Osterman, Paul. 1994. "How Common Is Workplace Transformation and Who Adopts It?" *Industrial and Labor Relations Review* 47, no. 2 (Jan.): 173–87.

Parker, Mike, and Jane Slaughter. 1994. *Working Smart: A Union Guide to Participation Programs and Reengineering.* Detroit: Labor Notes.

Phillips, Kevin P. 1990. *The Politics of Rich and Poor: Wealth and the American Electorate in the Reagan Aftermath.* New York: Random House.

Potter, Edward E., and Yi K. Ngan. 1996. *Estimating the Potential Productivity and Real Wage Effects of Employee Involvement.* Washington, D.C.: Employment Policy Foundation.

Prowse, Michael. 1992. "Is America in Decline?" *Harvard Business Review* 70, no. 4 (July–Aug.): 34–45.

Putnam, Robert. 1996. "The Strange Disappearance of Civic America." *American Prospect* 24 (Winter): 34–48.

Rifkin, Jeremy. 1995. *The End of Work: The Decline of the Global Labor Force and the Dawn of the Post-Market Era.* New York: G. P. Putnam and Sons.

Rubinstein, Saul, Michael Bennett, and Thomas Kochan. 1993. "The Saturn Partnership: Reinventing the Local Union." In *Employee Representation: Alternatives and Future Directions,* ed. Bruce Kaufman and Morris Kleiner. Madison, Wisc.: Industrial Relations Research Association Press.

Schrank, Robert. 1979. *American Workers Abroad.* Cambridge, Mass.: MIT Press.

Sheehan, Maureen. 1993. "Keep It Complicated . . . What Unions Owe Local Leaders to Prepare Them for Their Role in Joint Programs and Work Restructuring." Feb. 23. Unpublished.

Sherman, Joe. 1994. *In the Rings of Saturn.* New York: Oxford University Press.

Shostak, Arthur B. 1991. *Robust Unionism: Innovations in the Labor Movement.* Ithaca, N.Y.: ILR Press.

Slater, Philip, and Warren Bennis. 1990. "Democracy Is Inevitable." *Harvard Business Review* 68, no. 5 (Sept./Oct.): 167–76.

Uchitelle, Louis, and N. R. Kleinfield. 1996. "On the Battlefields of Business, Millions of Casualties." *New York Times,* Mar. 3.

U.S. Census Bureau. 1994. *1994 Statistical Abstract of the United States: USA Statistics in Brief.* Washington, D.C.

U.S. Department of Labor. 1993. Bureau of Labor Statistics. *Multifactor Productivity Trends, 1993: Tables 1–2.* Washington, D.C.

———. 1994. Commission on the Future of Worker-Management Relations. *Report and Recommendations.* Washington, D.C.

———. 1995a. Federal Mediation and Conciliation Service. *Guidelines: Innovative Collective Contract Provisions.* Washington, D.C.

———. 1995b. Office of the American Workplace. *Guide to Responsible Restructuring.* Washington, D.C.

Vroom, Victor, and Arthur Jago. 1988. *Leadership: Managing Participatively in Organizations.* Englewood Cliffs, N.J.: Prentice Hall.

Vroom, Victor, and Phillip Yetton. 1973. *Leadership and Decision Making.* Pittsburgh: University of Pittsburgh Press.

Weil, David. 1994. *Turning the Tide: Strategic Planning for Labor Unions.* New York: Lexington Books.

Weisbord, Marvin. 1993. *Discovering Common Ground: How Future Search Conferences Bring People Together to Achieve Breakthrough Innovation, Empowerment, Shared Vision, and Collaborative Action.* San Francisco: Berrett-Koehler.

Winnick, Andrew J. 1989. *Toward Two Societies: The Changing Distribution of Income and Wealth in the U.S. Since 1960.* New York: Praeger.

Wolff, Edward N. 1995. *Top Heavy: A Study of the Increasing Inequality of Wealth in America.* New York: Twentieth Century Fund Press.

Wyatt Company. 1993. *Wyatt's 1993 Survey of Corporate Restructuring: Best Practices in Corporate Restructuring.* Chicago: Wyatt Company.

11

ADVANCING UNIONISM
ON THE NEW TERRAIN

MIKE PARKER AND JANE SLAUGHTER

What's the point of the 1994 report by the AFL-CIO's Committee on the Evolution of Work, *The New American Workplace?* For the last ten years a wave of employer "reorganization" programs has swept the workplace. Employers, consultants, politicians, and a number of labor leaders all urge unions to come along for the ride on the "new terrain." How should unions respond?

The introduction, conclusion, and general tone of the report reassure us that unions can take advantage of employer interest in reorganization. "An increasing number of employers . . . have been open to joining with unions . . . to create partnerships to transform the work system" (AFL-CIO Committee on the Evolution of Work 1994, 1). This in turn means new possibilities for worker opportunity, job satisfaction, and workplace democracy. Unions should embrace reorganization; just watch out for the rocks by following travel instructions carefully.

Yet in the details of the report we find a different reality. New work systems of the type endorsed by the Committee on the Evolution of Work "are exceedingly rare" (13). General employer strategy is to reduce pay levels. Indeed, the dominant management strategy seems to be the "quest for a union-free environment" (16).

208

The report's value lies in articulating five principles and four guidelines for work reorganization programs. For the most part we agree with the principles as outlined. But the report both reflects and helps deepen a serious confusion in the labor movement. It steers the movement away from identifying the real problems. We see these as: 1) The employer offensive against workers is not an irrational action changeable by expert advice, therapy, or better communication, but a set of logical actions driven by the requirement to make profits under changing global economic, social, and technological conditions. 2) Labor's lack of a strategic response to this offensive makes it worse. 3) Much of labor's weakness stems from loss of vision and purpose.

The authors of the report want labor-management partnership on terms reasonably favorable to labor. But employers overwhelmingly have shown that they are not on that program. Employers want a union-free environment, not cooperation with unions. Where they cannot (yet) get rid of unions they attempt to depower and coopt them.

Consider the test of guideline 1, "mutual recognition and respect": "An employer who extends one hand to the union while at the same time using the other hand to do everything possible to prevent the organization of other employees of the enterprise—as so many employers do—lacks a full commitment to partnership" (11).

The number of employers who pass this test could probably be counted on the fingers of a worker who has lost a hand in a workplace injury. AT&T builds subsidiary National Cash Register (NCR), which wages a vicious fight against a Communications Workers organizing effort. General Motors fights any attempt to organize its white-collar workers. Worst of all are the massive outside contracting, outsourcing, and privatization policies that are prevalent everywhere. Under this guideline alone, "partnership" should be dismissed as fantasy.

Any management "respect" for the union must start with respect for its power, which in turn depends on its members. Unions are effective when members are both clear about their potential power as a unified force and involved in the ongoing process of building their union. Unions' central job these days must be to rebuild themselves as a powerful social force.

But The New American Workplace (NAW) report takes a different approach. Lacking a perspective for gaining power to implement labor's conception of a reorganized workplace, the NAW authors depend instead on enlightened employer self-interest: the notion that partnership with a union and a high-wage, high-performance workplace will yield greater productivity, quality, competitiveness, and therefore profits. Clearly, this economic conception is attractive. If true, then the labor movement need only convince employers no longer to "fear the unknown" (12), to see their true interests and overcome short-term thinking.

209

This is wishful thinking. Employers have undertaken work reorganization in a manner directly opposite to the AFL-CIO's hopes because new technology, globalization, and market forces reward companies that reduce their workforces, tighten management control, use low-wage labor, and either keep unions out or convert them to enterprise unions. The fact that mismanagement is still, as always, rampant does not mean that a switch to "good management" will benefit unions. Rather, the executive consensus equates "good management" with speed-up, job cuts, and tighter management control.

A powerful union movement would mean demands for a bigger portion of the pie, a social and political counterbalance to business interests in society, and more concern for health and safety. Corporations naturally see these demands as counter to their long-term interests. Effective unions are good for workers and for society, but not for employers. A worker-oriented workplace can exist only when union power changes the economic equation. Employers understand this. Denying this fundamental fact can only further weaken the labor movement in the face of the deadly assault.

COMPARING THE MODELS TO THE PRINCIPLES

The NAW sidesteps discussing any real-world programs, in line with the AFL-CIO's policy of avoiding offense to any affiliated union. But the union movement desperately needs leadership: which, if any, of these programs are worthy models? For years, for example, unionists entering onto "the new terrain" have been taken on field trips to NUMMI, the General Motors-Toyota joint venture assembly plant in California, and to Saturn. NUMMI has been described by then United Auto Workers (UAW) regional director Bruce Lee as the achievement of union goals: "The workers' revolution has finally come to the shop floor. The people who work on the assembly line have taken charge and have the power to make management do their jobs right" (Lee 1988, F2). Both NUMMI and Saturn, as we will argue, along with the other stars touted by advocates of cooperation, utterly violate the CEW's own principles and have created serious problems for workers. By not challenging these models, the NAW perpetuates the confusion around what work reorganization is really about.

Few would disagree that workers should have more power over their jobs and their workplace lives, that job design should respect and increase worker skill and knowledge. These ideas are so popular that even the most antiunion employers claim to embrace them. But the union movement must discern which programs, if any, bear any resemblance to labor's principles. Using the NAW's five principles and two of its guidelines, let us turn to that question.

210

Principle #1. Rejecting the separation of "thinking" and "doing." Ever since Frederick W. Taylor championed time-and-motion study, management has sought ways to break jobs down to their smallest elements, determine the fastest method to perform an operation, and require workers to use those methods. At the same time, unions have found that decent working conditions require limiting Taylorism.

The unpopularity of Taylorism has long made it a ready target for promoters of every new work system. Most "authorities" portray modern work reorganization programs as a humanistic alternative to Taylor's "scientific management." Speaking of what is now called "lean production," *Business Week* editorialized on August 31, 1987: "Such team-based systems, perfected by Japanese car makers, are alternatives to the 'scientific management' system, long used in Detroit, which treats employees as mere hands who must be told every move to make." In fact, under lean production the tendency is the opposite: to specify every move a worker makes in far greater detail than ever before. The system intensifies Taylorism and increases management control by placing workers and the entire system under pressure—which is why we call it management-by-stress.

NUMMI is probably the most-visited factory in the United States, as the original exemplar of the Toyota Production System/"team concept"/ lean production in this country. As advertised, at NUMMI the jobs were in fact initially designed by "teams." But the members of these teams were engineers, supervisors, and management-selected team leaders. They "charted" the jobs by breaking every job down to its individual "acts," studying and timing each motion, and then shifting the work to make the jobs more or less equal. Jobs are reworked over and over to eliminate free seconds. A detailed written specification tells each team member how to do each job: exactly how many steps to take and what the left hand should be doing while the right hand is picking up the wrench. Regular workers, then, simply implement a system designed by others—except for finding ways to speed up the job even further through problem-solving circles.

Jobs are to be done in precisely the same way every time by every worker. The company explains that this is how quality is maintained, and sends workers to SPC training to prove scientifically how variation of procedure is the enemy.

The little influence workers do have over their jobs is that they are organized to time-study themselves, in a kind of super-Taylorism. This is the "kaizen," or continuous improvement, made famous by NUMMI. Two champions of NUMMI write: "Workers are taught how to time their own jobs with a stopwatch, compare alternative procedures to determine the most efficient one, document the standard procedure to ensure that everyone can understand and implement it, and identify and propose improvements in that procedure" (Adler and Cole 1993, 90).

General Motors, having used NUMMI as its laboratory, now requires employees in other plants to attend standardized operations workshops, where they fill out detailed sheets recording the "elements" of each job, how many seconds each element takes to perform—and whether each motion is "value added" or "non-value added."[1]

This is one sense in which workers' minds are valued in the new system. And it is one way in which NUMMI's lean production does differ from the original Taylorism. Taylor thought he could discover workers' secret knowledge all at once, and workers would then revert merely to hired hands. Japanese managers realized that those who perform the work continue to have knowledge denied to management—and therefore some power over production. Thus the goal is *continuously* to shift workers' knowledge to managers.

To accomplish this, the system uses team leaders, who know and perform all jobs in their teams. A key part of their task is to document worker knowledge. In addition, a worker who believes she knows an easier or better method must get the supervisor's approval to use it. Under these conditions, it is virtually impossible not to share labor-saving innovations with management.

Traditional workplace managers lacked detailed shop-floor knowledge; supervisors had to allow workers some job flexibility if anything was to get done. Lean production seeks to squeeze out and capture for management this small amount of worker autonomy and flexibility. This added knowledge allows management to increase its control over the finest details of production. While there is worker resistance to the tight control over jobs, without union support or some form of collective action it is not very powerful.[2]

Principle #2. More skill and more responsibility for workers. More than anything else, the ideas of more skill and more responsibility for workers have been used to sell the lean system. Former secretary of labor Ray Marshall and union-connected authors Barry and Irving Bluestone, for example, argue that the "high wage, high performance" workplace requires highly skilled workers (Marshall 1992; Bluestone and Bluestone 1992).

Yet consider the observations of Jack Gordon, editor of *Training* magazine. 1) High skills will not necessarily mean high pay. Gordon cites the case of Carrier Corporation, which opened a new 150-worker factory in Arkadelphia, Arkansas, in 1992. Before they were even guaranteed a job, applicants took six weeks of training in blueprint reading, math, statistical process control, computer skills, and interpersonal communication. This sounds like a high-performance workplace if there ever was one. Workers are "empowered" too, ordering their own supplies and granted the ability to stop the production line. The salaries of these skilled, responsible employees: $16,000-$17,000 a year.

2) Management is not looking for skill in the sense of experience. "In the recession of the early '90s," Gordon notes, "veteran workers and managers aged 35 to 54 have been hit with layoffs at double the rate of recessions in the 1970s. Companies getting rid of their most experienced employees are not looking for higher skills. They're looking for younger people who'll work cheaper."

3) Since most of the new jobs being created in the U.S. economy are low-skill service jobs, the fact that they may be performed by workers who have some advanced training is moot. Gordon concludes that "unless a lot more companies start finding ways to make productive use of people with higher skills, we'll just be training smarter workers for dumber jobs" (Gordon 1993, 29).

Finally, are "high skills," as currently defined, really high skills? Sophisticated equipment—a computer, for example—doesn't make the operator skilled. Consider this illustration. The National Association of Manufacturers has showcased machinery producer Universal Dynamics as a "high-performance" company. Universal's attitude toward high skills is described as follows:

> One key to its success: the use of sophisticated equipment by hourly factory workers who need no more than an eighth-grade education and few language skills to do the job. Some of [the company's] best workers, operating computerized equipment using statistical process controls, are immigrants who speak very little English. . . .
>
> [Company President Don] Rainville said that with the increased use of computers to run machines, it now requires much less skill to operate even the most sophisticated equipment. As with the instructions on the machines his own firm makes for worldwide distribution, Rainville said the written word is being replaced by pictures very much like those on the cash registers at a fast-food restaurant.
>
> If anything, Rainville sees less of a need for further education as companies turn increasingly to automation. "I see the trend going the other way," Rainville said. Rainville concedes that higher education is still very much needed for engineers and other technicians, but not on the factory floor. "What I'm looking for is enthusiasm," he said. (Swoboda 1994, 14)

Gordon's conclusions and those of the National Association of Manufacturers jibe with the theory and practice of lean production, which requires maximum management flexibility to change quantities produced quickly. Slowing the assembly line is one way to decrease production in slow times, but it creates idle worker time—and the lean system does not tolerate idle time. If management can remove workers and redistribute the tasks to the remaining team members, most idle time can again be eliminated. Speed in redistributing tasks determines how responsive the factory can be to shifting demand.

This management flexibility to redistribute tasks easily requires that 1) tasks be broken down into the smallest units possible, 2) each task be well defined so it can easily be reassigned, 3) the skill level required for each task be as low as possible, and 4) workers be able and willing to do any task assigned.

Management calls workers who are able to do and who are movable to any job "multiskilled," but a more accurate term for this setup is "multi-tasking." The *abilities* required to do several very short pre-scripted tasks are manual dexterity, physical stamina, and the ability to follow instructions. Each such task requires little acquisition of new skills in the usual sense of requiring training and specialized knowledge; rather it requires practice to learn to do it quickly enough.

Multiskilling thus has less to do with training than with overcoming barriers such as union contract provisions, classifications, and traditions that prevent workers from doing more than one job. Training, under lean production, focuses more on company procedures and values than on marketable technical skills.

At CAMI, the joint venture of General Motors and Suzuki in Ingersoll, Ontario, a union survey asked workers how much training it took to learn their jobs. They answered five minutes, twenty minutes, a couple of hours (CAW-Canada Research Group in CAMI 1993). At Auto Alliance International (AAI), the joint venture of Ford and Mazda in Flat Rock, Michigan, a union survey found that roughly half the workers rated the training they had received as poor or none, compared to Mazda's promises (Babson 1993).

Thus when hiring, lean factories have shown little interest in applicants' skills acquired from previous work and much more interest in attendance records, ability to follow directions, physical stamina, and attitude toward management (Parker and Slaughter 1988; Graham 1995). For the skilled trades (electricians, machine repair, and so forth), the lean system seeks to contract out the most skilled work: major construction and complex repairs. The in-plant skilled trades jobs are reduced as much as possible to predictable, standardized preventive maintenance tasks. This policy frequently meets with resistance from workers trying to protect their skills.

And what about more "responsibility" for workers? The management-by-stress system separates responsibility from authority. Some authority is shifted downward—but far less than the responsibility loaded on those at the bottom. And downward transfer of authority almost completely stops with the group leader, known as foreman before the newspeak. Workers are encouraged to suggest "improvements" to the work process, but rejection or acceptance belongs to the group leader (Babson 1995). Witness the Mazda manual: "Team members do not on their own judgment decide on different locations for parts other than the counts and locations already established" (Mazda 1986).

Workers' authority is further degraded when discretion is transferred from the individual to the machinery. Sensors or mechanical devices check for defects or for an accumulation of production; if found, the machine automatically shuts the operation down. This is a combination of what its proponents call "foolproofing" and *jidoka,* or "autonomation."

Thus authority is reduced, but worker responsibility is increased. Just-in-time production forces each individual to keep up. Without production buffers, any momentary problem or lapse may affect production up and down the line, purposely magnifying the results. Organized systems of peer pressure, monitoring systems, and "visual management" intensify the pressure. High responsibility with low authority is the classic formula for workplace stress.

Principle #3. Flatter management structure. Of course, it is often of benefit to workers to have fewer managers around. Many workers see the absence of herds of supervisors as one of the advantages of the night shift. But the promise of fewer middle managers may be used as a way to make worker layoffs more palatable. A typical scenario: The company announces plans to slim the workforce by 15 percent. Union leaders protest, demanding "equality of sacrifice." Management accepts with alacrity. Both workers and managers are laid off—and the company president is laughing all the way to the bank.

Also, the flatter structure may be partly illusion. Some of the managerial work (keeping records of materials, notifying workers of changes) becomes additional work assigned to "value-added" workers. The highly praised Japanese model makes part of the hierarchy seem to disappear by moving it out of the plant, in the form of multiple levels of subcontracting.

Alternatively, titles may change. For example, one federal agency is seeking to cut the workforce by adopting a team structure. Management would be cut, and the managers would bump back into the hourly force with no loss of pay. Team leader classifications with many former management responsibilities would be created, and probably filled with those experienced in doing this kind of work. Low-seniority workers would be "riffed," creating a "reformed" and "flattened" structure that is actually more top-heavy than before.

Principle #4. Union decision-making role at all levels. Saturn, a special GM subsidiary, is widely hailed as the most advanced U.S. example of union involvement in decision making, from the shop floor to the boardroom (Bluestone and Bluestone 1992; Rubinstein, Bennett, and Kochan 1993; Higgins 1990). Both management and union officials, especially UAW Local 1853's Mike Bennett, are popular speakers at many gatherings.

Saturn embodies jointness: most management officials have a union counterpart, and the two "partners" function together. Rather than the traditional management structure with a worker participation program grafted on later, Saturn was designed as a partnership from the start by a UAW-GM team. Saturn officials say this structure allows the union to be in on decisions in formation, rather than simply reacting afterward. Bennett writes,

> The partnership attempts to integrate labor into the organization's long range and strategic planning and day-to-day operational decision making. Unlike most labor-management efforts, Saturn's joint committees have responsibility for strategic-level decision making, and an even more radical departure from traditional organization has taken place at the shop floor and middle management levels. Saturn's workforce has been organized into self-directed work teams responsible to a middle management organization half of whom are local UAW members. In this way the local union is in fact *co-managing* the business . . .
>
> Traditionally the role of a local union was to represent and organize the membership while management managed the business. The local union at Saturn is attempting to break down this dichotomy. It seeks to share responsibility for both the effective use of capital and for meeting the economic and social needs of the labor force . . . Instead of a division of responsibility based solely on constituency, both [labor and management] are responsible for managing people and capital. (Rubinstein, Bennett, and Kochan 1993, 361)

Of course, when the union has "ownership" of such decisions, it is more willing to defend them and make them work (Rubinstein, Bennett, and Kochan 1993). Worker Terry Walton, who filed suit against Saturn for race discrimination, says, "Talking to Mike Bennett is like talking to [company president] Skip LeFauve. He is not in bed with management, he *is* management" (Hinkle 1993).

There is no question that some union leaders as individuals have more influence in Saturn's day-to-day decisions than in traditional factories. Are workers' needs therefore more strongly reflected in those decisions? We would argue instead that the Saturn partnership gives management a powerful tool for greater control over the workforce. It is telling that when sections of the union—from the rank and file to the UAW International—have resisted the totalitarianism inherent in the partnership, they have not tried to use and redefine Saturn's existing partnership structures. Apparently, they see those structures as too corrupt or too byzantine to be reformed. Instead they have looked to install traditional UAW methods of functioning (including, unfortunately, those that are not particularly effective or involving of the rank and file).

Saturn does not provide a model for strengthening union power, if that means something other than integrating union officials into manage-

216

ment. Saturn is structured so that line and many staff positions consist of both a "rep" and a "nonrep" partner. (The terms "union" and "management" are not commonly used. Employees are called "represented" or "nonrepresented.") Mike Bennett serves on the Manufacturing Advisory Council, the Local 1853 recording secretary works in corporate communications, and union vice presidents have been partnered with the heads of business units.

Critics ask why it takes two partners to do one job. Bennett responds that because each rep and nonrep pair of operations module advisors (OMAs—roughly equivalent to general foremen) advises one hundred or so production workers, and because the work units are essentially self-managing, the ratio of indirect labor to direct labor is actually lower than in Japanese plants. But Bob Hoskins, an OMA who once ran against Bennett for union president, says, "Sometimes I'm in meetings, in humongous meetings, and I can't believe it—all these damn people there, and none of them contributing"—that is, none of them building cars.

Rank-and-filer Diane Fitzgerald sums up the union's "power": "Sometimes I think some of the union positions are just maybe a little bit . . . show. You've got these two people doing this job; one person does the job, and the other person represents the union. I interviewed for a job one time where the union person would have a non-rep partner, and they asked me how would I feel about doing the same job as this non-rep person and making less money. And I thought, 'That says something right there.' "

Saturn workers are a mixture of those who welcome the greater variety of work through job rotation and being team "point person" for housekeeping, safety, or quality; those who would rather work be as hassle-free as possible; and those who are sick of the Saturn rhetoric ("are you willing to change?"). For the former group, there has been much to like about the self-directed work teams, although management is rapidly moving to diminish the teams' responsibilities. Many workers liked having a role in hiring new members for their teams, for example—but that function has now been bumped up to the "module" level.

Rank-and-file members interviewed in April 1994 clearly felt no more involved in their union than they had at their previous GM plants, and usually much less so. Views expressed ranged from "it feels like we don't have a union here" to "you only see the union at election time" to "politics as usual," referring to the battles among different slates. As in more traditional UAW plants, "the union" means "the officials"; the difference is that at Saturn they are seen as part of the management structure, as in fact they are.

The UAW's vision at Saturn was union representation *in* decisions, rather than as a result of decisions. Union involvement would give workers a voice where and when it could matter, rather than too late. One

217

example is the choice to build a station wagon rather than a more prestigious convertible, because a station wagon would sell more (Rubinstein, Bennett, and Kochan 1993, 350).

This degree of union power sounds good. But the union is explicit that its role is not to represent workers' interests. Rather the union's job is "balancing the needs of the business with the needs of the people." In a traditional, arm's-length union-management relationship, this balance comes about through the process of negotiation and compromise. But at Saturn, the union has made meeting the needs of the business *its* business. This means that there are two parties looking after management's interests (or one and a half), and only half a party looking after the members' interests (unless, of course, you buy the idea that GM management truly makes decisions with workers' concerns in mind). One die technician said, "The intention was good down here, but some of it they've gone overboard on. Management is for the business, the union should be for the people. There's a gray area in the middle where they can work together. Here the union doesn't just work in the gray area—it's on the management side of the gray area."

Using the win-win philosophy, union officials argue that there is a single solution for any problem that is objectively, logically the "best." Denise Harding, an appointed health and safety official, says: "The union now has to put on a different hat. We have to have facts and figures, review the data. We don't come in like a bulldog anymore. We put on our good business hat; we're not really union or management—we advocate for a good business decision." Bennett describes the contrast: "Before, management decided on manpower and the union had to take an adversarial stance to get more. Now, really you let information make the decisions" ("Working Together" 1994). As an example, Bennett has spoken proudly of the union's choice of nonunion suppliers over union ones, for quality reasons (Hage 1990).

Further, union officers encourage workers to see their future tied to Saturn's success as a competitor of other UAW-organized plants. Mike Bennett has specifically advocated that unions pursue their interests at the local level and avoid solidarity with other workers. In 1992, GM's Lordstown, Ohio, stamping plant went on strike over contracting out. GM wanted to move some of the stamping plant's parts production, most of it for Saturn, to nonunion shops, at a loss of 160 jobs.

The strike quickly shut Saturn down, along with eight other assembly plants. Bennett complained to the press that the International union should have allowed Lordstown workers making Saturn parts to cross the picket line. Bennett said a local union's role should be to help its own company "explore opportunities to compete. I don't support the current process [the strike]. We can't continue to remove wages from competition in the international economy" ("Labor's Days at GM" 1992, A8). (Compare this view with the NAW's statements on the necessity of removing wages from competition.)

In 1994–95, Bridgestone/Firestone waged a vicious assault on its union, including hiring permanent striker replacements. Throughout the strike, Saturn continued to buy tires from the struck company. Whether this was because the union lacked power to stop such purchases or because it chose not to exercise its power is not clear. Either explanation is damning.

Paradoxically, the Saturn project—seen by many as a prounion American alternative to the Japanese model—ends up creating something very close to the enterprise unions of Japan.

Finally, how much say does the union really have in running Saturn? Union officials did have considerable input into the plant design, the labor relations system, and the contract. But the brass at GM are making the decisions about Saturn's future. Throughout 1994, speculation raged about whether GM would decide to expand Saturn. The company cannot make a profit unless it can produce 500,000 cars a year, and current capacity, even working twenty hours a day, six days a week, is 322,000. In early 1995, GM announced that, rather than expand the Tennessee plant as the local had strongly urged, the company would build a car called a Saturn at its Wilmington, Delaware, facility.

When it comes to building *union* strength—in the sense of a conscious membership, ready and able to be mobilized collectively in their own behalf—Saturn clearly fails. The auto workers' unions at Japanese-managed CAMI in Ontario and AAI in Michigan, mentioned above, make no pretense of partnership and operate under a tight lean-production regimen. But they are far stronger than UAW Local 1853.

Principle #5. Equitable distribution of the rewards for better performance. Under this heading, the NAW covers two issues. The first is job and income security, both of which are explicitly under attack by the new work systems. The gurus of the newest and most honest version, reengineering, are explicit that the goal is to "obliterate jobs" (Hammer and Champy 1993). Reengineering makes a principle of the "clean sheet" approach to job design: eliminate any commitments to processes or people.

The second compensation issue is sharing the rewards of increased productivity. Here the NAW suggests that the method of distributing economic benefits, whether through base wages, profit sharing, gainsharing, or stock ownership, is not important as long as the union negotiates the agreement. We disagree: methods of economic distribution have a profound effect on unionism. In Japan, merit pay, bonus pay, and seniority pay may account for a majority of a worker's paycheck, giving the supervisor tremendous power and dividing workers. In contrast, the relatively flat basic wage system in union industries in the United States is one of the strengths of the American working class and helps to maintain solidarity.

Gainsharing schemes are often rigged to give workers incentives to cut jobs or to undermine safety. Drawing workers into "sharing" the successes and failures of the firm reinforces worker identity with the firm. It undermines union efforts to create industry-wide standards, portability of benefits, or political action to restrict corporate power.

Guideline #4. Agreed-upon goals, reflecting mutual interests. The notion that employers and workers (and their unions) have mutual interests is the foundation of the AFL-CIO's approach. The argument for mutual interests goes something like this:

> Perhaps the adversary relationship between labor and management made sense some 50 years ago. But the situation has changed. New technology requires a higher level of skill, working together, and communication. The high levels of competition, particularly from abroad, and customers' demands for higher quality require that we work together. These days, we have more in common in than we have in conflict.
>
> Therefore the old style of adversarial bargaining is inappropriate. The main task is to "problem solve." The parties start from the overall principle of mutual interests, gather the facts in some objective manner, and then deduce the objectively best solution for the problem.

Our approach is different. We believe the conflict of long-term interests between companies and their workers is both fundamental and primary. Some mutual interests do exist, but they are outweighed by underlying conflict. This is not a question of goodwill but of bottom-line interests. Management aims to maximize profits, and "good" management (from a stockholder point of view) does this by any means necessary. The union aims to secure a better life for workers. Both parties use the means they think appropriate to meet these bottom-line goals.

Observers often confuse tactics and goals. But when particular *tactics* of labor and management coincide, the convergence is likely to be temporary, dependent on changeable conditions, and not based on a harmony of overall aims.

Improving quality, for example, could seem to be a win-win situation. But often the company insists that to get quality, it must keep the same worker on the same job every day, though most workers prefer to rotate. Union officials accept this demand in hopes that improved quality will enhance job security. But management's attention to quality can very soon revert to the usual push for quantity. When that happens, will the union be able to get rotation back?

The point is that management has options, and will choose based on the prevailing management fad, the economic situation, and the strength of the labor movement. Managers are not committed to quality or productivity for their own sakes but according to whether and how much they increase profitability.

Thus the union should never give up its ability to use its own means to pursue its own separate goals. This is especially true in the arena of changing work methods and work relations. Once management gets what it wants, the promises, the sweeteners, and the idea of a trade-off seem to disappear.

Guideline #2. Based on a collective bargaining relationship. Here we will turn to our own recommendations for carrying out this excellent guideline.

Union success on the dangerous terrain of labor-management cooperation programs depends on a well-thought-out strategy based on thoroughly understanding that the two sides' interests in the program are different, rather than searching for a flimsy common ground. Accepting the program on the employer's terms is like accepting all the employers' demands at the bargaining table without counterdemands.

In the "collective bargaining model," the union side has its own agenda and its own proposals. Indeed, the union should organize member involvement in every level of participation programs as if they were an extension of collective bargaining. Then union members think in terms of we/they, not jointness. Every union participant regards her/himself as part of the union collective, not simply as an individual with good ideas (the mindset promoted by management).

Here we suggest demands for structuring a participation program and ideas on how to organize members.

Keep the structure as simple as possible. Avoid creating an unwieldy bureaucracy of functionaries who become committed to the program as an end in itself. The chance to appoint lots of union members may seem inviting, but if their jobs and perks depend on the program, they could become a fifth column. In addition, creating a participation bureaucracy will shift the responsibility and initiative away from the membership, to a few officials acting *for* the membership. The appeal of these programs is that workers finally get to be involved, so help members to be involved, the union way.

Negotiate a sunset clause for all committees and other structures so that none has an existence independent of or beyond the contract.

In teams or participation groups, *union members must have the right to call a time-out and caucus among themselves.* They should also have the right for union-only planning time before the joint meeting.

Be cautious about management's favorite problem-solving procedures. Brainstorming is best limited to union-only meetings. Differences among union members should be resolved before approaching management as a unified group. Likewise, the requirement to achieve consensus can create intolerable peer pressure. Avoid an atmosphere of the good old boys and girls sitting around working out their internal differences.

Reject any structure or training that makes facilitators responsible to both management and the union. The union must have the exclusive right to select its facilitators. They are representing union interests in the program, not the interests of "the process" or of some vague notion of jointness. Some locals have the facilitators take the union oath of office.

Because of the heavy co-optive pressures on facilitators, the union should *have procedures worked out in advance for appointment or election and removal.* Facilitators are part of the union leadership and union structure. They should get union training in the contract, grievance procedure, and union history, and should meet regularly with leadership bodies. In any case, the facilitators' job should not be so attractive that it "spoils" them. The "no loss, no gain" position may be best for most locals.

Beware of "neutral" consultants. Many consultants claim to be able to represent both sides, but most come from a probusiness background. Management pays the high consultant fees, and he who pays the piper calls the tune.

Consultants are invested in the program itself. Their pay comes from keeping the program going, no matter what. If consultants are necessary, then let the union and the company each have its own.

Resist blanket confidentiality agreements. Secrecy puts a barrier between leaders and members. The entire membership has a right to know what is going on in the participation program.

Treat all union participants as representatives of the union. Have them take the union oath of office. Members who have a healthy skepticism about the program should be encouraged to take assignments. They should go to their coworkers regularly for advice and instructions.

Assign an organizer for the union side, to oversee the union's involvement. This might be a key union officer or a program facilitator working with an officer. This person can make sure that union participants are briefed in a timely fashion on key issues that arise in the program. Where there are disputes he or she should bring participants together to resolve them.

Set up regular communication between participants in teams or circles and the union structure. "Team stewards" could meet regularly with the union leadership, the organizer, or an oversight committee.

Take the initiative, or be "proactive," to use the participation terminology. View joint meetings as the place to press the union's overall agenda, not simply to respond to management initiatives.

Put on a union orientation to the participation program, completely separate from any company training. In this training, you should "inoculate" members against the company messages they will receive.

Find resources for the union, to lessen dependence on management's ex-

perts. These could include other unions, labor studies programs, and your own members. You may be surprised how many people already have expertise in computers or accounting, for instance—if only they were asked.

Avoid off-site joint meetings or investigative trips. They can look like junkets: officers playing golf while not helping members deal with problems. Management also uses such trips as a sort of bonding experience, to get union leaders to like the way management does things.

Arrange activities that bring members in contact with members of other unions in the company/industry/area, especially unions that are trying a mobilized approach.

Above all, *maintain the union's willingness and ability to get out of the program.* If the union can't withdraw from the program in a unified and organized way, then leaders are in a weak position to deal with management in the program. Management won't take seriously the union's ability to pull out if it knows that patronage keeps some on board.

Choose a specific issue close to the membership's heart, and *build an aggressive campaign* around that. This last point is perhaps the most important—and the least often carried out. It is more effective to campaign around something the membership cares about—and show the connection of that issue to the participation program—than to mount a more abstract educational program about the dangers of participation. The campaign could be a fight to save a particular work rule or a full-fledged contract campaign. But it must be about something that the union can show directly affects members' lives.

In *Working Smart,* we discuss possible mobilization issues. Among these are a union approach to quality, fighting stress, resisting job documentation, defending work rules, fighting contracting out, and maintaining the right to challenge workload standards.

CONCLUSION

There is now a visible stirring in the official labor movement, as evidenced by the open struggle for leadership of the AFL-CIO in 1995 and the mergers of a number of internationals. Open recognition of the problem is certainly a step forward. ("Labor has lost all of its vigor and vitality and there is no bubbly to it," as Steelworkers president George Becker put it [Sabath 1995].) So also are steps to eliminate costly and enervating turf wars and to increase resources for organizing.

But ultimately the issue is whether the labor movement can mobilize its members, which is where the real power lies. Employers recognize this and work hard to separate members from their unions. When union leaders sign on to employer work reorganization campaigns as junior partners, in the hopes that they can get a free ride, they undermine the union's strength.

223

Work reorganization does provide possibilities for labor. But the possibilities do not lie in the merging of employer and union interests, as the AFL-CIO's report suggests. Rather, the possibilities come about because the new systems unintentionally provide the union with new levers of power—if it is organized. Just-in-time production makes management more vulnerable to surgical union actions. New technology means high capital investment and therefore increased need to keep equipment running. Lower tolerances in the systems, and even "foolproof" devices, add power to work-to-rule campaigns. Team meetings create opportunities to wage union battles. (For an extended description of such tactics see La Botz 1991, chs. 3, 5.) But exercising this potential power depends on a union-conscious membership and a union leadership that keeps everyone's eyes on the prize.

NOTES

1. For an example of a worksheet at a GM parts plant, see Parker and Slaughter 1994, 77. The manager of manufacturing engineering explained: "The worksheets will be posted on the job so that anyone can walk up to the job and perform with a minimum of break-in time."

2. Resistance is much more difficult in nonunion workplaces. Usually it requires some form of collective activity—i.e., the essence of unionism. See Graham (1995) for descriptions of resistance at Subaru-Isuzu.

BIBLIOGRAPHY

Adams, Larry. 1994. "Mail Handlers Resist QWL." In *Working Smart: A Union Guide to Participation Programs and Reengineering,* by Mike Parker and Jane Slaughter. Detroit: Labor Notes.

Adler, Paul S., and Robert E. Cole. 1993. "Designed for Learning: A Tale of Two Auto Plants." *Sloan Management Review* 34, no. 3 (Spring): 85–94.

AFL-CIO Committee on the Evolution of Work. 1994. *The New American Workplace: A Labor Perspective.* Washington, D.C.: American Federation of Labor-Congress of Industrial Organizations.

Asher, Robert, and Ronald Edsforth, eds. 1995. *Autowork.* Albany, N.Y.: State University of New York Press.

Babson, Steve. 1993. "Lean or Mean: The MIT Model and Lean Production at Mazda." *Labor Studies Journal* 18, no. 2 (Summer): 3–24.

———. 1995. "Restructuring the Workplace." In *Autowork,* ed. Robert Asher and Ronald Edsforth. Albany, N.Y.: State University of New York Press.

Banks, Andy, and Jack Metzgar. 1989. "Who Will Win Control of Shopfloor Knowledge?" *Labor Research Review* 8, no. 14 (Fall): 5–55.

Bluestone, Barry, and Irving Bluestone. 1992. *Negotiating the Future: A Labor Perspective on American Business.* New York: Basic Books.

CAW-Canada Research Group in CAMI. 1993. *The CAMI Report: Lean Production in a Unionized Auto Plant.* Willowdale, Ont.: Canadian Auto Workers.

Gordon, Jack. 1993. "Into the Dark: Rough Ride Ahead for American Workers." *Training* 30, no. 7 (July): 21–29.

Graham, Laurie. 1995. *On the Line at Subaru-Isuzu: The Japanese Model and the American Worker.* Ithaca, N.Y.: ILR Press.

Hage, Dave. 1990. "Saturn Plant Is GM's Laboratory for Testing New Ways of Working." *Minneapolis Star-Tribune,* Oct. 21.

Hammer, Michael, and James Champy. 1993. Interview in *Across the Board,* June.

Higgins, James. 1990. "Line Workers Really Do Help Make Decisions." *Detroit News,* May 13.

Hinkle, Don. 1993. "Saturn Suit Charges Racial Discrimination." *Columbia Daily Herald,* May 20.

"Labor's Days at GM." 1992. *Wall Street Journal,* Sept. 4, A8.

La Botz, Dan. 1991. *A Troublemaker's Handbook: How to Fight Back Where You Work and Win!* Detroit: Labor Notes.

Lee, Bruce. 1988. "Worker Harmony Makes NUMMI Work." *New York Times,* Dec. 25, F2.

Marshall, Ray. 1992. "Work Organization, Unions, and Economic Performance." In *Unions and Economic Competitiveness,* ed. Lawrence Mishel and Paula Voos. Armonk, N.Y.: M.E. Sharpe.

Mazda. 1986. *MMUC Production System: Concept and Outline.* Mazda Motor Manufacturing (USA) Corporation. Flatrock, Mich.: Mazda.

Mishel, Lawrence, and Paula B. Voos, eds. 1992. *Unions and Economic Competitiveness.* Armonk, N.Y.: M.E. Sharpe.

Parker, Mike, and Jane Slaughter. 1988. *Choosing Sides: Unions and the Team Concept.* Detroit: Labor Notes.

———. 1994. *Working Smart: A Union Guide to Participation Programs and Reengineering.* Detroit: Labor Notes.

Rubinstein, Saul, Michael Bennett, and Thomas Kochan. 1993. "The Saturn Partnership: Co-Management and the Reinvention of the Local Union." In *Employee Representation: Alternatives and Future Directions,* ed. Bruce E. Kaufman and Morris M. Kleiner. Madison, Wisc.: Industrial Relations Research Association.

Sabath, Donald. 1995. "USW President Seeking Members to Energize Union." *Cleveland Plain Dealer,* Aug. 5.

Swoboda, Frank. 1994. "Manufacturing Success." *Washington Post,* Apr. 11, bus. sec., 1, 14–15.

"Working Together: Saturn and the UAW" (video). 1994. Hohokus, N.J.: Merrimack Films.

CONTRIBUTORS

LEE BALLIET currently works as director of the Indiana State Employee Labor-Management Project. He is also an Associate Professor Emeritus at Indiana University, Bloomington, where he served as director of the IU Division of Labor Studies from 1982 to 1992.

DAROLD T. BARNUM teaches negotiation and conflict resolution, and organizational strategy at the University of Illinois at Chicago. He was the founding director of the Center for Human Resource Management at the University of Illinois and the Public Employee Relations Project at Texas Tech University. He has also served as a facilitator for union-management cooperative efforts.

PETER DOWNS is a thirty-eight-year-old union activist and writer with over 200 published articles to his credit. A twelve-year member of the United Auto Workers and employee of General Motors, Downs is a former Recording Secretary of UAW Local 2250 and thrice was elected international convention delegate. He is a member and former leader of the New Directions Movement in the UAW. Downs's union career has included membership in the United Brotherhood of Carpenters and the Amalgamated Clothing Workers of America (later merged into the Amalgamated Clothing and Textile Workers), and affiliations with the International Association of Machinists and the Farm Labor Organizing Committee.

ADRIENNE E. EATON is an Associate Professor and Director of Credit Programs in the Labor Studies and Employment Relations Department of the School of Management and Labor Relations, Rutgers University. She conducts research on workplace democracy, the "new" labor relations, and employee involvement with a particular focus on the role of and impact on unions. Her research on these topics has been published in *Industrial and Labor Relations Review, Labor Studies Journal,* and *Advances in Industrial and Labor Relations.* She served as chair of the University and College Labor Education Association Worker Participation Task Force from 1992–96.

JIM GRATTAN is a degreed software engineer who has worked in decidedly nonunion, high-tech industry in the Atlanta, Georgia, area for over twenty years. He is an outspoken advocate for workplace democratization with articles appearing in local publications. He is currently completing his bachelor's degree in Labor Studies from Indiana University with the goal of obtaining a position in the labor movement to advance the cause of working men and women.

MAE M. NGAI is Director of Research and Policy at the Consortium for Worker Education, a nonprofit organization which provides schooling, training, and reemployment services for union members in New York City. She is a Ph.D. candidate in history at Columbia University, where she is writing a dissertation about United States immigration policy and racial formation in the first half of the twentieth Century.

PETER LAZES, Ph.D., is a member of the faculty at Cornell University, New York State School of Industrial and Labor Relations. At Cornell, he founded and is the director of Programs for Economic Transitions, and Strategic Planning Programs for Unions. Lazes also founded and directed Programs for Employment and Workplace Systems (PEWS), and cofounded the Center for Participative Management and Industrial Democracy in Lodz, Poland. He has established Workplace Systems, Inc., a consulting firm which has assisted labor and management in creating new work systems since 1981.

BRUCE NISSEN is a Program Director at the Center for Labor Research and Studies at Florida International University in Miami. He is the author of *Fighting for Jobs: Case Studies of Labor-Community Coalitions Confronting Plant Closings* (SUNY Press, 1995), and the coeditor of *Grand Designs: The Impact of Corporate Strategies on Workers, Unions and Communities* (ILR Press, 1993) and *Theories of the Labor Movement* (Wayne State University Press, 1987).

MIKE PARKER is coauthor with Jane Slaughter of *Working Smart: A Union Guide to Participation Programs and Reengineering* and *Choosing Sides: Unions and the Team Concept,* both published by Labor Notes. He has also written many other books and articles on unions, work organization, and

quality and has worked with unions and companies in developing training plans and programs for new technology and as an industrial electri-
cian and a consultant to business on industrial computer machine
control.

JANE SAVAGE, MPPM, is a senior consultant at Workplace Systems, Inc.,
working with unions and management to design new work systems and
implement quality processes in the automotive supply and chemical manufacturing industries. Savage has also led private workshops for internal
union and management consultants and has aided in the design and implementation of modular manufacturing units and new compensation
systems within the apparel industry. She has worked as an engineer and
was a member of a designers' and drafters' union.

MAUREEN SHEAHAN has been the Executive Director of the Labor-Management Council for Economic Renewal since 1990. She has worked as a
UAW/Ford education advisor; general manager of a unionized, nonprofit,
worker-owned and managed print shop; coordinator of a consumer-
owned food co-op; secretary; and secondary English teacher. Sheahan
was a member of the International Typographers Union and is currently
with the National Writers Union, UAW Local 1981. She also coordinates
the work of the Region's International Labor Solidarity Network and is
active with the local COSH group.

JANE SLAUGHTER is coauthor with Mike Parker of *Choosing Sides: Unions
and the Team Concept* and *Working Smart: A Union Guide to Participation
Programs and Reengineering*, both published by Labor Notes. She covered
the automobile industry for Labor Notes for sixteen years and has spoken
on labor-management cooperation and other issues throughout the
United States and Canada, as well as in Mexico, England, Germany, Gua-
temala, and Puerto Rico. Her articles, often coauthored with Mike Parker,
have appeared in *Technology Review, Industrial and Labor Relations Report,
The New York Times, Labor Research Review, The Witness, The Progressive,*
and *Multinational Monitor.*

EDWARD L. SUNTRUP teaches labor relations, collective bargaining, and
dispute resolution tactics in the College of Business Administration, University of Illinois at Chicago. He has been a long-time arbitrator and me-
diator in both the private and public sectors and has been involved in the
federal government's reinvention program as a facilitator.

INDEX

Abramson, Jerry, 163
absenteeism at the workplace, 10, 14, 103, 166; not tolerated at NUMMI, 83
adversarial attitudes, 13, 50, 111, 160; as basis of private sector labor law, 23, 81–82; and cooperation, 39, 49, 124–26; debate over, 27, 117, 220; disrupting cooperative programs, 171; in the federal sector, 151, 249. *See also* alienated consciousness of workers; attitudes of U.S. workers
AFL-CIO (American Federation of Labor-Congress of Industrial Organizations): Center for Workplace Democracy, 20, 59, 72; Committee on the Evolution of Work, 18–29, 37, 58, 79, 93, 94, 103, 110, 208, 210; corporate affairs department, 59; education department, 59; opposition to repeal of NLRA Section 8(a)(2), 22, 135; perspective on involvement programs, 18–20, 22, 36–54, 79; public employee department, 150; role in NLRA reform, 89–90; role in workplace change, 25, 182, 201–4. *See also New American Workplace AFL-CIO News*
alienated consciousness of workers, 10. *See also* adversarial attitudes; attitudes of U.S. workers
alternative dispute resolution (ADR), 164

Amalgamated Clothing and Textile Workers Union (ACTWU), 17, 58, 111, 117, 119, 199. *See also* International Ladies Garment Workers Union (ILGWU); Union of Needletrades, Industrial, and Textile Employees (UNITE)
Amalgamated Transit Union (ATU), 166
American Federation of Government Employees (AFGE), 148, 150
American Federation of Grainmillers (AFGM), 18, 116, 199
American Federation of State, County, and Municipal Employees (AFSCME), 111, 165, 167, 169; District Council, 62, 167
American Federation of Teachers (AFT), 168, 199
American Postal Workers Union (APWU), 17
apparel industry. *See* garment industry
apprenticeship programs, 41, 203; in Germany, 65
assembly line, 9; disciplining effects of, 10
associational unionism, 87
AT&T, 209
attitudes of U.S. workers, 26–28; contradictory aspects of, 88–89; fearing the demands of new work systems, 50, 134; in Indiana state public sector,

231

99–100, 201, 214; in unionized plants, 13, 81, 183–84, 186–91

works councils: in Germany, 11, 63–65; potential for U.S., 204; statutorily mandated, 27, 87

work teams. *See* team production

work week. *See* hours of work

Xerox Corporation, 45, 117